ABBREVIATIONS
& ACRONYMS

KIP SPERRY

REVISED 2ND EDITION

ABBREVIATIONS
ACRONYMS

KIP SPERRY

A Guide for Family Historians

Ancestry.

Library of Congress Cataloging-in-Publication Data

Sperry, Kip.
  Abbreviations & acronyms : a guide for family historians / compiled by
Kip Sperry.— 2nd rev. ed.
      p. cm.
  ISBN 1-59331-026-9 (alk. paper)
  1. Genealogy—Dictionaries.   2. Abbreviations.   3. Acronyms I.
Title: Abbreviations and acronyms. II. Title.

CS6.S64 2003
929'.1'03—dc21

                                                              2003005903

Ancestry.com
An imprint of Turner Publishing Company
4507 Charlotte Ave., Suite 100
Nashville, TN 37209
www.turnerpublishing.com

10 9 8 7 6 5 4 3 2

INTRODUCTION

ALL FIELDS OF STUDY HAVE THEIR OWN UNIQUE abbreviations, acronyms, alphabetic symbols, initials, contractions, and shortenings of words. Genealogy and history are certainly no exception. Perhaps even more abbreviations are used in these two disciplines than one can imagine.

This book lists abbreviations and acronyms alphabetically as found in genealogical and historical sources—both in original records and in printed sources. Included is a brief explanation or description of the abbreviation, acronym, or initials.

This work is intended as a reference source for genealogists, historians, reference librarians, and others searching for the meaning of an abbreviation or acronym. Such references might be found in federal population census schedules, Soundex indexes, mortality schedules, court records, original records on microfilm or in archives or courthouses, or in printed sources, such as compiled genealogies, periodical articles, newspapers, and other sources. Abbreviations of many institutions, publishers, and organizations are also included, and some show their address. Internet addresses have not been included since they change frequently.

Most of the abbreviations refer to the United States and Canada, although others are found in British sources and sometimes other countries as well. Generally this guidebook does not include foreign language abbreviations, such as German, Greek, and so forth. Some basic computer terms are included; however, other manuals better explain computer terms in greater detail. A bibliography of reference titles and related Internet Web pages concludes this work. One may question why medical and other abbreviations are identified here. Knowing the meaning of these abbreviations may be helpful when researching mortality schedules, death records, court records, and other similar records used by genealogists, historians, and other researchers.

It is realized that not every abbreviation and acronym found in genealogical and historical sources is identified here. That would be an overwhelming task. Many county and local genealogical and historical organizations and libraries have their own unique abbreviations, as do compiled genealogies and other publications. Generally, periods have not been used in the abbreviations. Thus, C.G. is listed in this work as CG. Board for Certification of Genealogists is a registered service mark, and the following are service marks of the Board for Certification of Genealogists: Certified Genealogist, CG; Certified Genealogical Instructor, CGI; Certified Genealogical Lecturer, CGL; Certified Genealogical Records Specialist, CGRS; and Certified Lineage Specialist, CLS.

Appreciation is extended to the following individuals who assisted with typing the manuscript: Emily C. Allen, Melissa E. Finlay, Robin Lewis, Amber Ostler, Angie Rasmussen, Marta M. Smith, and Marta E. Taylor. The following individuals served ably as research assistants: Misty C. Armstrong, Susan Howell, Emily Carrie Hunter, Kirsha Johnson, Julie Kaufman, Echo King, Melissa Law, Amy J. McLane, Sherri Padgette, Marci Anne Powell, Brandy Lynn Sago, and Jennifer Stoker. I am grateful to Brigham Young University, Provo, Utah, for providing secretarial and editorial services. Special appreciation to Matt Wright and Jennifer Browning at Ancestry for their assistance.

—Kip Sperry

A

a (1) about (2) abstract (3) acre(s) (4) administration (5) adultery (6) against (7) age (8) analysis (9) annual (10) *annus* (age[d]) (11) ante (before) (12) archives (13) aunt (14) sealing conversion

a. after

A (1) Agder-Aust'Agder (2) Alien (3) Aunt

A/ acting

A&A *Abbreviations & Acronyms: A Guide for Family Historians*, compiled by Kip Sperry (Provo, UT: Ancestry)

AA (1) Agricultural Adjustment (2) American Archivist (3) Associate of Arts (4) Australia (5) Automobile Association (British) (6) Automatic Archives

AAA Ancestral American Associates

AAAL American Academy and Institute of Arts & Letters

AAAW Advanced Air-launched Anti-Armour Weapon

AAC Administrative Advisory Council

AAC *Anno Ante Christum* (in the year before Christ)

AAC Archives Advisory Commission (Massachusetts), Massachusetts Historical Records Advisory Board, Massachusetts State Archives, 220 Morrissey Blvd., Boston, MA 02125

AAC Army Air Corps

AACD American Association for Counseling and Development

AACR *Anglo-American Cataloging Rules* (American Library Association)

AACR2 *Anglo-American Cataloging Rules* (American Library Association, 1990)

AACSB American Assembly of Collegiate Schools of Business

AAF Army Air Force

A-Ag Aust-Agder, Norway

AAG Association of American Geographers

AAG Association of Accredited Genealogists, Utah, P.O. Box 4043, Salt Lake City, UT 84110-4043

AAG Assistant Adjutant General

AAGG African-American Genealogy Group, P.O. Box 1798, Philadelphia, PA 19105-1798

AAGHS African-American Genealogical and Historical Society

AAGHSC Afro-American Genealogical and Historical Society of Chicago, P.O. Box 37-7651, Chicago, IL 60637

AAGHSTN African American Genealogical and Historical Society of Tennessee

AAGRA Australasian Association of Genealogists and Record Agents

AAGSC African American Genealogical Society of Cleveland

AAGSNC African-American Genealogical Society of Northern California, P.O. Box 27485, Oakland, CA 94602-0985

AAGSSC African-American Genealogy Society of Sacramento California

AAHE American Association for Higher Education, One Dupont Circle, Suite 360, Washington, DC 20036-1110

AAHGS Afro-American Historical and Genealogical Society, P.O. Box 73086, Washington, DC 20056-3086

AAI Automated Archives, Inc.

AAL Aid Association for Lutherans

Aalb Aalborg, Denmark

AALE American Academy for Liberal Education

AAM American Association of Museums, Washington, DC

a.a.O at the place quoted

AAONMS Ancient Order of Nobles of the Mystic Shrine

AAP *Ancestors of American Presidents*, by Gary Boyd Roberts

AAP Assessment of Achievement Programme (Scottish)

aar against all risks

AAR Air-to-Air Refueling

aar/Aarn year

Aarhus Aarhus, Denmark

AARs After Action Reports

AAS American Antiquarian Society, 185 Salisbury Street, Worcester, MA 01609-1634

AASK Adoption Answers Support Kinship, 8 Homestead Drive, South Glastonbury, CT 06073-2804

AASLH American Association for State and Local History, 1717 Church Street, Nashville, TN 37203-2991

AASP *American Antiquarian Society Proceedings*

AASR Ancient Accepted Scottish Rite (Masonic)

AAUP American Association of University Professors, 1012 14th Street NW, Suite 500, Washington, DC 20005-3465

ab (1) abbey (2) about (3) abridgement (4) abstract (5) administrator's bond (6) appeal against bastardy

a & b assault and battery

Ab Abe, Abel, Abraham

AB *Artium Baccalaureus* (Bachelor of Arts)

AB/Alta Alberta, Canada

ABA American Bar Association, 750 N. Lakeshore Dr., Chicago, IL 60611

aban abandoned

A Barb Anna Barbara

A'Bard Auster'Bardastrandarsysla

abba an abbey

abbr/abbrev (1) abbreviated (2) abbreviated form (3) abbreviation

Abby Abigail

ABC Adoptee-Birthfamily Connection, P.O. Box 22611, Fort Lauderdale, FL 33335-2611

ABC Advisement by Computer

abd (1) abdicated (2) abroad

Abd/ABD/Abdns Aberdeenshire (Scotland)

ABD Aberdeen, Scotland

Abe Abraham, Abram

ABE American Board of Education

ABELL *Annual Bibliography of English Language and Literature*

ABER Anhalt Bernburg

Aberd/ABER Aberdeen, Scotland

Abg Aldonberg

ABI *American Biographical Index*

ABIGAIL Massachusetts Historical Society Online Catalog

ab init *ab initio* (from the beginning)

abl ablative

Ab^m Abraham

ABMC American Battle Monuments Commission, ABMC Courthouse Plaza II Ste. 500, 2300 Clarendon Blvd., Arlington, VA 22201

ab *nepos* (great-great grandson)

ab *neptis* (great-great granddaughter)

abot abbot

Abou/Abu literally, father; the first element in many Arabic proper names; sometimes abbreviated to Bu

Abp Archbishop

abr (1) abbreviation (2) abridged (3) abridgment

Abr/Abram/Abrhᵐ Abraham

abs (1) abscond (2) absent (3) abstract

ABS American Bible Society, 1865 Broadway, New York, NY 10023-7505

ABSEES *American Bibliography of Slavic and East European Studies*

abst absent

abstr abstract(s)

abt about

ABWE Association of Baptists for World Evangelism, P.O. Box 8585, Harrisburg, PA 17705-8585

Aby Abraham, Abram

ac (1) acres (2) adopted child (3) *anni currentis*, current year (4) archives case (5) attested copy

Ac (1) acres (2) adopted child

AC (1) Air Corps (United States) (2) Alsace Loraine (3) ancestor chart (4) *Ante Christum* (before Christ) (5) appellate court (6) Assumption College

A/C (1) according to (2) account (3) account of

ACA American Congregational Association, Congregational Library and Archives, 14 Beacon Street, Boston, MA 02108

ACAD (1) academic (2) academy/ies

Acad Academy, Academic

ACASA Archives of Czechs and Slovaks Abroad, Regenstein Library, 1100 East 57th Street, Chicago, IL 60637-1502

ACBLF Association canadienne des bibliote-caires de langue française

acc (1) accommodation (2) accompanied (3) according (to) (4) account (5) accusative

ACC American Computing Centers

ACC Anglican Catholic Church

accomptᵗ (1) accomptant (2) account

accon/accot/acct/acompt account

accordᵍ according

accoᵗ**/acc**ᵗ account or accompt

acct (1) account (2) accountant

Acctcy Accountancy

Acctg Accounting

accu accurate

ACCUS American Catholic Church in the United States

ACD *Adams County Democrat*, West Union, Adams County

ACE Allied Command Europe

ACG American College of Genealogy

ACGS American-Canadian Genealogical Society, P.O. Box 6478, Manchester, NH 03108-6478

ACGS Ashtabula County Genealogical Society, 860 Sherman St., Geneva, OH 44041-9101

ACGSI Allen County Genealogical Society of Indiana, P.O. Box 12003, Fort Wayne, IN 46862

achd adopted child

achiev achievement

ACIR Advisory Commission on Intergovernmental Relations

ackd/acknowled/acknowd/acknown acknowledged

ACLIN Access Colorado Library and Information Network, Colorado State University, 201 East Colfax Ave., Denver, CO 80203

ACLMA Association of Canadian Map Libraries and Archives Association

ACLS American Council of Learned Societies, 228 East 45th Street, New York, NY 10017-3398

ACLU American Civil Liberties Union, 125 Broad St., 18th Floor, New York, NY 10004-2400

ACN All concerned notified

acnt account

ACO Air Cadet Organisation (British)

ACORN Akron Community Online Resource Network (Akron, Ohio)

acpj archives common pleas journal

ACPL Allen County Public Library, 900 Webster Street, Fort Wayne, IN 46802

Acq Acquisition Librarian, Acquisitions

ACS American Community Survey

ACSS audio cascading style sheet

act (1) acting (2) active

actg acting

Actg Acting

Activ Activities

ACV Armoured Combat Vehicle

ACW American Civil War

ad (1) administrated (2) administrator (3) administration docket (4) adopted (5) adopted daughter (6) adulterer, adultery (7) *ante diem* (before the day) (8) Archdeacon (9) archdeaconry

ad/add *addatur* (let there be added, addition)

Ad (1) Adam (2) Adopted (3) Adult Services Librarian

AD (1) adopted daughter (2) *anno Domini* (in the year of the Lord) (3) Archdeaconry/ies

A&D Ancestors and Descendants, 10714 Hepburn Circle, Culver City, CA 90232-3717

Ada Adelaide

ADA Americans with Disabilities Act

Adau/AdD adopted daughter

ADC Aide-de-Camp

adcl/AdCl adopted child

adcon archdeacon, archdeaconry

add addition

Add Address

AdD adopted daughter

Addie/Addy Adelina

addl additional

Add.MS Additional Manuscripts (British Library, London, England)

addn addition

Addr Address

ADE Aden

Adel Adelaide

Adelh Adelheid, Adelheit

ADES Anhalt Dessau

AdGcl adopted grandchild

ADH *aus dem Hause* (out of the house)

ADI Area of Dominant Influence (such as newspaper or other media)

ad inf *ad infinitum* (to infinity)

ad init *ad initium* (at the beginning)

ad int *ad interim* (in the meantime)

adj (1) adjective (2) adjoining (3) adjoint(e) (4) adjourned (5) adjuster (6) adjunct

adj/adjt adjutant

Adj Gen Adjutant General

ad lib *ad libitum* (at will)

ad loc *ad locum* (at the place)

ad locum *ad loc* (to or at the place)

adm (1) administrator (2) Admiral (3) Admiralty (England) (4) admission (5) admitted (e.g., to church) (6) letters of administration

adm admitted to communion (church)

adm/admin/admin^(ion)/adminism/admon/admn/adn (1) administration (2) administrative (3) administrator

Adm admiral

Ad M adopted mother

Adm Co Administrative County (British)

adminr/admn/admr(s)/admor/adm'r/ adnors (1) administrative (2) administrator(s)

admin administrative

Admin Administration, Administrative

adminstr administrator(s)

Administr Administrator

Administrv Administrative

Adminr Administrator

Admis Admissions

admix/adminx administratrix

Admon (1) administration (2) letter(s) of administration

admor administrator (probate)

admr administration

admrx/admx/adm'x administratix

admstr administers

ADN *Ancestry Daily News* (online newsletter)

adnors administrators

a dnt attendant

Adolph Adolphus

adop adopted

Adop Adoption

ador administrator (probate)

adp adoption

ADP automatic data processing

ad patres gathered to his father's, dead

adpt adopted

adptn adoption

adptr adoptor

Adr Adrian

ads (1) *adversus* (the opposite of versus) (2) advowson (3) autograph document signed

AdS adopted son

ADSL Asynchronous Digital Subscriber Line

adtrix administratrix

adv (1) adverb (2) adversus (against) (3) advertising (4) advised (5) advisor (6) advisory

Adv Advisor, Advisory

Advan Advanced, Advancement

Advert Advertising

AdvGen Advocate General

advr (1) adviser (2) advisor (3) advisory

advt advertisement

ADY Alderney

æ/aet/aetat/aetatis (1) age (2) aged

aet *aetatis* (aged)

ae(t)/aeb (1) at the age of, aged (2) each (3) one (4) one of several administrator's and executor's bonds

aed administrator's and executor's docket

AEF *before ab initio* (before abate)

aegidius Giles

A El Anna Elisabeth

AELC Association of Evangelical Lutheran Churches

Aelizia Alice

aeltester/aelteste oldest, eldest, elder

Aeron Aeronautical, Aeronautics

Aerosp Aerospace

aet/aetat/aetas *aetatis, aetatis* (aged, generation, lifetime, of age)

aetatula very tender childhood

AEW Airborne Early Warning

a.f. *L. anno futuro*, next year

af/aff'dt affidavit

Af/Afr Africa

AF Africa

AF *Ancestral File* (database in FamilySearch™)

A-F Anglo-French

AF&AM Ancient Free and Accepted Order of Masons

AFB Air Force Base

afds aforesaid

Aff (1) Affairs (2) Affidavit

aff'dt/afft affidavit

affin (1) affinity (2) affinitive

Aff Liver Affection of Liver

affl affluent

Aff Rec Affiant's Record

AFG Afghanistan

AFGE American Federation of Government Employees, 80 F Street, NW, Washington, DC 20001

AFHS Alberta Family Histories Society, P.O. Box 30270, Station B, Calgary, Alberta, Canada T2M4P1

AFIHC American Family Immigration History Center (Ellis Island)

AFN/Afn Ancestral File Number (FamilySearch™)

aforsd/afsd/aforesd/afors/aforsd/forsd aforesaid

AFPRB Armed Forces Pay Review Body

Afr Africa

AFr Anglo-French

AFR/AFRI/Afric Africa

AFRA American Family Records Association, P.O. Box 15505, Kansas City, MO 64106-0505

AFRC American History Research Center, University of Akron, OH 44325-1702

aft (1) after (2) afternoon

AFT (1) *Ancestry Family Tree* (genealogy software from Ancestry.com) (2) Ancestry Forum Trainee

ag (1) age (2) Agreement

Ag August

AG^{SM} Accredited Genealogist. One who has passed the rigorous tests administered by ICAPGen, P.O. Box 970204, Orem, UT 84097-0204

AG (1) Adjutant General (2) Attorney General (3) Attorney General's Office

AG/Arg Argentina

AG:ABC "American Genealogy: A Basic Course," NGS' home-study course

AGBI *The American Genealogical-Biographical Index* (Middletown, Conn.: Godfrey Memorial Library). Formerly known as Rider's Index.

AGCI *Australian Genealogical Computer Index*

AGCIG Arizona Genealogical Computer Interest Group, P.O. Box 51498, Phoenix, AZ 85076-1498

agcy agency

AGD (1) Adjutant General's Department (2) adopted granddaughter

AGE (1) Assembly of Governmental Employees (2) Association for Genealogical Education (organization no longer meeting)

agee aged

AGES Accelerated Genealogical Endexing Schedules (Salt Lake City, UT)

Aggie/Aggy Agatha, Agnes

AGI Archivo General de Indias, Seville

Agl Anglesey, Wales

Ag Lab agricultural laborer

AGLL American Genealogical Lending Library, P.O. Box 329, 593 West 100 North, Bountiful, UT 84011-0329

AGM *American Genealogy Magazine*, P.O. Box 1587, Stephenville, TX 76401

AGM Annual General Meeting

agmt agreement

Ag^n Augustin

agncy agency

agnt agent

AGO Adjutant General's Office

Agr (1) agricultural laborer (2) agriculture

AGRA Association of Genealogists and Record Agents, 29 Badgers Close, Horsham, West Sussex, England RH12 5RU

agric/agrl agriculture

Agric Agricultural, Agriculture

Agron Agronomy

agrt agreement

AGS adopted grandson

AGS Alabama Genealogical Society, P.O. Box 2296, Samford University Library, 800 Lakeshore Drive, Birmingham, AL 35229-0001

AGS American Genealogical Society, Depository and Headquarters, Samford University Library, Box 2296, 800 Lakeshore Drive, Birmingham, AL 35229

AGS American Geographical Society

AGS Anchorage Genealogical Society, P.O. Box 212265, Anchorage, AK 99521-2265

AGS Arkansas Genealogical Society, P.O. Box 908, Hot Springs, AR 71902-0908

AGS Association for Gravestone Studies, 278 Main Street, Suite 207, Greenfield, MA 01301

AGS Augusta Genealogical Society, P.O. Box 3743, Augusta, GA 30914-3743

AGSC American Geographical Society Collection

agt agent

agt/agst against

agt brewry agent for the union brew

agy agency

AGY Anglesey

AH (1) *Anno Hebraico* (in the Hebrew year) (2) *Anno Hegirae* (in the year of the Hegira)

AH *Agricultural History*

AHA American Historical Association, 400 A Street SE, Washington, DC 20003-3889

A&HA Ancient & Honorable Artillery Company of Massachusetts

AHC Arkansas History Commission and State Archives

AHD *American Heritage Dictionary of the English Language*

AHFA Adam Hawks Family Association

AHH Arthur H. Hughes

ahl *ad hoc locum* (to this place)

AHN Archivo Histórico Nacional, Madrid

AHQ *Alabama Historical Quarterly*

AHR *American Historical Review*

AHS Alaska Historical Society, P.O. Box 100299, Anchorage, AK 99510-0299

AHS Arizona Historical Society, 949 East Second Street, Tucson, AZ 85719

AHS Atlanta Historical Society, Atlanta History Center, Library/Archives, 3101 Andrews Drive, NW, Atlanta, GA 30305

AHSGR American Historical Society of Germans from Russia, 631 D. Street, Lincoln, NE 68502-1199

A'Hun Auster'Hunavatnssysla

AI (1) *Annals of Iowa* (2) appreciative inquiry (3) artificial intelligence

aib archives inventory book

AIC American Institute for Conservation of Historic and Artistic Works

AIC Army Invalid's Certificate

AID Adoptees Identity Discovery, P.O. Box 2159, Sunnyvale, CA 94087

aid Aid of execution (court record)

AIG Adjutant-Inspector-General

AIGI Amelia Island Genealogical Society

AIHS American Irish Historical Society, 991 Fifth Avenue, New York, NY 10028

AIIM Association for Information and Image Management

Ailie Alice, Alison, Helen

AIM (1) Academic Information Manager (2) America Online Instant Messenger

AIS Accelerated Indexing Systems (publisher of printed census indexes and compiler of U.S. census indexes on microfiche)

AIS Adoptees in Search, P.O. Box 41016, Bethesda, MD 20824

AIS Archival Information System (National Archives and Records Administration, Washington, DC)

AISI Accelerated Indexing Systems International (publisher of printed census indexes and compiler of U.S. census indexes on micro-fiche)

aj (1) adjutant (2) associate judge

AJAG Assistant Judge Advocate General

ajcc associate judge county court

AJGS Association of Jewish Genealogical Societies

AJHS American Jewish Historical Society, New York, NY, and Waltham, MA

AJHSQ *American Jewish Historical Society Quarterly*

AJKids Ask Jeeves for Kids

AJLH *American Journal of Legal History*

AJR *American Journalism Review*

AK/Ak Alaska

Aka/AKA also known as (often used before a name to indicate that the name is an alias)

AKC Associate, King's College, London, England

Akhs Akershus, Norway

al/AL (1) alias (2) alien (not naturalized, foreign born person of another country, abbreviation often found in U.S. census schedules) (3) alley (4) aunt-in-law (5) autographed letter unsigned (often a draft in the author's hand-writing)

Al Aunt-in-law

Al Alice, Allan, Allen

AL (1) Alaska (2) American Legion

A/L Archives/Library

AL/Ala Alabama

ALA ALA filing rules (American Library Association)

ALA American Library Association, 50 East Huron, Chicago, IL 60611

AlA&ML Alabama Agricultural and Mechanical State University Library, P.O. Box 908, Normal, AL 35762

Alab agricultural laborer

ALARM Alliance of Libraries, Archives and Record Management

Alas Alaska

Alb (1) Albert (2) Albier

ALB (1) Albania (2) Alberta, Canada

Albq Albuquerque, NM

Albr Albrecht

ALC (1) Adult Learning Center (2) American Lutheran Church

ALCTS Association for Library Collections and Technical Services

ald alderman

Ald Aldenberg

ALD Alderney

AlDAR Alabama Daughters of the American Revolution

Aldern Alderney, Channel Islands

Alec/Aleck Alexander

aleg/alleg allegation, allegiance

Alex/Alex^r Alexander

Alf Alfonso, Alfred

Alfie Alfred

Alg (1) Algiers (2) Algonquin dialect

ALG/ALGE Algeria

ALHN American Local History Network

Alia Alias

ALIC Archives Library Information Center (National Archives and Records Administration), 700 Pennsylvania Ave. NW, Washington, DC 20408

Alick Alexander

all (1) alley (2) alliance (3) allow

ALL Academy of Lifelong Learning, University of Delaware

ALL All countries

All Allegany

Alld Allied

Allie/Ally Alice, Alison

ALMA Adoptees Liberty Movement Association, P.O. Box 727, Radio City Station, New York, NY 10101-0727

alne alone

ALOH American Legion of Honor

ALOR Alsace Lorraine

alph alphabetically

ALPLI Allen County Public Library, 900 Webster Street, Fort Wayne, IN 46802

als alias

ALS/a.l.s. autographed letter signed

als/alsoe *alius* (the second, also)

ALS/al(s)s autographed letter(s) signed

Als/ALS Alsace/Alsem

ALS Adult Learning Service

ALSA/Alsac Alsace

AlSAr Alabama Department of Archives and History, 624 Washington Ave., Montgomery, AL 36130-0100

AlsK Alsies Kohem

als wt alias writ

alt (1) Alter, age (2) alternate (3) altitude

Alta Alberta, Canada

altm at liberty to marry

Alum Alumni

Alvsbg Alvsborg, Sweden

Alx Alexander

aly alley

Am American

AM (1) *anno mundi* (in the year of the world) (2) *ante meridiem* (before noon) (3) *Artium Magister* (Master of Arts)

AM/AME/Amer (1) America (2) American

AMA American Medical Association (*see* especially Deceased Physician File, National Genealogical Society, Arlington, VA)

AMAE Archives Du Ministère Des Affaires Étrangères, Paris, France

A Magd Anna Magdalena

Aman almsman

Am. Antiq. American Antiquarian Society, 185 Salisbury Street, Worcester, MA 01609-1634

A Mar Anna Maria

Amb (1) Ambassador (2) Ambrose

AMC Anna Maria College

AMC (1) Archival and Mixed Collections (2) Archives and Manuscripts Control

AME African Methodist Episcopal Church

amend amendment

Amer (1) America (2) American

AMG (Annapolis) *Maryland Gazette*

AMICUS National Library of Canada online database

AML Association for Mormon Letters

AMLCD Active Matrix—LCD

AMLS Master of Arts in Library Science

AMORC Ancient Mystical Order Rosae Crucis (Rosicrucians), 1342 Neagles Ave., San Jose, CA 95191

AMRAAM Advanced Medium-Range Air-to-Air Missile

AmRC Amistad Research Center, New Orleans, LA, ARC, Tilton Hall, Tulane University, 6823 St. Charles Ave., New Orleans, LA 70118

Ams Amsterdam

AMS American Ship

Amst assistant master

Amste Amsterdam, Netherlands

amt amount

AMtr assistant matron

AMVETS American Veterans of World War II, Korea and Vietnam,

AMVETS National Headquarters, 4647 Forbes Blvd., Lanham, MD 20706-4380

an (1) accession number (2) *annus, anno* (in the year)

a.n. above named

An Ann, Anne

AN (1) Anglo-Norman (2) Archives Nationales, Paris, France (3) Arapahoe Nation (4) Austria-Netherlands

Ana Anna

Anat Anatomy

ANB *American National Biography*, 24 vols. (New York: Oxford University Press)

anc (1) ancestor(s) (2) ancestral (3) ancestry

Anc Ancestry

anc ch ancestor chart

Anc Co ancient county (British)

Anc File Ancestral File (genealogical database in FamilySearch™)

Anc & Hon Ancient and Honorable Artillery Company of Massachusetts

And Andrew

AND Andorra

An Do/AnoDom *Anno Domini* (in the year of the Christian era)

Andr Andreas

Andr^w/And^w Andrew

ANep adopted nephew

Ang (1) Angur (2) Angus, Scotland

ANG American Newspaper Guild

Angl (1) Anglican (2) Anglicized

Angl/ANGL Anglesey, Wales

ANGU Angus, Great Britain

ANHA Anhalt

anie adopted niece

AniMap *AniMap* locality software (The Gold Bug, Alamo, CA)

Anl Annual Report

ann (1) annotated (2) annual (3) annum (4) annuity

Ann Annual, Annually

Anniv./anniv Anniversary

annl annual

annot annotated

annu/ annuit annuitant (has yearly fixed sum)

annul annulment

ano (1) annus (year) (2) another

ano/an year, as in "Ano 1683"

anon anonymous

ans answer

ANS Angus, Scotland (*see* Forfar, Forfarshire)

ANSRS Adoption Network for Search, Reunion, and Support

ant (1) antiquary (2) antonym

Ant (1) Anthon, Anthony, Anton (2) Antrim, Northern Ireland (3) Antsovlerberg

ANT Antigua, West Indies

ante (1) before, or prior to (2) in front, forward

Anthro Anthropology

Anthrop Anthropology

anti against

ANTI Antigua

antiq (1) antiquarian (2) antiquary (3) antiquities (4) antiquity

Antiq Antiquarian

Ant°/Ant^a Antonio/Antonia

Anul Annulment

anx annex

ao (1) Anno (year) (2) account of

AO (1) Archives of Ontario, Toronto, Ontario (2) Atlantic Ocean (3) Audit, Exchequer and Public Record Office, Kew, England

AO12, AO13 American Loyalists' Claims, 2 series, Public Record Office, Kew, Richmond, Surrey, England TW9 4DU

AOC Atlantic Ocean

AOF Ancient Order of Foresters

AOH Ancient Order of Hibernians

AOL America OnLine (commercial computer online service)

AOKMC Ancient Order of Knights of Mystic Chain

AONS Association of One-Name Studies

AOP American Order of Pioneers

Aôut August

AOUW Ancient Order of United Workmen

ap (1) a prefix meaning "son of" (2) appraiser (3) apprentice

Ap (1) Apostle (2) Apprentice

Ap/Apr/Aprill April (month) Abrill

AP (1) ancient parish (British) (2) Associated Press

apb archbishop

APB Archives de la Marine, Brest, France

apd (1) appealed (2) appearance docket (3) appointed (4) attending places of division

APDU Association of Public Data Users, Division of Business & Economic Research, University of New Orleans, New Orleans, LA 70148

APG Association of Professional Genealogists, P.O. Box 350998, Westminster, CO 80035-0998

APGI Association of Professional Genealogists in Ireland

APG-L Association of Professional Genealogists Electronic Chapter

APGQ *Association of Professional Genealogists Quarterly*, P.O. Box 350998, Westminster, CO 80035-0998

APH Association of Personal Historians

API Associated Press International

APJI Association for Protection of Jewish Immigrants

apk archives, packet

apl Appeal

APL Service historique de la Marine, Archives du Port de Lorient, Lorient, France

APLIC Association of Parliamentary Librarians in Canada

APM Assistant Provost Marshal

apmt appointment

APO Air Force Post Office, Army Post Office

APOLROD Association for the Preservation of Ontario's Land Registry Office Documents, 251 Second Street, Stouffville, Ontario L4A1B9

apoth apothecary

app (1) apparent (2) appendix (3) application (4) appointed (5) appraisement record (inventory) (6) apprentice (7) approach (8) appropriation (9) approximately

app blksmt apprentice blacksmith

appc apprentice

app carptr apprentice carpenter

app cbntmkr apprentice to cabinet maker

appd (1) appeared (2) appointed

App Div Appellate Division

app'dt appointed

append appendix

appl/applic (1) applied (2) application

Appl Applied

appls/applls appeals, as in law

Appop Appoplectic

app prntr apprentice printer

appr (1) appearance (2) appellor (3) appraisement (4) appraisal (5) apprentice

apprd (1) appeared (2) appraise

Approp Appropriation

approx approximately

Approx Approximate, Approximately

apprs appriser

appt (1) apparently (2) appointed (3) appointment

Appt Appointment

app't appointed

apptd/appted appointed

appur/appurts appurtenances

appwagnmkr apprentice to wagon maker

appx appendix

Apr April

APS American Philosophical Society, 104 South 5th Street, Philadelphia, PA 19106-3387

APSDS Association de personnel de services documentaires scolaires

APSECS Australasian and Pacific Society for Eighteenth-Century Studies

APSG Association for the Promotion of Scholarship in Genealogy, Ltd., 255 North 200 West, Salt Lake City, UT 84103-4545

apt appointed

apt(s) apartment(s)

APVA Association for the Preservation of Virginia Antiquities, 204 West Franklin Street, Richmond, VA 23220-5012

AQ *Ancestral Quest* (genealogy software program)

AQMD Assistant Quartermaster-General

aqs autograph quotation signed. Usually a verse or statement or a few bars of music written out and signed.

a quo from whom

ar record of administration

Ar Arthur

AR (1) *Alabama Review* (2) Annual Report (3) Appeal against Removal (4) AR (Anno Regni), the year of the reign of (5) Alien Registration

AR/Ark Arkansas

ARA/ARAB Arabia

Arab Arabia, Arabian, Arabic

ARAM Association of Records Management and Administration

arb arbitrator, arbitrate, arbitration

arc arcade

ARC American (National) Red Cross

ARC Archival Research Catalog (National Archives and Records Administration)

ARC Area Research Centers

ARC Automated Resource Center, Family History Library, 35 North West Temple Street, Salt Lake City, UT 84150 (no longer in use)

ArCat Archives Computer Catalog

arch (1) archaeological (2) architect (3) architecture (4) architectural (5) archives

Arch Archibald

Arch. Archbishop

Archaeol Archaeology

Archd Archdeaconry

Archeol Archaeological, Archeology

archit architectural

Archit Architectural, Architecture

Archiv (1) *Achiv für das Studium der Neueren Sprachen und Literaturen* (2) Archives

archt architect

ArcM Master of Architecture

ARCS Admiralty Raster Chart Service

Arfr Artificer

arg (1) argent, silver (heraldry) (2) argentum blue (a silver color)

Arg Argyllshire, Scotland

ARG/ARGE/Argt Argentina

ARGUS *ARGUS*, Marysville, Union Co. newspaper

ARGY/ARL Argyllshire, Great Britain

Argyll Argyll, Scotland

ArHQ *Arkansas Historical Quarterly*

ARI Automated Research Inc., 1160 South State St., Suite 220, Orem, UT 84097

Ariz/AZ Arizona

Ark Arkansas

Ark & Dove Society of the Ark and the Dove

ARL Argyll, Scotland

ARL Ancestry Reference Library (CD-ROM)

ARL *Ancestry Reference Library*, MyFamily.com, Inc., P.O. Box 990, Orem, UT 84059

ARL Association of Research Libraries, 21 Dupont Circle, Washington, DC 20036

Arm/Armagh Armagh, Ireland

ARM/ARME Armenia

ARMA Association of Records Managers and Administrators

Armr Armorer

Armst Armstadt

Arnold James N. Arnold, *Vital Record of Rhode Island, 1636-1850*

ARP Applied Research Programme

ARPA Advanced Research Project Agency (Department of Defense)

arprt airport

arr (1) arranged (2) arrangement (3) arrival (4) arrived

AR REC Archive Records (family group record in the Archive Section of the Family Group Records Collection, Family and Church History Department, Salt Lake City, UT)

ARR *Anno Regina Register*

ARRC Allied Command Europe Rapid Reaction Corps

arrv arrived

ARS Automated Records System (General Land Office), GLO Records Access Staff, Bureau of Land Management, Eastern States, 7450 Boston Boulevard, Springfield, VA 22153-3121

arsl arsenal

art article

art/Art/artill/arty/artl artillery

Arth/Art'/Arth' Arthur

arti/artif artificer

Artl Artillery

ArUS Arrived in the United States

Arvl Arrival

ARVN Army of Republic of Vietnam

a/s aux (bons) soins (de)

As Asian, Asia, Asiatic

AS (1) Adopted Son (2) Alsase, France (3) Anglo-Saxon (4) *anno salutis* (in the year of salvation) (5) at Sea (6) Azores

AS/ASM American Samoa

ASA Advertising Standards Authority (of England)

A-Sbg Aabenraa, Sonderborg

ASC (1) Army Service Corps (2) Army Survivor's Certificate (3) Isle of Ascension (4) *The Anglo-Saxon Chronicle*

ASCAP American Society of Composers, Authors, and Writers

ASCII American Standard Code for Information Interchange (a common communications format for personal computers)

AscM assistant schoolmaster/mistress

ASEA At Sea

Aser agricultural servant

ASF Archivio di Stato, Florence, Italy

ASF American Sephardi Federation, 305 Seventh Ave., New York, NY 10001

ASFHS Association of Scottish Family History Societies

ASG American Society of Genealogists, P.O. Box 1515, Derry, NH 03038-1515

ASGR Association of Germans from Russia

ASGRA Association of Scottish Genealogists and Record Agents, P.O. Box 174, Edinburgh, Scotland EH35QZ

13

ASGS Arizona State Genealogical Society, P.O. Box 42075, Tucson, AZ 85733-2075

ASHM American Swedish Historical Museum

ASI (1) Adopted Sister (2) Asia

ASIA Asia

ASJA *American Society of Journalists and Authors*

asm assignment

Asmb (1) assemblies (2) assembly

asmblr assembler

ASN Archivio di Stato, Naples

Asn Association

A-Sndr Aaberaa, Denmark

Asnmt Assignment

asoc associate

ASon adopted son

asr assessor

ASRAAM Advanced Short-Range Air-to-Air Missile

assd assigned

assgn (1) assign (2) assignee

assist/asst assistant

assn/assoc/assocn association

asso/assoc (1) associate (2) association (3) associé(e)

Asso Associates

Assoc Associate

AssocSc Associate in Science

Asso.Pres.Ch Associated Presbyterian Church

asst/Asst assistant

Ass't Q.M. General Assistant to Quarter Master

assy assembly

ASTED Association des sciences et des techniques de la documentation, 3414, avenue du parc, Suite 202, Montréal, Québec, Canada H2X 2H5

Astl Australia

ast mrshll assistant marshal

Astron Astronomy

Astrophys Astrophysical, Astrophysics

ast srvyor assistant surveyor

A Sus Anna Susanna

ASV Archivio di Stato, Venice, Italy

ASW Anti-Submarine Warfare

at (1) archives, testamentary record (2) attendant (3) shows that the person named was "at" the location given during the year shown

At Attendant

A-tapes Audio tapes

atba able to bear arms

ATBL American Trust for the British Library (London)

Atch assistant teacher

ATG Applied Technology Gallery (GENTECH, etc.)

Athl Athletic

Atl Atlantic Ocean

at lge at large

Atmos Atmospheric

atndt attendant

a&tr administration and testamentary record

ATS Aviation Training Ship

ATS at Sea

att (1) attached, attached to (2) attest

att/atty attorney

attn attention

Attr Attribute

attt/attachmt/attachm attachment, as in law

attrib attributed to

ATTU Atlantic To The Urals

atty attorney

ATut assistant tutor

au (1) aunt (2) author (3) gold

AU (1) Aunt (2) Austria

auc *ab urbe condita* (from the founding of the city, i.e., Rome, in 753 B.C.)

AUC Atlantic Union College

aud/Aud auditor

Audiol Audiology

Aug August, Augustus, Augustine

Aug/Augs/Augst/Ag August

AUH Austria Hungary

AUM Ancient Order of Mysteries – Masonic Order

AunL aunt-in-law

AUP Acceptable Use Policy

AUS Arm of the United States

AUS/Aust/Austr/OES Austria

AUS/AUSL/Austl/AUT Australia

Austin John Osborne Austin, *The Genealogical Dictionary of Rhode Island*

Aut Austria

AUT Australia

auth authorized

auto autobiography

aux auxiliary

Aux Sons of Union Auxiliary to Sons of Union Veterans of the Civil War

av (1) *annos vixit* (he lived [so many] years) (2) availability

av/aver average

a/v *ad valorem* (tax on goods)

Av/Ave avenue

AV Audiovisual, Audiovisual Materials

AV Ancestry View

AV Appeal against vagrancy

ava/us grandmother/father

avail available

ave avenue

Ave Avenue

AVGS Antelope Valley Genealogical Society, P.O. Box 1049, Lancaster, CA 93584-1049

AVI Audio Video Interleaved (Microsoft)

Aviat Aviation

AVLB Armoured Vehicle Launcher Bridge

Avr April

AW Arizona and the West

awc admon (letters of administration) with will and codicil annexed

AWC Army Widow's Certificate

AWD Ancestry Weekly Digest

AWE Atomic Weapons Establishment

AWmn almswoman

AWOL absent without official leave

AWT *Ancestry World Tree* (Ancestry.com)

Ayr/AYR Ayrshire, Scotland

AYR Ayr, Scotland

Az/az azure (a blue color) (heraldry)

AzGAB Arizona Genealogical Advisory Board, P.O. Box 5641, Mesa, AZ 85211-5641

AzHS/AHS Arizona Pioneers Historical Society, 949 East Second Street, Tucson, AZ 85719

AzMBL Arizona Mesa Branch Genealogical Library, Mesa, AZ (Family History Center)

AZO/ AZOR Azores

Aztec Club Aztec Club of 1847

B

b (1) bachelor (2) baptism, baptême (French) (3) birth (4) book (5) born (6) bride (7) brother (8) on maps and charts: Bay or Bayou (9) burial

b. before

B (1) Baptist (2) Black (3) Born (4) British (language) (5) Brother (6) Burial Register (7) Burials

ba Bastardy

ba/bach bachelor

ba/bap/bapt baptized

Ba (1) Bastard (2) Bavaria, Germany

BA (1) Bachelor of Arts (2) Bahamas (3) Bastard (4) Bastardy Allegation (5) Bavaria (6) Boston Athenaeum

BAAF British Agencies for Adoption and Fostering, 11 Southwark Street, London, England SE1 1RQ

Bab/Babs Barbara

baby baby

Bacc Baccalaureate

bach/bachr bachelor

BACSA British Association for Cemeteries in South Asia

Bad/BAD/BADE Baden

BAE Bureau of American Ethnology

bag baggage

BAg/BAgr Bachelor of Agriculture

BAH/BAHA Bahamas

BAI Bahama Islands

Bai Baierne/Bairn/Baier

BaiD bailiff's daughter

Baier Baiern

Bail bailiff

Bair (*see* Bai)

BaiS bailiff's son

BaiW bailiff's wife

bakr baker

bal balance

bal/ball an account balance

Balth Balthasar

BAM British America

Ban (1) Banel (2) Bangor, Bantu

BAN Banffshire, Scotland

BAN/BANF Banff, Scotland

B and S Bargain and Sale

bank cashr cashier of the Alton Bank

bank intrp interpreter in bank

bank tellr teller in bank

bap/bp baptize/d

Bapl Baptism (LDS)

Bapm Baptism

Bapt/bapt (1) Baptist (2) baptized

bar (1) baron (2) baroness (3) bartender (4) boar

Bar (1) Barisha (2) Bartender (3) Baron, Baroness

BAr/BArch Bachelor of Architecture

BAR/BARB Barbados

BarA bar assistant

Barb/Barb·/Barbie Barbara

bark bar keeper

Barm Bar Mitzvah

BarM barmaid, barman

Baronial Ord Baronial Order of Magna Charter

bart/bt baronet

Bart Bartholemew

Bart^me Bartomone

BarW barwoman

Bas bastard

BASc Bachelor of Applied Science

Basm Bas Mitzvah

Bat Battery (military regiment)

BAT Batavia

batch bachelor

batln/bat/batt battalion

BATSUB British Army Training Support Unit Belize

BatM bath man

batt battery

BAUS Bingham Association in the United States

Baut·, B^t Bautista

Bautzn Bautzen, Saxony

Bav/Ger/Bava Bavaria, Germany

BAV/BAVA Bavaria (Bayern)

Bay Bayden

BB (1) Bail Bond (2) Barbados (3) Bastardy Bond

b/b Buried beside

BBA Bachelor of Business Administration

BBC British Broadcasting Corporation

BBCS Bulletin of the Board of Celtic Studies

Bbd Bombardier

BBI *British Biographical Index*

Bbl Bible

bbl(s) barrel(s)

B Boy bound boy

BBS Blairs' Book Service, 1661 Strine Drive, McLean, VA 22101

BBS Bulletin Board System; Bulletin Board Service (users exchange files and leave messages)

Bc Bachelor

BC/B.C. (1) bachelor (2) Bachelor of Chemistry (3) Bail Court (4) Bas-Canada (i.e., Lower Canada or Québec) and British Columbia, Canada in 1881, 1891, and 1901 (5) Becker College (6) before Christ (7) Bible Church (8) Borough Council (9) British Columbia, Canada (10) Vancouver Island, Canada

BCC Bellevue Community College, 3000 Landerholm Circle, Bellevue, WA 98007

BCC British Council of Churches (*see* CCBI)

BCC/UCF Brevard Community College, University of Central Florida, 1519 Clearlake Rd., Cocoa, FL 32922-6597

BCCFA British Columbia Cemetery Finding Aid (Canada)

BCD (1) binary code decimal (2) Bristol County, Massachusetts, Deeds

BCE (1) Bachelor of Chemical Engineering (2) Bachelor of Civil Engineering (3) before the Christian Era (4) before the common era

b/cer birth certificate

BCG® Board for Certification of Genealogists®, P.O. Box 14291, Washington, DC 20044

BCGS British Columbia Genealogical Society, P.O. Box 88054, Lansdowne Mall, Richmond, BC, Canada V6X3T6

bch beach

Bch Bachelor of Surgery

BCHS Bucks County Historical Society, 84 South Pine Street, Doylestown, PA 18901-4999

BCL Bachelor of Civil Law

BCMS Bible Churchmen's Missionary Society

bd (1) birth date (2) board (3) boarder (4) bond (5) binding, bound (6) buried

Bd (1) Baden, Germany (2) Bedfordshire, England (3) Boarder

BD Bachelor of Divinity

Bda. Arch. Bermuda Archives, Hamilton, Bermuda

Bdau boarder's daughter

bde brigade

BDF Bedfordshire, England

bdl bundle

Bdle beadle

BDN Baden

bds (1) beds (2) boards

BDS Bachelor of Dental Surgery

bdt birthdate(s)

Bdx Bourdeaux

Bdy Broadway

BE (1) Bastardy Examination (2) Belgium

BE/BEd (1) Bachelor of Education (2) Bachelor of Engineering

Bea/Beattie/Beatty Beatrice

Beat Beatrice

BEA Bureau of Economic Analysis

bec became

BECPL Buffalo and Erie County Public Library, 1 Lafayette Square, Buffalo, NY 14203

BEDF/Beds (1) Bedford, England (2) Bedfordshire, England

BEE Bachelor of Electrical Engineering

bef before

BEF British Expeditionary Force(s)

beh beheaded

Behav Behavioral

BeHLUM Bentley Historical Library, University of Michigan, 1150 Beal Ave., Ann Arbor, MI 48109-2113

Bei Beirn/Biern/Beiyens

BEK Berkshire, England

bel believed

Bel/BEL/Belg Belgium

Bel/Bell/Belf Belfast, Ireland

Bell/Bella/Belle Arabella, Isabella

Ben Benjamin

Bened Benedikt, Benedict

BENG Bengal

Benj/Benjᵃ/Benjⁿ/Benjᵐ Benjamin

BEO Board of Economic Operation

beq (1) bequeathed (2) bequest

Ber (1) Berlin/Bernstadt (2) Bermuda (3) Berne (4) Berwickshire, Scotland

BerG Berlin, Germany

Bergen Bergen, Norway

Behav Behavior, Behavioral

BERK/Berks Berkshire (England)

Berl/Berli Berlin

BERM/Berm Bermuda

Berndo Bernardo

Bert Albert, Bertram, Herbert, Hubert, Robert

Bertie/Berty Albert/a, Bertha, Herbert, Robert/a

Berw Berwick, Scotland

BER Bermuda

BERW Berwick, Great Britain

bet/betw between

Bev Beverly

BEW (1) Berwickshire (2) Berwick, Scotland

Bey Beyens

bf (1) before, such as before 1850 (2) black female (3) boldface type

BF (1) Bachelor of Finance (2) Bachelor of Forestry

BFA Bachelor of Fine Arts

B&FUA British and Foreign Unitarian Association

bg big

BG (1) Bugler (2) burial grounds (3) Burg

Bgd Brigadier

BgdMaj Brigade Major

BGen Brigadier General

bgemn baggageman

Bgg/Mstr Baggage Master

B Girl bound girl

BGL Branch Genealogical Library of The Church of Jesus Christ of Latter-day Saints (known as Family History Center)

bglr bugler

BGMI *Biography and Genealogy Master Index* (Detroit: Gale Research Co., 1975-)

BGS Buckinghamshire Genealogical Society, Mrs. Eve McLaughlin, Varneys, Rudds Lane, Haddenham, Bucks, England HP17 8JP

BGS Bachelor of General Studies

BGSU Center for Archival Collections, Bowling Green State University, Bowling Green, OH

b.h. boarding house

BH (1) Bohemia (Böhmen) (2) Board of Health

BHC British High Commission

BHC Burton Historical Collection, Detroit Public Library, 5201 Woodward Ave., Detroit, MI 48202

Bhlm Bornholm, Denmark

BHM *Bangor Historical Magazine*

BHN British Honduras

bhpric Bishopric

BHR *Business History Review*

BHS Bahamas

BHS Beverly Historical Society, 117 Cabot Street, Beverly, MA 01201

BHU/Bhu Bhutan

BI British Isles

Bia Bian

BIA Bureau of Indian Affairs

Bib (1) Bible (2) Biblical

bibl *bibliotheca* (library)

bibl/bibliog bibliography, bibliographer, bibliographical

Bibliog/Bibliogr Bibliography

Bic Bickerburg

BIC born in the covenant (LDS)

Bicent Bicentennial

BIDC Business/Industry Data Center

Biddy Bridget

bien biennial

Biera Bieran

Biern Bierne/Bierren

BIFHS British Isles Family History Society

BIFHSGO British Isles Family History Society of Greater Ottawa

BIGWILL British Isles Genealogical Society of Wisconsin and Illinois

BIGHR British Institute of Genealogy and Historical Research

BIGR *British Isles Genealogical Register* (project of the Federation of Family History Societies)

BIGRA British Isles Genealogical Research Association

BIGWILL British Interest Group of Wisconsin and Illinois

BIHR *Bulletin of the Institute of Historical Research* (British)

Bil Bilafelt

b-i-l brother-in-law

Bill/Billie/Billy William

Bills Colic Billious Colic

Bills Fev. Billious Fever

bi-m every two months

bio/biog/biogr (1) biographical (2) biography

Bio biographical sketch of a person's life

Biochem Biochemical, Biochemistry

biog biography, biographer, biographical

Biog biographical, biographically, biography

biol (1) biological (2) biologist (3) biology

Biol Biological, Biology

Biomed Biomedical

Biophys Biophysics

Bir (1) Birmingham (2) Biron

BIR birth

BIRDIE British Isles Regional Display of IGI Extracts

Birt/BIRT birth

BIS Bachelor of Independent Studies

bish bishop

BITNET because it's time network

bi-w biweekly

BJ Bachelor of Journalism

BJS Bureau of Justice Statistics

bk/bks (1) bank (2) barracks (3) block (4) book(s) (5) brook

Bk (1) Black (of African American descent) (2) Book (3) Buckinghamshire, England

BK *Brother's Keeper* (genealogy software program)

bkbndr bookbinder

Bklyn Brooklyn

BKM Buckinghamshire, England

Bkmobile Bookmobile

bkpr bookkeeper

Bkrpt Bankruptcy

bksm blacksmith

bk statnry book and stationery

BKW *Brother's Keeper for Windows* (genealogy software program)

Bl (1) British Library (2) Brother-in-law

BL (1) Bachelor of Law (2) Belgium (3) British Library, London, England (4) brother-in-law

Blaw by law

Bldg Building

bldg(s)/blg building(s)

bldr builder

Blek Blekinge, Sweden

blf bluff

BLG Belgium

BLit(t) (1) Bachelor of Letters (2) Bachelor of Literature

blk (1) black (2) block

blksmith/Blk Smth blacksmith

BLM Bureau of Land Management, U.S. Department of the Interior, Eastern States Office, 7450 Boston Blvd., Springfield, VA 22153. *See also* GLO

BLN Bounty Land Number

bl reg bounty land rejected

blrmkr boilermaker

BLS (1) Bachelor of Library Sciences (2) Bureau of Labor Statistics

Blsl Blessing (LDS)

bltd billeted

Blu Blumberg

Blvd Boulevard

BLW/BLWT Bounty Land Warrant (a right to free land in the Public Domain)

bm (1) *beatae memoriae* (of blessed memory) (2) bi-monthly (3) black males (4) bondsman

BM (1) Bachelor of Medicine (2) Bench Mark used in surveying land (3) Bermuda (4) Brigade Major (5) British Museum

BMA Bureau of Missing Ancestors (Everton Publishers, Logan, UT)

BMAA Baptist Missionary Association of America

BMan (1) bar manager (2) bondsman

BMD births, marriages, deaths

BMD Ballistic Missile Defence

bmdr bombardier

bmo business machine operator

Bmot boarder's mother

BMP Bit-mapped graphics format (Windows Bitmap)

BMR British Mission Registers (LDS)

BMS Boston Marine Society, Charleston Navy Yard, Boston, MA 02129

BMSGH Birmingham and Midland Society for Genealogy and Heraldry

bmt basement

BMus Bachelor of Music

bn birth

Bn (1) Battalion (2) births

BN Baden, Germany

BNA British North America

bnd (1) bend (2) bond (marriage)

bndsmn bondsman

Bnf Banffshire, Scotland

BNR Body Not Recovered

Bnq Bibliotheque nationale du Québec

bns banns (marriage)

bo (1) Boarder (2) born (3) bottom (4) bought (5) bound

b/o brother of

Bo (1) Boarder (2) Bound

BO (1) as found in land records of colonial period, probably means British Oak or Bur Oak, inferred from WO meaning White Oak (2) Bohemia

boat ngner engineer on boat

Bodl. Libr. Bodleian Library, Oxford England; Bodleian Library, Broad Street, Oxford, England OXI 3BG

Boe Boehm/Boern

Boh/Bohe Bohemia

Bohme Bohmen/Bahmen/Böhmen

Bol Bolivar, Bolvia

BOL Bolivia

Bom Bombay (India)

bona goods, chattels, moveable property

boot boots

bor borough

BOR (1) Borough (2) Island of Borneo

BorB boarder's brother

BorC boarder's child

Bord boarder/boardress

BorD boarder's daughter

BorG boarder's grandson

BorN boarder's niece

BORO Borough

BorS boarder's son

BorW boarder's wife

Bos/Carp Boss Carpenter

Bosn Boatswain

BOSN Bosnia

bot bought

Bot Botany

BotB boat boy

BotM boatman

botp both of this parish

BoU Boston University, Boston, MA

boul boulevard

boy boy

Boyds *Boyd's Marriage Index*

bp (1) baptized (2) before the present (3) birthplace (4) bishop

Bp Bishop

BP Black Polls

BPd/BPe Bachelor of Pedagogy

BPE Bachelor of Physical Education

BPh/BPhil Bachelor of Philosophy

bpl birthplace

BPL Boston Public Library, 700 Boylston Street, Copley Square, Boston MA 02117

BPOE Benevolent and Protective Order of Elks

BPOEW Benevolent and Protective Order of Elks of the World

BPP British Parliamentary Paper

bps bits per second (computer term)

bpt baptized

Bpt/Mins Baptist Minister

bq *bene quiescat* (may he rest well)

BR90 Bridging for the Nineties

br brought

br/bro brother

Br (1) Branch (2) Britain (3) British

BR (1) Book of Remembrance (2) Branch (3) Brazil (4) Bremen, Germany (5) British (6) British Rail (7) Bromskirchen (8) Brother

Bra Bradenburg/Braunsweig

BRA/Braz Brazil

BRA British Record Association

Brain Fev Brain Fever

Brain Inf Brain Infirmation or Inflamation

BraL Braslaw

BRAN/Brand Brandenburg

Brassfnshr brass finisher

BRAZ (1) Brazil (2) Brazilian

BRBL Beinecke Rare Book and Manuscript Library, Yale University, New Haven, CT 06520

BRC (1) Boston Record Commissioners (2) British Channel

brd buried

BRD Germany (1991)

Brdbg Brandenburg, Prussia

brdng hs boarding house

Bre (1) Brecknockshire, Wales (2) Breman

Bre/BREC (1) Brecknock, Wales (2) Brecon, Great Britain

BRE (1) Bachelor of Religious Education (2) Breconshire (3) Bremen

Brec Bible record

Breme/BREM Bremen

Brev Brevet

brew brewer

brg (1) bridge (2) burg

BRG British Guiana

BrHCDPL Burton Historical Collection, Detroit Public Library, Detroit, MI

bri bridge

BRI British East Indies

brick brnr brick burner

Brid Bridget

Brid^a Brigida

BriE Bristol, England

Brig (1) Brigade (2) Brigadier

Brig Gen Brigadier General

Brig Insp Brigadier Inspector

Brig Q.M. Brigadier Quarter Master

br-in-l brother-in-law

Brio Brion/Briosson

Bris Brisen

Brisb Brisbane

Brist Bristol

Brit. (1) Britain (2) British (3) Briton (4) Great Britain

Brit Col British Columbia, Canada

Brit. Mus. British Museum, London, England

Brit Ref British Reference

brk brook

Brk Berkshire, England

brklyr bricklayer

brkmn brakeman

BrLD brother-in-law's daughter

BrLS brother-in-law's son

BrLW brother-in-law's wife

Brm Bermby

BRM Business Reply Mail

BRN born

bro brother(s)

br/o brother of

Bro (1) Bromane (2) Brother

Broadcast Broadcasting

BroD brother's daughter

BroL/bro-i-l/bro-il brother-in-law

bro/o brother of

BroR brother in religion

bros/bro(s) brothers

BroS brother's son

BroW brother's wife

BRP British Province

BRS Belarus (Belorussia)

BRS British Record Society

BrSi boarder's sister

Bru/Brun/Bruns/Brunsw Brunswick (Braunschweig), Germany

BRU Brunei

Brum Birmingham

Brunsw Brunswick

Brvt Brevet

Bryn Bryan Public Library, 107 East High Street, Bryan, OH 43506

bs Blacksmith

bs/B/S bill of sale

Bs Stllr Boss Stiller

BS (1) Bachelor of Science (2) Bahamas (3) British Standard

BSA Boy Scouts of America

BSA Bukovina Society of the Americas

BSAg Bachelor of Science in Agriculture

BSBA Bachelor of Science in Business Administration

BSc Bachelor of Science

BSch boarding scholar

BSE Bachelor of Science in Engineering

BSEd Bachelor of Science in Education

Bser bakery servant

bshp bishop

bshp tr bishop's transcript(s)

Bskd Buskerud, Norway

BSL Bachelor of Science in Law

BSN Bachelor of Science in Nursing

BSnL boarder's sister-in-law

BSPI *Bayou State Periodical Index*

Bt (1) Baronet (2) Beat (3) Brevet

BT (1) Bishop's Transcript(s) (England) (2) Board of Trade, Public Record Office, Kew, England

BT/BTh/B Theology Bachelor of Theology

BTA British Tourist Authority (formerly British Travel Association)

btch butcher

Bte Buteshire, Scotland

btlr butler

BtlS butler's son

BtlW butler's wife

btm bottom

Btm Boatman

Btry/Bttry/Bty Battery (army unit)

BT(s) Bishop's Transcript(s)

Btss Baronetess

bttn battalion

BTU British thermal unit(s)

btw (1) bulletin board (computer) abbreviation (2) between (3) by the way

btwn between

bu (1) burial (2) buried (3) bushel

Bu butler

BU Baptist Union of Great Britain and Ireland

BUCH Buchau

Buck/Bucks/BUK Buckinghamshire, England

BUD Budapest

Buf Buffalo, NY

BUGB Baptist Union of Great Britain

bul/bull bulletin

BUL/BULG Bulgaria

Bull. AASLH *Bulletin of the American Association for State and Local History*

Bulletin *Genealogical Forum of Oregon quarterly*, 2130 SW 5th Avenue, Suite 200, Portland, OR 97201-4934

Bunty Barbara

BUP British United Press

BUPNS *Bulletin of the Ulster Place-Name Society*

bur (1) bureau (2) burial (3) buried

BUR/BURM Burma

Bur Bureau

Bur Gr burying ground

Buri Burial

Burkh Burkhard, Burkhart

Bur Plot burial plot

Bürg Bürger, citizen

burs bursar

bus/busn business

Bus Business

BUS Business Services

BUT Bute, Scotland

BUT Buteshire

Bute/BUTE Bute, Scotland

bv *beide von* (both from)

BV Bavaria

BVI British Virgin Islands

BVM Blessed Virgin Mary

BVR Bureau of Vital Records

BVRHS Bureau of Vital Records and Health Statistics

Bvt Brevet

bw bi-weekly

b/w black and white

BW Brunswick

BWI British West Indies

Bwid brother's widow

BWO Books We Own

bx box (archival)

Bx Beatrix

Bye Byern

byp bypass

Byr (1) Byrne/Byren/Byern/Bayern (2) Byron/B'yror

byu bayou

BYU Brigham Young University, Provo, UT 84602

C

c/ca. *circa* (about, frequently used before an uncertain or approximate date, around), e.g., c. 1790 or ca. 1790.

C/c (1) Baptisms (2) Cambridgeshire, England (3) came to the area shown (4) case number (5) Celtic (6) cemetery record (7) centigrade (8) century (9) Chancery (10) chapter (in law citations) (11) child (12) christened (13) Christening Register (14) *circa* (about) (15) Colored (16) Contintental Census (17) controlled extraction (LDS) (18) copyright (19) Corporal (20) cousin (21) indicates christenings (or births) extracted in Controlled Extraction Program of the LDS Church (22) name cleared for LDS temple (23) 1890 Union pension census (24) cousin (25) means man served in Confederate Army

C./Ct. court

c. baptized

C1 First Corporal

C2 Second Corporal

C3 Third Corporal

C4 Fourth Corporal

C5 Fifth Corporal

C6 Sixth Corporal

C7 Seventh Corporal

C8 Eighth Corporal

C21 Command, Control and Intelligence

ca. (1) *circa* (approximately) (2) about

Ca/Can Canada

CA (1) Central America (2) Chartered Accountant (3) Coast Artillery (4) Commonwealth Award (Virginia Genealogical Society) (5) Court of Appeals

CA Church Archives, Historical Department of The Church of Jesus Christ of Latter-day Saints, 50 East North Temple, Salt Lake City, UT 84150

CA/Ca/Calif California

CAA Civil Aviation Authority

C of A Coat of Arms

CaAR California State Archives, 1020 "O" Street, Sacramento, CA 95814

cabtmkr cabinetmaker

CAC Center for Archival Collections, Bowling Green State University, Jerome Library, Bowling Green, OH 43403-0175

CACC Council for the Accreditation of Correspondence Colleges (British)

Cache Cache Genealogical Library, Logan, UT

CAD Canadian dollars

CAD Certificate of Arrival Division, Ellis Island

cadet cadet

CAE Caenarvonshire, Wales

CAEDM Computer Aided Engineering Design and Manufacturing

CAER/Caerns Caernarvon, Wales

CAGG Computer-Assisted Genealogy Group

CAI/CAIT/Caith Caithness, Scotland

CAI (1) Caithnesshire (2) Canary Islands

CAILS Certified American Indian Lineage Specialist (Board for Certification of Genealogists, P.O. Box 14291, Washington, DC 20044). *See* CLS

cal calculated (date)

Cal (1) California (2) calendar

calc calculated

Calg Calgary, Canada

CALG Certified American Lineage Genealogist

Calif California

Calif Pioneers Society of California Pioneers, The Alice Phelan Sullivan Library and Archives, 300 4th Street, San Francisco, CA 94107-1272

CALS Certified American Lineage Specialist (Board for Certification of Genealogists, P.O. Box 14291, Washington, DC 20044). Now known as Certified Lineage Specialist[SM] (CLS).

CALUPL Council of Administrators of Large Urban Public Libraries (Canada)

Calv (1) calvary (2) Calvin

CAM/Camb/Cambs Cambridgeshire, England

CAM Central America

Camb/Cambs (1) Cambridge, England (2) Cambridgeshire

CAME Central America

CAMLS Cleveland Area Metropolitan Library System (Cleveland, Ohio), 20600 Chagrin Blvd., Ste 500, Shaker Heights, OH 44122-5334

campn campaign

Can Canada, Canadian

CAN canceled

CAN/CANA (1) Canada (2) Canadian

Cana Canada

CanaW Canada West

cand candidate

Can$ Canadian dollar

CanP Canadian Press

Cantab Cantabrigiensis (of Cambridge)

CAO (1) Chief Administrative Officer (2) Conference of Administrative Officers

cap (1) capital (2) capitalized

cap/capt/capt[n]**/Capt** Captain (military)

Cap (1) Cape Britton (2) Capital (3) Captain

CAP (1) Cape Colony (2) Catalog of American Portraits

CAP/CAPE Cape of Good Hope

CAPG Colorado Chapter, Association of Professional Genealogists, P.O. Box 40817, Denver, CO 80204-0817

capt (1) captive (2) captured

Capt Captain

CaptLt Captain Lieutenant

Car Charles

Car/CAR Carlow, Republic of Ireland

CAR Caribbean

CAR Children of the American Revolution

CarC care child

card carder

Card Cardiganshire, Wales

CARD/Cards Cardigan, Wales

CARI Caribbean Islands

CARL Canadian Association of Research Libraries

CARN County Archives Research Network (British)

Carls Carlsruhe (Karlsruhe)

Carm Carmarthenshire, Wales

CARM/Carms Carmarthen, Wales

Carn Carnarvonshire

CARN County Archives Research Network (British)

Caro/Carol Carolina

carp/carpt carpenter

carpt jonr carpenter & joiner

carr carriage

carr drvr carriage driver

carr mkr carriage maker

carr trmr carriage trimmer

cart carter

Carvan Carvan, Ireland

Cas Cassel (Kassel)

CAS California African-American Society

cash cashier

casl casual

CaSL/CSL California State Library, Sacramento, CA Library and Courts Building, 914 Capitol Mall, Sacramento, CA 95814

CASLIS Canadian Association of Special Libraries and Information Services

CaSlSu California State Library, Sutro, CA

CASOM Conventionally-Armed Stand-Off Missile

Casp Kaspar, Caspar

Cast Caste

CAST Center for Applied Special Technology

cat (1) catalog (2) catalogue

Cat (1) Cataloging Librarian (2) Catalogs

cath cathedral

Cath (1) Catharina (2) Catharine (3) Catherine (4) Catholic (5) Katharina

Cath/Cathie/Cathy Catherine, Katherine

cath bshp Catholic Bishop

cathclergy Catholic clergyman

Cathⁿ Cathrine, Cathryn

cathpriest Catholic Priest

CATNYP Catalog of the New York Public Library, New York, NY

Catt Cattaraugus County, NY

Caus Cause

cav. Cavalry (military regiment)

Cav Cavan, Republic of Ireland

Cawel Cawell

Cay Cayuga

cb (1) chain bearer (2) county borough

Cb Cuba

CB (1) Bachelor of Surgery (2) Christenings & Burials (3) Color Bearer (4) Companion of the Order of the Bath (5) Court Baron (England)

CBA Council for British Archaeology

CBDE Chemical and Biological Defence

CBE Commander of the Order of the British Empire

Cbern Canton Berne, Switzerland

CBI China, Burma, India

CBIL Computer Based Instruction Lab

CBKA Commander Benevolent Knights Association

CBL C. Belles

Cbnt Mkr Cabinet Maker

Cboy cart boy

CBT Computer-based training

cc (1) carbon copy (2) category codes (3) county census (4) cubic centimeters

CC (1) chain carrier (2) Clerk of Court (3) Community College (4) Company Commander (5) Country Club (6) County Clerk (7) County Commissioner (8) county coordinator (USGenWeb Project) (9) County Court

C of C (1) Chamber of Commerce (2) Community of Christ (formerly RLDS)

CCAP Circuit Court Automation Program

CCAPG Colorado Chapter, Association of Professional Genealogists (APG), 19341 Knotty Pine Way, Monument, CO 80132-9438

CCAT Center for Computer Analysis of Texts (University of Pennsylvania)

CCBI Council of Churches for Britain and Ireland Inter-Church House, 35–41 Lower Marsh, London, England SE1 7RL

CCC (1) Civilian Conservation Corps (2) Clerk of the County Court (3) Copyright Clearance Center (4) Chapman County Codes (British)

CCCGS Contra Costa County Genealogical Society, P.O. Box 910, Concord, CA 94522

CCCO Central Committee for Conscientious Objectors

CCD (1) census county divisions (2) Computer Council of Dallas, TX (3) Charged Coupled Device

CCEL Christian Classics Ethereal Library

CCF Collections Control Facility (Library of Congress)

CCG Connecticut Coordinated Genesearch, P.O. Box 757, Watertown, CT 06795

CCGS Chautauqua County Genealogical Society, P.O. Box 404, Fredonia, NY 14063

CCGS Clark County Genealogical Society, P.O. Box 2728, Vancouver, WA 98668-2728

CCGS Coctaw County Genealogical Society, P.O. Box 1056, Hugo, OK 74743

CCGS Colorado Council of Genealogical Societies, P.O. Box 24379, Denver, CO 80224-0379

CchD coachman's daughter

CChem Chartered Chemist

Cchm coachman

CchS coachman's son

CchW coachman's wife

CCN *Century Cyclopedia of Names*

CCNGS Clark County Nevada Genealogical Society, P.O. Box 1929, Las Vegas, NV 89125-1929

CCP Court of Common Pleas

CCPL Cuyahoga County Public Library, 2111 Snow Road, Parma, OH 44134-2792

CCRA Certified Clinical Research Assistant

CCTAS Crusaders–Catholic Total Abstinence Society

cd (1) civil docket (2) Contrary to the Discipline (Quaker)

CD (1) Canada (2) compact disc, i.e., CD-ROM

Cda Canada

CDA Colonial Dames of America

CDA Centre for Defence Analysis

CDEC Combined Document Exploitation Center

CDF Channel Definition Format

CDIB Certified Degree of Indian Blood

CDIC Combat Data Information Center

CDL California Digital Library

cdn canadien

cdne canadienne

CDP census designated place

Cdr Commander

CD-R compact disc – recordable

Cdre Commodore

CD-ROM compact disc, read only memory

CD-RW compact disc – recordable rewritable

CD XVII Colonial Dames of the Seventeenth Century

CDV *carte de Visite* (1800s photo)

CE (1) Canada East (i.e., Canada-East or Québec) (2) Caveat Emptor (3) Central America (4) Central Europe (5) Chief of Engineers (6) Christian Era (7) church extension (8) Church Elder (9) Church of England (10) Civil Engineer (11) common era

C of E Church of England

CEB Census Enumeration Book

CEF Canadian Expeditionary Force

CEGEP College d'Enseignement General et Professional

cem/Cem cemetery

CEM Central America

Ceme Cemetery

Cem Rec cemetery record, such as burial book or card file

cen/cens census

CEng Chartered Engineer

cent (1) centennial (2) centigrade (3) centimeter (4) central (5) century

Cent Central

CEO Chief Executive Officer

cer/cert (1) certain (2) certificate(s) (3) certified (4) certify

Cest Cheshire, England

CEU Continuing Education Unit(s)

CEY/CEYL Ceylon, Sri Lanka

cf (1) cardboard file box (2) *confer* (compare)

CF (1) Connecticut Firelands (2) Chaplain to the Forces

CFA Canadian Field Artillery

CFAR Church Unit Checking Account (LDS Family History Center term)

CFB Canadian Forces Base

CFE Conventional Armed Forces in Europe

CFGFHS Canadian Federation of Genealogical and Family History Societies

CFHG Center for Family History and Genealogy, Brigham Young University, Provo, UT 84602

CFI *Computer File Index* (now known as *International Genealogical Index* and the *Ordinance Index*, part of FamilySearch™)

CFL (1) Consortium of Foundation Libraries (2) Council of Federal Libraries (Canada)

CFO Chief Financial Officer

CFQ Competing For Quality

cft croft

cftr confectioner

CGˢᴹ Certified Genealogist (Board for Certification of Genealogists, P.O. Box

14291, Washington, DC 20044). One who has passed the rigorous tests administered in this specialty by BCG.

CG (1) Coast Guard (2) Color Guard

CG *The Computer Genealogist*, New England Historic Genealogical Society, 101 Newbury Street, Boston, MA 02116-3007

CGA Church Genealogical Archives (Genealogical Society, Salt Lake City, UT)

CGA Color Graphs Adapter

CGC Council of Genealogy Columnists (now ISFHWE)

CG(C) Certified Genealogist (Canada)

CGE Centennia Genealogy Edition, Clockwork Software, Inc. P.O. Box 148036, Chicago, IL 60614

CGH Cape of Good Hope

CGIˢᴹ Certified Genealogical Instructor (Board for Certification of Genealogists, P.O. Box 14291, Washington, DC 20044). One who has passed the tests administered in this teaching specialty by BCG.

CGI Common Gateway Interface (Internet Web page scripts)

CG-Intern Certified Genealogist-Intern (a term formerly used by the Board for Certification of Genealogists)

CGLˢᴹ Certified Genealogical Lecturer (Board for Certification of Genealogists, P.O. Box 14291, Washington, DC 20044). One who has passed the tests administered in this teaching specialty by BCG.

CGL Computerized Genealogical Library

CGN Cardiganshire, Wales

CGN Connecticut Gravestone Network

CGNDB Canadian Geographical Names Database

CGPR Canadian Genealogical Projects Registry

Cgr/Mkr Cigar Maker

CGRSˢᴹ Certified Genealogical Records Specialist (Board for Certification of

Genealogists, P.O. Box 14291, Washington, DC 20044). One who has passed the tests administered in this specialty by BCG. (Formerly known as Certified Genealogical Records Searcher).

CGS California Genealogical Society, P.O. Box 77105, San Francisco, CA 94107-0105

CGS Cape Cod Genealogical Society, P.O. Box 906, Brewster, MA 02631

CGS Chicago Genealogical Society, P.O. Box 1160, Chicago, IL 60690

CGS (1) Chief of the General Staff (2) *The Companion to Gaelic Scotland*

CGS Colorado Genealogical Society, P.O. Box 9218, Denver, CO 80209-0218

CGSSD Computer Genealogy Society of San Diego, P.O. Box 370357, San Diego, CA 92137-0357

CGSI Czechoslovak Genealogical Society International

CGT Compagnie Generale Transatlantique (ship line)

ch (1) change (2) chemin

Ch (1) Cheshire, England (2) Children's Librarian, Children's Services

Ch/ch (1) Chancery record, Common Pleas Court (2) chaplain (3) chapter (4) chief (5) child/children, issue, offspring (6) church (7) courthouse (8) custom house

CH (1) Chancery record, Common Pleas Court (2) Chaplain (3) China (4) Chinese (5) county court houses (6) Couer Hessen (7) Switzerland

Cha chamber maid

CHA Canadian Historical Association

Cha'/Char'/Chas Charles

Chaut Chautauqua County, NY

CHAI Channel Islands

chan (1) chancel (2) chancery

Chan Change

Chanc Chancellor

Chanc. Chancellor, Chancery

Chan. Proc. Chancery Proceedings

chap (1) chaperon (2) chaplain (3) chapter

char charwoman

Char Character

CHAR Charleston

Charlie/Charly/Chas Charles

chauf chauffeur

ChB Bachelor of Surgery

Ch Ch Christ Church

chd child

ChD Doctor of Chemistry

CHD County Health District

ChE Chemical Engineer

Ch E Chemical Engineer

Checklist *Checklist of United States Public Documents, 1789-1909* (1911, repr. 1953)

Chelsea P Chelsea pensioner (sometimes Chelsea out pensioner) (Scotland)

chem (1) chemical (2) chemist (3) chemistry

Chem (1) Chemical, Chemistry (2) Chemung

Chen Chenago

Ches/CHES Cheshire, England

CHess Corhessen

chf chief

chg chargeable

chh church

CHH Carmarthenshire, Wales

CHH Cincinnati Historical Society, Museum Center, 1301 Western Avenue, Cincinnati, OH 45203-1129

ChHS Chicago Historical Society, Clark Street at North Avenue, Chicago, IL 60614

Chi (1) Chicago (2) child (3) children (4) China

CHI (1) Channel Islands (2) China

Chil Child

child children

Children, Amer National Society Children of the American Colonist

CHIN/CHN China

chkr checker

CHL/CHIL Chile

chld child

chldn/chn (1) children (2) condemned his/her misconduct

chm chairman

ChMd chambermaid

chmn chairman

Chmn Chairman

Chmntz Chemnitz, Saxony

chn children

CHN China

Chnd chandler

chng change

ch/o, c/o child/children of

ChoB choirboy

CHODs Chiefs of Defence Staff

Chol Inf Cholera Infantum

ch of nm change of name

chp chaplain

Chp/Chpn chaplain

chpt chapter

chr charter

chr/chrs church(s)

Chr (1) Christening (2) Christian (3) Chronic

CHR/chr/chris (1) christened (2) christening (a child is baptized and named)

CHR *Catholic Historical Review*

CHRA Canadian Human Rights Act

chrg charge

chris christened

Christ Christopher

chrm chairman

chron chronologically

Chron Chronicles

Ch' Charles

CHS Cheshire

CHS Chicago Historical Society, Clark Street at North Avenue, Chicago, IL 60614-6099

CHS Connecticut Historical Society, 1 Elizabeth Street at Asylum Avenue, Hartford, CT 06105

CHS Cincinnati Historical Society, Museum Center, 1301 Western Avenue, Cincinnati, OH 45203-1129

CHSA Chinese Historical Society of America, 650 Commercial Street, San Francisco, CA 94111

ChsM cheese man

CHSRS Canadian History and Society Research Service, National Library of Canada, 395 Wellington Street, Ottawa, Ontario, Canada K1A 0N4

ChsW cheese woman

CHSW Collections of the State Historical Society of Wisconsin, 816 State St., Madison, WI 53706

Cht Charts

CHUG Computing in the Humanities Users Group

ch w church warden

Chwm Chairwoman

chyd churchyard

CI Channel Islands

CI Civilian Internee

Cia Compañia (company)

CIBS Canadian Information by Subject

Cic Cicely

CIC Committee on Institutional Cooperation

C.I.C. Clerk of the Inferior Court

CID (1) Center for Instructional Design (2) Confidential Identification Number

CIDG Civilian Irregular Defense Group

Cie Compagnie (company)

CIE Companion of the Order of the Indian Empire

CIG Computer Interest Group, e.g, (name of society) Computer Interest Group

CIHM Canadian Institute for Historical Micro-reproductions, 395 Wellington, Room 468, Ottawa, Ontario, Canada KIA ON4

cil/Cil cousin-in-law

CILLA Coordinated Inter Library Loan Administration (Canada)

CIMA Committee for Instructional and Media Arts

CIMO Cimorelli Immigration Manifests Online

CIMS Centre for Immigration and Multicultural Studies

C-in C Commander-in-Chief

Cinci/Cinn/CinO Cincinnati, OH

CINCPAC Commander in Chief of the Pacific Command

CIO Congress of Industrial Organizations

CIP (1) Cataloging in Publication (Library of Congress) (2) Cataloguing in Publication (National Library of Canada)

CIP Critical Infrastructure Protection

CIPO Canadian Intellectual Property Office

cir circle

cir/circ (1) *circa* (about, around) (2) circulation

circ circus

Circ Circulation

Cis/Cissie/Cissy Cecilia

C Is Cannel Islands

CIS Cataloguing-in-Source

CIS Conference in the States (National Genealogical Society annual conferences)

CIS Congressional Information Service

CIS Central Index System

Cisco San Francisco, CA

CISE Computer and Information Science and Engineering

CISL Canary Islands

CISTI Canada Institute for Scientific and Technical Information

cit (1) citato (work cited) (2) citizen

Cit Citizen

Citn Citation

City Clk City Clerk

city hospkp keeper of city hospital

city recdr city recorder

civ/civl civil

CivW Civil War

cj (1) chief justice (2) county jail (3) county judge

CJHS Columbus Jewish Historical Society, 1175 College Ave., Columbus, OH 43209-2890

CJTF Combined Joint Task Force

ck (1) check (2) cook (3) creek

CK Cape Kennedy

CK of A Catholic Knights of America

cl (1) carload (2) child (3) class (4) colonel

Cl child

Cl classical

CL (1) came and left the area (2) Colonial (3) Continental Line (4) Courier of Liberty, West Union, Adams Co. (5) William L. Clements Library, University of Michigan, Ann Arbor, MI (6) Continental

Cla Clare, Republic of Ireland

CLA Clare

CLA California Library Association, 717 K Street, Ste 300, Sacramento, CA 95814-3477

CLA Canadian Library Association, 200 Elgin Street, Suite 602, Ottawa, Ontario, Canada K2P 1L5

CLA Cemetery Listing Association

CLAC/Clack Clackmannan, Scotland

ClaI Clare County, Ireland

CLAL Cancer Longevity, Ancestry and Lifestyle study

Class Classical, Classics

clb club

CLB Columbia

cl cts clerk of courts

CLE cleared

Clem Clement, Clementia, Clementine

Clem' Clement

Cler Clerical Staff

clerk clerk

cler serv clerical survey

Clev/Cleve Cleveland, OH

CLF Clayton Library Friends, P.O. Box 271078, Houston, TX 77277-1078

clfs cliffs

clg (1) clergyman (2) college

Cliff Clifford

Clin Clinical

clk clerk

Clk/CLK Clackmannan, Scotland

Clk/Clke/Cl/Cl Ct/Clrk/Clr Clerk (of a court or county)

Clk Chan Ct Clerk of Chancery Court

Clk Cir Ct Clerk of Circuit Court

Clk Cts Clerk of Courts

Clk Dis Ct Clerk of District Court

Clk/Mkr/Clk M clockmaker

Clk of Peace Clerk of the Peace

Clk Sup Ct Clerk of Superior Court

Cllr Councillor

Clmt/Ccpl Clermont County Public Library, 180 South 3rd Street, Batavia, OH 45103

cln cleaning, cleaner

clo (1) close (2) clothing

clos closing

cloth drsr clothe dresser

clothng mct clothing merchant

clr clear

Clrg clergyman

clrgymn ME clergyman Methodist

clrgymn RC clergyman Roman Catholic

CLRO Corporation of London Record Office

CLSᴿᴹ Certified Lineage Specialist (Board for Certification of Genealogists, P.O. Box 14291, Washington, DC 20044). One who has passed the tests administered in this specialty by BCG.

CLS Charleston Library Society, 164 King Street, Charleston, SC 29401

CLSP Center for Life Stories Preservation

clth clothier

CLTL Central Library Training Lab

cm (1) catholic missionary (2) centimeter (3) christenings & marriages (4) church membership mentioned (5) Commissary

c/m Chinese male

Cm Central America

CMA Census Metropolitan Area

CMA Clan McAlister of America

Cman cellarman

c marshall city marshall

CMB (1) all types of parish registers (2) christenings, marriages, and burials

cmd command

CMC (1) Certified Management Consultant (2) christening, marriage, and cemetery records

CMD Collections Management Division (Library of Congress, Washington, DC)

cmd'd commanded

cmdg commanding

cmdr commander

Cmdt Commandant

CME Cambridge Medieval History

CMG Companion of the Order of St. Michael and St. George

CMGS Central Massachusetts Genealogical Society, P.O. Box 811, Westminster, MA 01473-0811

CMH Center of Military History

CMIC Combined Military Interrogation Center

Cmkr cheesemaker

Cmman Court Martial man

CMN Carmarthenshire, Wales

CMOf Court Martial Officer

cmpy company

CMS (1) *Chicago Manual of Style* (2) Collection Management Services

CMSR Compiled Military Service Records (National Archives, Washington, DC)

Cmsry Commissary

cmst chemist

Cmty Community

CMW Complete Maps of the World (Hammond, Inc.)

cn (1) census (2) concubine (3) conference

Cn concubine

CN (1) Capital News (2) Carolina (3) *Church News* (4) Cherokee Nation (5) Continental Navy

CNAD Conference of National Armaments Directors

CN/CND (1) Canada (2) Canadian

CNGF Common New Generation Frigate

CnHS Connecticut Historical Society, 1 Elizabeth Street at Asylum Avenue, Hartford, CT 06105

CNI Coalition for Networked Information

CNRI Corporation for National Research Initiatives

CNS (1) Catholic News Service (2) Copley News Service

CnSL Connecticut State Library, 231 Capitol Ave., Hartford, CT 06106

cn soapmn candle & soap man

Cnt Cornet

cntb constable

Cntrctr Contractor

CntS canteen steward

cnty county

cnty clerk county clerk

CNY Canary Islands

c/o (1) in care of (2) child of (3) children of

co county office/officer

Co (1) Cornish (2) Cornwall, England

Co (1) Company (2) County

Co/co (1) chosen overseer (Quaker) (2) company (3) county (4) cousin

Co./co. country

CO (1) Chief of Ordnance (2) Colonial Office, Public Record Office, Kew, England (3) Commanding Officer (4) company (5) conscientious objector (6) County (7) cousin

CO/Colo Colorado

coa/Coa coachman

COA Coat of Arms

coal drvr driver in coal tank

Co Asr County Assessor

Co Aud County Auditor

CobG Coburg Gata

COBRA Counter Battery Radar

Cobug Cobugh

Co Clk County Clerk

cod codicil

COD (1) cash on delivery (2) collect on delivery

COED Census of Overland Emigrant Documents

co/f colored female

Coff chief officer

coffehskpr coffee house keeper

cog consent of guardian

coh co-heir, co-heiress

Co Health County Health Department

CoHu cook's husband

COI Central Office of Information (British)

Co Judge County Judge

col (1) collection (2) colonel (military) (3) colony/-ial (4) colored (5) column

Col College

col/cold abbreviation for Negro or African American person, often found in legal documents and censuses

COL/Clmb/COLO Columbia

ColC (1) college cook (2) Columbia, CT

col^d colored

Col Dames of Amer Colonial Dames of America

Col Dames XVII Cent National Society Colonial Dames of the Seventeenth Century

Col Dau, XVII Cent National Society Colonial Daughters of the Seventeenth Century

Colg colleague

Colket Meredith B. Colket, *Founders of Early American Families* (Cleveland: Founders' Project, 1985)

Coll collections

coll (1) college (2) collegiate

coll/colln/Col (1) collection(s) (2) collector

collect collection

colloq (1) colloquial (2) colloquialism (3) colloquially

Col Lords of Manors Order of Colonial Lords of Manors in America

collr collector

colls collaterals

coll/stu college student

ColM college matron

Colo (1) Color (2) Colorado

COLO Colombia

Col Ord Colonial Order of the Crown of the Crown

ColP college porter

Cols/Colum Columbus, the state capital of Ohio

ColS college student

Col Soc of Pa Colonial Society of Pennsylvania

com (1) comitatus (2) county as used in English visitation pedigrees (3) command, commander (4) commentary (5) commerce (6) commission, commissioner (7) committee (8) commodore (9) common, commoner (10) communicate (11) companion (12) complain, complained of (13) complete

co/m colored male (African American)

Com (1) companion (2) commercial

COM Comoro Islands, Africa

COM (1) completed (2) Component Object Model (3) Computer Output Microform

comd command

comdg commanding

comdr commander

comdt commandant

coml commercial

Coml Commercial

comm (1) commander (2) commissary (3) commissioner(s) (4) committee (5) commodore (6) community

Comm (1) Comment (2) Committee (3) Communication

com. mer. commission merchant

commiss (1) commission (2) commissioner

commn commission

commn'd commissioned

Commo Commodore

commr commissioner

Commun Community

Comms Communications

comn commission

Comn Commission

comnr commissioner

comp/comps (1) accompt (account) (2) company (3) companion (4) comparative degree (5) compater, sponsor(s) (6) compilation (7) compiler(s), compiled by (8) complained, complained of (9) compositor

Comp Composition

compar comparative

Compar Comparative

Com Pleas Ct Common Pleas Court

complt (1) complainant (2) complaint

compt account

compt comptroller

Comput Computer, Computing

comr commissioner

comssn mct commission merchant

Comt Committee

Com^te Committee

con (1) condemned (2) conjunx (3) consent (4) *contra* (against) (5) country

Con Constance

CON (1) Consular (British) (2) Cornwall

Conc (1) Concatenate (2) concubine

Concep^on Concepcion

cond conditional

condr conductor

conf (1) confederate (2) conference (3) confirmed

Conf Confirmation

Conf Chills Confective Chills

confect confectionary

confectnr confectioner

Confed Confederate

confedn confederation

confest confessed, as in confession of a judgement

confr confectioner

cong (1) congregational (2) congress (3) congressional

Cong Congressman, Congress, Congressional

Cong Brain Congestion of the Brain

Cong Lungs Congestion of the Lungs

congl congressional

conj (1) conjunction (2) conjugation

Conl Confirmation (LDS)

Conn/CT Connecticut

ConnHS/CHS Connecticut Historical Society, 1 Elizabeth Street at Asylum Avenue, Hartford, CT 06105

ConnSL/CSL Connecticut State Library, History and Genealogy Unit, 231 Capitol Avenue, Hartford, CT 06106

con/o consent

Conr Konrad, Conrad

cons (1) consonant (2) consultant (3) consultative (4) consulting

consang consanguinity

Conserv Conservation

cons/o consort of

consol consolidated

const (1) consistory (2) constitute (3) constitution(al)

Constit Constitution

constl constitutional

constn construction

constr (1) construction (2) constructor

Constr Construction

Consult Consultant

Consumpt Consumption

consv conservation

Consv Conservatory

cont (1) continued (2) contract (of marriage) (3) contesting

Cont Continuation

Cont/Contl Continental

contd/cont'd continued

Contin Continuing

contl continental

contr (1) contract (2) contractor (3) contraction (4) contrast (5) controlled

conv (1) convention (2) convict

COO Chief Operating Officer

CooD cook's daughter

COOF Catholic Order of Foresters

cook cook

Cook Cook Islands

coop cooperative

Coop Cooparates, Cooperating, Cooperation

co-op co-operative

Co Ord County Ordinary

coord (1) coordination (2) coordinator

Coordr Coordinator

cop consent of parents

cop copy service

Coph Copenhagen, Denmark

Coph Roskilde, Denmark

Copp^r Cooper

copr copyright

cor/cors corner(s)

cor/corr/corresp (1) correspondence (2) correspondencing

COR Corfu Island

COR Cork

COR/Co. R Costa Rica

Corbin Corbin Collection (New England Historic Genealogical Society, Boston, MA). Microfilmed.

CORC Cooperative Online Resource Catalog

Co Rcdr County Recorder

CORDS Civilian Operations and Rural Development Support

Corn/CORN/Cornw Cornwall, England

corp/corpl corporal

Corp/CORP (1) Corporal (2) Corporation

corpn corporation

corr (1) correction (2) correspond (3) correspondence (4) correspondent

corres (1) correspondence (2) correspondent (3) corresponding

Corresp Mem. Corresponding Member

Cor^s Cornelius

Cors Corsica

Cor(s) corner(s)

cort/crte court

cos (1) cousin(s) (2) counties

COS (1) Chief of Staff (2) Commercial Online Service (3) Costa Rica

COSHRC Council of State Historical Record Coordinators

CosM costume maker

CoSn cousin's son

COT *Chronicle of the Times*, Batavia, Clermont County

cotts cottages

CoU Colorado University, University of Colorado at Boulder, Boulder, CO 80309

Couc cousin's child

CouD cousin's daughter

CouH cousin's husband

CouL cousin-in-law

coun/counc council

Coun Council

cou/o cousin of

couns (1) counsellor (2) councillor

Couns Counseling

Court of P's and Q's Court of Common Pleas and Quarter Sessions

Court Rec Legislative Records of the Governor's Council (Massachusetts Archives)

cous/coz/csn cousin

cous-i-l cousin-in-law

CouW cousin's wife

cov entered into covenant without coming to communion (church)

CowB cowboy

CowL cow lad

CowM cowman

CowS cowman's son

CowW cowman's wife

cp (1) camp (2) civil parish (British) (3) compare (4) cooper (5) country of publication

CP (1) Cape of Good Hope & Cape Province (2) case postal (3) Catholic Priest (4) Common Pleas (Court) (5) common progenitor (6) G. E. Cokayne, *Complete Peerage*

CPA Certified Public Accountant

cpad Common Pleas Court Appearance Docket

CPC Canterbury Prerogative Court, London, England

CPC Cumberland Presbyterian Church

CPCGN Canadian Permanent Committee on Geographical Names

CPCt Common Pleas Court Record

cpe cape

CPE Continuing Professional Education

cpl/Cpl Corporal (military)

CPL Cleveland Public Library, 325 Superior Avenue, NE, Cleveland, OH 44114-1271

cpmb Common Pleas Court Minute Book

CPNS Soldier's Children Were Pensioned

CPO Chief Petty Officer

cpob Common Pleas Court Order Book

CPR (1) Calendar of Patent Rolls (2) Civilian Personnel Records

cprb Common Pleas Court Record Book

Cprv Provost of college

cptn captain

CPU central processing unit (computer hardware)

CPX Command Post Exercise

CQ (1) *Congressional Quarterly* (2) Congressional Quarterly Service

cr criminal or criminal court case

cr/CR (1) church record(s) (2) court record (3) created (4) credit, creditor (5) creek

Cr Creek

CR (1) Carolina (2) carriage return on your computer, or press Enter (3) Costa Rica (4) County Recorder

CRA Church Records Archives of the LDS Church, Family History Library, Salt Lake City, UT

Crd Cardiganshire, Wales

CRE Crete

CRE Commission for Racial Equality

cred creditor

crem cremated

cres crescent

crft crofter

CRI Civil Registration Index(es)

CRIC Costa Rica

crim criminal

Crim Criminal

Criminol Criminology

CRIMP County Records of Indian Microfilm Project

crk creek

Crk Creek

Crk Cork, Republic of Ireland

CRL Center for Research Libraries (a cooperative library)

Crm Carmarthenshire, Wales

Crn Caernarvonshire, Wales

CrnS crown servant

CRO/C.R.O. County Record Office (England)

CRO/CROA/Croat Croatia

CRP Corporate Research Programme

crpl corporal

Crpntr Carpenter

Crrg/Mkr Carriage Maker

Crrg/Smth Carriage Smith

crs/crspd correspond, correspondence

CRT Canadian Refugee Tract

CRT cathode-ray tube

Crte Curate

CRW Custom Report Writer (*The Master Genealogist*)

cs census

CS (1) Civil Service (2) Church of Scotland (3) Color Sergeant (4) County census

CS/CZ/Cze/CZE/CZH Czechoslovakia

C of S (1) Chief of Staff (2) Church of Scotland

CSA (1) Confederate States Army (2) Confederate States of America; the southern states that succeeded from the U.S. before the Civil War

CSAEFC Colorado Stake Archives Education Fund Committee

CSB Bachelor of Christian Science

CSC Carl Sandburg College, 2232 South Lake Storey Road, Galesburg, IL 61401

CSC (1) Clerk of Superior Court (2) Corsica

CSCC Chapter Support Committee Chairman

CSer college servant

CSG Connecticut Society of Genealogists, P.O. Box 435, Glastonbury, CT 06033-0435

CSGA California State Genealogical Alliance, P.O. Box 311, Danville, CA 94526-0311

CSi CompuServe Interactive (online service)

CSIM CompuServe Instant Messenger

CSL California State Library

CSL Connecticut State Library, History and Genealogy Unit, 231 Capitol Avenue, Hartford, CT 06106

CSM *Christian Science Monitor*

csn cousin

CSN Confederate States Navy

CSNEH Center for the Study of New England History

CSP Christian Science Practitioner

CSPI Canadian Studies Publisher, 519 Mill St., P. O. Box 336, Lockport, NY 14095

CSR (1) Computer Services Representative (2) Computer Support Representative

CSS cascading style sheet

CST (1) Central Standard Time (2) *Chicago Sun Times*

C/S/Tch C. S. Teacher

cstm h of Custom House Office

CT/Conn Connecticut

C^t court

Ct/ct court

ct(s) (1) Captain (2) cent(s) (3) certificate/certificate to (4) county (5) court(s)

cta *cum testamento annexo* (with will attached)

CTAHS Commerce Township Area Historical Society, 207 Liberty Street, P.O. Box 264, Walled Lake, MI

CTAS Catholic Total Abstinence Society

CTBT Comprehensive Test Ban Treaty

CTC Certified Travel Consultant

Ctchg Cutchogue

Ctgr cottager

CTGS Cumberland Trail Genealogical Society, P.O. Box 576, St. Clairsville, OH 43950-0576

Ctkr caretaker

ctl central

ctl/ctrl control key (on computers)

CTBNYT *Chicago Tribune—New York Times*

ctr (1) center (2) cutter

Ctr Center

ct.r. court record

ctre centre

CtRec court record

CtrM counterman

Ctry Country

CTSSAR Connecticut Society of the Sons of the American Revolution, P.O. Box 270275, West Hartford, CT 06127-0275

cttee committee

cty county

cty crtclk city court clerk

CtyLt County Lieutenant

cu cubic

Cu (1) Cumberland, England (2) Cumbric (language)

CU (1) Cambridge University (England) (2) Clark University, 950 Main Street, Worcester, MA 01610

CU/CUB/CUBA Cuba

CUL Columbia University Library, 612 West 115th St. New York, NY 10025

CUL Cumberland

Cultur Cultural

Cumb/CUMB/Cumbld Cumberland, Great Britain

CUP (1) Cambridge University Press, 40 West 20th St. New York, NY 10011-4211 (2) Canadian United Press

CUPP Canada-Ukraine Partners Program

cur curate

Curon curation

curr/cur current, now

Curric Curriculum

custdn custodian

Cutoff Yr Cutoff year

Cutr cutter

Cuyu Cuyahoga County, Ohio

cv/c.v. (1) cove (2) curriculum vitae

cv commercial venture/business

CVB Convention and Visitors Bureau

CVGA Central Virginia Genealogical Association, Inc., P.O. Box 5583, Charlottesville, VA 22905-5583

CVI Cape Verde Island

CVO Commander of the Royal Victorian Order

CVR Connecticut Vital Records

CVS Aircraft Carrier

cw case will

CW (1) Canada West (i.e., Ontario) (2) carriage wheels (3) Church Warden (4) Choctaw Nation (5) Civil War (6) Civil War Families, Ohio Genealogical Society, 713 S. Main St., Mansfield, OH 44907-1644 (7) Colonial Williamsburg, Williamsburg, VA

CWAAS Cumberland and Westmorland Antiquarian and Archaelogical Society

Cwdr chief warder

CWFO Society of Civil War Families of Ohio, Ohio Genealogical Society, 713 South Main Street, Mansfield, OH 44907-1644

CWLD Civil War Letters and Diaries

cwo cash with order

CWom chairwoman

CWR Connecticut Western Reserve (northeastern Ohio)

CwrD chief warden's daughter

CWrd chief warden

CWrS chief warden's son

CWRU Case Western Reserve University, Cleveland, OH 44106

CWrW chief warden's wife

CWSAC Civil War Sites Advisory Commission

CWSS Civil War Soldiers and Sailors System (Civil War military database)

cwsy causeway

cwt a hundredweight, one hundred and twelve pounds, e.g., "The inventory revealed three cwt of bronze."

cy (1) city (2) county

cyn canyon

CYP/CYR Cyprus

CZ Territory of Canal Zone

CZ/CZH/Czec/Czech Czechoslovakia

CZR Czech Republic

D

d (1) daily (2) date (3) daughter (4) day (5) death or mortality censuses (6) *décès* (death) (7) *decessit* (died) (8) deed (9) died (10) ditto (11) *dorso* (back) (12) Old penny, denarius

d/ daughter of

-d ("-" is a number) penny, pence (Penny is used to show the size of nails.)

D (1) Daughter (2) Democrat, Democratic (3) deputy (4) Devon, England (5) died (6) District (7) divorced (8) docket (9) Doctorate (in) (10) *Dominus* (the Lord) (11) Duke (12) Dutch

d or das day(s)

d.s.p. died without issue

d.y. died young

D197101 110 year file (Family History Department)

da (1) daughter (2) day(s)

DA (1) Dakota (2) Daughter (3) *Journal of the Devonshire Association of Art, Sciences, and Literature*

D.A. District Attorney

Dª Doña [title]

DAAG Deputy Assistant Adjutant General

DAB *Dictionary of American Biography*

DAC Dominion (Public) Archives of Canada, Ottawa, Canada

DAC National Society Daughters of the American Colonists, Alabama Society, 433 West Vista Court, Mobile, AL 36609

DAG Deputy Adjutant General

DakT Dakota Territory

Da Labor Day Laborer

DAL Dalmatia

DalD daughter-in-law's daughter

DalF daughter-in-law's father

DalH daughter-in-law's husband

DalM daughter-in-law's mother

DALM Dalmatia

DalS daughter-in-law's son

DalU daughter-in-law's uncle

Dames, Court of Honor National Society of the Dames of the Court of Honor

Dames of Loyal Legion Dames of the Loyal Legion of the United States

DAMRUS *Directory of Archives and Manuscript Repositories in the United States*

Dan/Danl/Danˡ/Danny Daniel

Dand/Dandie Andrew

Dar (1) Darmstadt (2) Darnsted

DAR National Society, Daughters of the American Revolution, 1776 D Street NW, Washington, DC 20006-5392

DAR Official Rosters, Revolutionary Soldiers in Ohio

DARL Daughters of the American Revolution Library, 1776 D Street NW, Washington, DC 20006-5303

Darm Darmstadt, Germany

DAR Misc Rec Daughters of the American Revolution, Miscellaneous Records

DAS *Directory of American Scholars* (Gale Group)

DaSS daughter's stepson

dat (1) date (2) dated (3) dative case

DAT Digital audiotape

dau/daur(s)/dau^r/dau(s) (1) daughter(s) (2) daughter(s) of

Dau Daughter

dau/o or d/o daughter of

Dau Barons of Runnemede National Society Daughters of the Barons of Runnemede

DauC daughter's child

Dau of Col Wars National Society Daughters of Colonial Wars

DauD daughter's daughter

Dau of 1812 National Society United States Daughters of 1812

Dau Founders The National Society of the Daughters of Founders & Patriots of America, 706 Woodlawn Avenue West, North Augusta, SC 29841-3372

DauH daughter's husband

dau-i-l daughter-in-law

DauL daughter-in-law

Dau Rep of Tex Daughters of the Republic of Texas, DRT Library, P.O. Box 1401, San Antonio, TX 78295-1401

daus/daut daughters

DauS daughter's son

Dau Union Veterans Daughters of Union Veterans of the Civil War 1861-1865, 503 S Walnut St., Springfield, IL 62704-1932

Dau of Utah Pioneers National Society of the Daughters of Utah Pioneers, 300 North Main, Salt Lake City, UT 84103-1699

Dav/Dav^d/Dave David

DAV Disabled American Veterans

db (1) deed book (Recorder's Office) (2) domesday

Db Derbyshire, England

DB (1) database (2) Deed Book (3) *Divinitatis Baccalaureus* (Bachelor of Divinity) (4) Domesday Book

dba doing business as

DBA Doctor of Business Administration

DBE Dame Commander of the Order of the British Empire

DBF database file

DBG Denbighshire, Wales

dbn *de bonis non administratis* (concerning goods not settled by preceding administrator)

dbncta de bonis non cum testo annexo

DBY Derbyshire, England

dc (1) deceased (2) docket

DC (1) District of Columbia (Washington) (2) Doctor of Chiropractic

D & C Dean and Chapter

d & coh daughter & coheiress

DCB *Dictionary of Canadian Biography*

DCC Society of Descendants of Colonial Clergy

DCC Digital compact cassette

dce *Writ of diem clausit extremum* (he has closed his last day)

DCE Division of Continuing Education

DCG Descendants of Colonial Governors

DCGS Douglas County Genealogical Society, P.O. Box 3664, Lawrence, KS 66046-0664

DCGS Dutchess County [NY] Genealogical Society, P.O. Box 708, Poughkeepsie, NY 12602

DCH (1) Dames of the Court of Honor (2) Diploma in Children's Health

DCHS Dutchess County Historical Society, P.O. Box 708, Poughkeepsie, NY 12602

DCJ District Court Judge

DCL (1) Dartmouth College Library, Hanover, NH (2) Doctor of Canon Law (3) Doctor of Civil Law

DCM Distinguished Conduct Medal

DcoPL Denver Public Library, 10 West Fourteenth Ave. Pkwy., Denver, CO 80204

DCSPER Deputy Chief of Staff for Personnel

DCW National Society Daughters of Colonial Wars

dd (1) dated (2) *de dato* (on this date) (3) death date (4) deed (5) died

dd. death date

DD (1) deaths (2) dishonorable discharge (3) *Divinitatis Doctor* (Doctor of Divinity)

DDC Dewey Decimal Classification

DDR (1) Death Duty Register(s) (British) (2) German Democratic Republic (formerly East Germany)

DDS (1) Dewey Decimal System (2) Doctor of Dental Surgery

de (1) day (2) dead (3) descriptors (4) docket of estates (5) God (6) of (7) to die

DE/Del Delaware

de & De from

Dea/Deac/Deacn Deacon

dean dean

Deat Death

Debrett's *Debrett's Genealogical Peerage of Great Britain and Ireland*

debt debtor

dec (1) deacon (2) deceased (3) decimal (4) declare

DEC means that the person was deceased

dec/decla/declae declaration

decd/dec^d/deced/dcd/dec'd/d'd deceased

decd. deceased

Decmb/Dec/Dcmbr/D December

D. Ed Doctor of Education

def (1) defense (2) definite (3) definition

def/deft defunt (deceased – masculine), defunte (deceased – feminine)

def sen definitive sentence

deft/defendt/defend/defdt defendant

del (1) delegate (2) delivery

Del/Delaw/DL/De (1) Delaware (2) Delaware, Ohio

Del. Delaware

DEL Delaware-Genealogical-Data-Bank

deld delivered

deleg delegate, delegation

DelHS/DHS Delaware Historical Society, 505 Market Street, Wilmington, DE 19801

Deln Delegations

DelPAr/DPA Delaware Public Archives, Dover, DE, Hall of Records, 121 Duke of York St., Dover, DE 19907

Dem Democratic

DEM Germany Deutsche Marks

demi/dem/di/d one half or smaller than

Den Denbighshire, Wales

Den Denominational

DEN/DENM Denmark

Denb/DENB Denbigh, Wales

DEng Devonshire, England

Denny Denis, Dennis

DENRAH Digital Encyclopedia of Railroad History

Dent Dental, Dentistry

dep (1) deposed (2) depot

Dep (1) Depository (2) Deputy

dep/depty deputy

depo/depot/depos deposition

dept (1) department (2) deputy

Dept Department

DEQ National Society Descendants of Early Quakers

DERA Defence Evaluation and Research Agency (British)

DERB/Derby/Derbys Derbyshire, England

deriv derivative

Dermatol Dermatology

Derry Londonderry, Ireland

des designate

desc/desct (1) descend (2) descendant(s) (3) descended (4) descends (5) descents

DESCEND *Descendant Chart* (genealogy software program)

Desc of Col Clergy Society of the Descendants of the Colonial Clergy

Desc of Col Governors Hereditary Order of the Descendants of Colonial Governors

Desc, Founders of Hartford Society of the Descendants of the Founders of Hartford

Desc, Sons & Dau of Kings of Britain Descendants of the Illegitimate Sons and Illegitimate Daughters of the Kings of Britain

Desc Knight of Most Noble Ord of the Garter Society of Descendants of Knights of the Most Noble Order of the Garter

Desc of Lords of Md Manors National Society of Descendants of Lords of the Maryland Manors

Desc, Loyalists Amer Rev Hereditary Order of Descendants of the Loyalists and Patriots of the American Revolution

Desc, NJ Settlers Descendants of the New Jersey Settlers

Desc of Signers of Decl of Indep Descendants of the Signers of the Declaration of Independence

descr describe(d), description

descs descendants

DesL Doctor of Letters (French)

Des News *Deseret News*, Salt Lake City, UT

desr desire

DesS Doctor of Science (French)

DESSAR Delaware Society of the Sons of the American Revolution

Dest Destination

Det/Detch Detachment

DETC Distance Education and Training Council

DetM Detroit, MI

Deu Deutschland (Germany)

dev (1) developing (2) development

DEV/DevE/DEVO/Devon Devonshire, England

Devel Development, Developmental

Develop Development

DEW distant early warning

DFA Descents from Antiquity

DFA Dragoo Family Association

DFAW Descendants of the Founders of Ancient Windsor

DFC Distinguished Flying Cross Society, 8430 Production Ave., San Diego, CA 92121

DFHS Dutch Family Heritage Society, 2463 Ledgewood Drive, West Jordan, UT 84084

Dfnc Defiance Public Library, 320 Fort Street, Defiance, OH 43521

DFPA National Society, Daughters of Founders and Patriots of America, National Headquarters, Park Lane Building, Suites 300–05, 2025 Eye Street, NW, Washington, DC 20006

DFS Dumfries, Scotland

DFS Dumfriesshire, Scotland

dft defendant

dg degree of gift

dg/d.of.g deed of gift

DGP Defence Group on Proliferation

DGS Dallas Genealogical Society, P.O. Box 12446, Dallas, TX 75225-0446

DGS Delaware Genealogical Society, 505 North Market Street, Wilmington, DE 19801-3091

DGSJ *Delaware Genealogical Society Journal*

dh *das heißt* (namely)

DH (1) *Delaware History* (2) Doctor of Humanities

DHCP Dynamic Host Configuration Protocol

DHD Daughters of Holland Dames

DHE Defence Housing Executive

DHFS Department of Health and Family Services

DHHS New Hampshire Department of Health and Human Services

di (1) das ist (that is) (2) demi (one-half)

DI (1) Declaration of Intent (2) Deseret Industries

dia^d diamond

dial (1) dialect (2) dialectical

diam^d diamond

Dick/Dickie/Dickon/Dicky Richard

dict dictionary

dietn dietitian

Dij Dijon (France)

dil daughter-in-law

dim diminutive

dio/dioc diocese

dip FHS Diploma in Family Historical Studies (Australia). Awarded by the Society of Australian Genealogists to those who take its course of study and subsequently pass its exams.

dir (1) directeur (trice) (2) director

Dir Director

direct directory

dis disowned, disowned for

Dis Diseases

DIS Defence Intelligence Staff

dis/disc discharge(d)

disb disbursement

disc disciples

disch/dischd/discd discharged

Dis Ct District Court

disp (1) dispensation (for marriage) (2) dispenser

dispr dispatcher

diss dismissed (church)

diss (1) dissertation (2) dissolved

dist (1) distinguished (2) distributor (3) district

Dist/DIST District

distrib (1) distribute (2) distribution

Ditto, Do a repeat of what was previously written

div/DIV (1) divide (2) divided (3) divinity (4) division (5) divorce (6) divorced

Div (1) Division (2) Divorce

DIV Divorced wife of a veteran

Divf Divorce filling

div. divorced

divnl divisional

divs divisions

DJ Dow Jones

DJAG Deputy Judge Advocate General

Djur *Doctor Juris* (Doctor of Law)

DK (1) Dakota Territory (2) Denmark

dl dale

Dl/DL (1) daughter-in-law (2) daughter lawful

DL Delaware

DL (1) Deputy Lieutenant (2) Doctor of Laws

DL Old Dartmouth Historical Society, New Bedford, MA 02740

Dla day laborer

DLC Donation Land Claim (e.g., Oregon Donation Land Claim)

dld delivered

DLit/DLitt (1) Doctor of Letters (2) Doctor of Literature

DLP (1) Descendants of Loyalists and Patriots (2) Digital Library Program

DLP Hereditary Order of the Descendants of the Loyalists and Patriots of the American Revolution, 608 South Overlook Drive, Coffeyville, KS 67337-2531

DLPS Digital Library Production Service

dlr dealer

DLS Doctor of Library Science

dm (1) dam (2) domestic

Dm domestic

DM Denmark

DM Double Marker (gravestone)

DM Draper Manuscripts, State Historical Society of Wisconsin, Madison, WI

DM/DrmMaj Drum Major

DMAF Defence Military Assistance Fund

Dmag dairy manager

DMD Doctor of Dental Medicine

DMF *Death Master File* (Social Security Administration)

Dmf Dumfriesshire, Scotland

Dmi *Domini*

Dmkr dressmaker

DMn Doctor of Ministry

dmnstr demonstrator

DMR/Dm. R Dominican Republic

Dmstc Domestic

DMus Doctor of Music

DMV Double marker-veteran (gravestone)

DMV Research Center-Delmarva History and Culture

DMWV Descendants of Mexican War Veterans, P.O. Box 830482, Richardson, TX 75082-0482

d-m-y day, month, year

DMZ demilitarized zone

DN (1) Denmark (2) *Deseret News*, Salt Lake City, Utah (3) Dominica, Sunday (4) *Dominus Noster* (Latin) Our Lord

Dⁿ Don [title]

DNA deoxyribonucleic acid (molucular basis of heredity)

DNB Dunbarton, Scotland

DNB *Dictionary of National Biography*

Dnca Dominica, Sunday

DNK Denmark

DNM deceased non-member

DNS Domain Name Server (connected to the Internet), Domain Name System

DNS do not seal (LDS)

do/do° (1) ditto (the same), used in many older records (2) same as above

d/o, da/o, dau/o daughter of

Do Dorset, England

DO Doctor of Osteopathy

DOA dead on arrival

dob/DOB date of birth

doc (docs) document(s)

Doc Document

doc est docket of estates

doct doctor

dod date of death

Dod/Doddy Georgy

DOD Department of Defense

d of g degree of gift

DOI Department of the Interior

d.of.t/dt deed of trust

dol dollar

dol/$ U.S. dollar, Spanish milled dollar, and occasionally an early Peso

Doll/Dolly Dorothy

dom date of marriage

DOM Document Object Model

dom domicile

dom/domc/Dom domestic

Dom Dominic, Dominick

Dom (1) Dominica, Sunday (2) *dominus master* (used as a title)

DOM Dominica

Dom/Dut Domestic Duties

DOMS Diploma in Ophthalmic Medicine and Surgery

dom serv domestic servant

Don Donegal, Republic of Ireland

DON Donegal, Ireland

Donca Dominica, Sunday

Doneg Donegal, Ireland

Dor (1) Dorian (2) Dorothy

DOR/Dors Dorsetshire, England

Dora Dorothy

DORIS Department of Records and Information Services, Municipal Archives, New York, NY

Doroth Dorothea

DORS/Dors Dorset, England

DOS Disk Operating System

dow dowager

DOW died of wounds

DOW Down

doz dozen

dp (1) death place (2) dropped plain dress and/or speech

DP (1) data processing (2) Delaware Patron (3) displaced person (4) National Archives and Records Administration descriptive pamphlet/publication

DPA Delaware Public Archives

DPA Doctor of Public Administration, Hall of Records, 121 Duke of York Street, Dover, DE 19901

DPCN Decentralized Program for Canadian Newspapers

Dpen dependent

DpGv deputy governor

DPh/DPhil Doctor of Philosophy

DPH Diploma of Doctor of Public Health

DPI/dpi dots per inch

dpl (1) death place (2) diploma

DPL Dallas Public Library, 1515 Young Street, Dallas, TX 75201

DPL Denver Public Library, Genealogy Division, Western History Collection, 1357 Broadway, Denver, CO 80203-2165

DPL Dover Public Library, 525 North Walnut Street, Dover, OH 44622

DPMO Department of Defense POW/MIA Office

dpo depot

dpob date, place of birth

Dprt Departure

DPS Dead People's Society

dpt department

DPT desktop publishing program(s)

Dr/dr (1) as now, a debtor, debt, debit, or indebted to, especially in account ledgers (2) daughter (3) doctor (4) dram (5) drain (6) drive (7) when found in Quaker records this term stands for drinking spiritous liquor to excess

Dr./Dr doctor, physician, or surgeon

DR (1) Darmstadt, Germany (2) death record (3) The National Society Daughters of the Revolution of 1776

DR/Drm Drummer

DRA Defence Research Agency

dram pers *dramatis personae*

DRAM Dynamic Random-Access Memory

drap draper

drct director

Dresdn Dresden, Saxony

drest dressed (as in meat)

drftsmn draftsman

Drgns Dragoons

dr-in-l daughter-in-law

driv driver

Dr. Jur Doctor of Laws or Jurisprudence

DRL Dutch Reformed Church

drm drummer

DrmMaj Drum Major

DrnM drawing master

DRO Diocesan Record Office (England)

Dro Brain Dropsy of the Brain

Dro Heart Dropsy of the Heart

DROPS Demountable Rack Off-loading and Pick-up System

drov drover

drpd dropped

drsmkr dressmaker

Drsr dresser

DRSW Documentary Relations of the Southwest

DRT Daughters of the Republic of Texas, Caddel-Smith Chapter, 909 South Park, Uvalde, TX 78801

drum drummer

DryB dairy boy

drygds&gro dry goods & groceries

drygoodmct dry good merchant

DryM dairymaid, dairyman

DryS dairy servant

ds (1) deserted (2) died single (3) document signed

DS/d(s)s document(s) signed

DS Democratic Standard

DS/DSc Doctor of Science

DSC Distinguished Service Cross

Dscr Description

DSDI *The Genealogical Register of the Descendants of the Signers of the Declaration of Independence*

Dser domestic servant

DSGR/DSGRM *The Detroit Society for Genealogical Research Magazine*, Detroit Society for Genealogical Research, Inc., Detroit Public Library, Burton Historical Collection, 5201 Woodward Avenue, Detroit, MI 48202

DSL Digital Subscriber Line (technology)

DSL State Library of Delaware, 43 South Dupont Highway, Dover, DE 19901

DSM (1) Digital Sanborn Maps (2) Distinguished Service Medal

DSO Companion of the Distinguished Service Order

dsp/DSP *decessit sine prole* (died without issue)

dspl/dspleg/dsp legit *decessit sine prole legitima* (died without legitimate issue)

dspm *decessit sine prole mascula* (died without male issue)

dspms *decessit sine prole mascula superstite* (died without surviving male issue)

dsps *decessit sine prole supersite* (died without surviving issue)

DSS Dead Sea Scrolls

DSSSL Document Style Semantics and Specification Language (computer term)

DST (1) Daylight Saving Time (2) District

dt (1) date(s) (2) daughter(s), daughter of (Quaker) (3) delirium tremens

DT (1) Dakota Territory (2) Darmstadt, Germany (3) deed of trust (4) document type (5) Donation Tract

dtd dated

DTD Document Type Definition

DTER Dakota Territory

DTEO Defence Test and Evaluation Organisation

dth death

DTh/DTheol Doctor of Theology

dto ditto

DTP desktop publishing

dtr (1) daughter (2) doctor

Du Durham, England

Dub/DubI/DUB Dublin, Ireland

Dubester Henry J. Dubester, *State Censuses: An Annotated Bibliography of Population after the Year 1790 by States and Territories of the United States* (1948, repr. 1969), Henry J. Dubester, *Catalog of United States Census Publications, 1790-1945* (1950) (repr. U. S. Bureau of the Census, *Bureau of the Census Catalog of Publications, 1790-1972* (1974)

DUF Dumfriesshire, Scotland

DUL Duke University Library, Durham, NC

dum/d.unm died unmarried

Dumb Dumbarton, Scotland

Dumf/DUMF Dumfries, Scotland

DUN Dunbartonshire

Dunb/DUNB Dunbarton, Scotland

dunm died unmarried

DUP duplicate

dur during

DUR/Durh/DURH Durham, Great Britain

Dutch Col Soc of Del Dutch Colonial Society of Delaware

DuU Duke University, Durham, NC

DUV Daughters of Union Veterans of the Civil War

DUVCW Daughters of Union Veterans of the Civil War, National Headquarters, D.U.V. Registrar's Office, 503 South Walnut Street, Springfield, IL 62704

DV *Deo volente* (God willing), found in cemeteries

DVB *Dictionary of Virginia Biography*

DVD (1) Digital Versatile Disk (2) digital video disk

dvm *decessit vita matris* (died in the lifetime of the mother)

DVM (1) Doctor of Veterinary Medicine (2) *Verbi Dei minister* (Minister of the Word of God)

dvp *decessit vita patris* (died in the lifetime of the father)

DVR Society of the Descendents of Washington's Army at Valley Forge

dvu *decessit vitae uxoris* (died in the lifetime of the husband/wife)

dw/Dw dishwasher

DWB *Dictionary of Welsh Biography*

dwi died without issue

DWL Dr. Williams' Library, 14 Gordon Square, London, England WC1H OAG

dwli died without legitimate issue, also dsp (leg)

dwmi died without male issue

Dwn Down, Northern Ireland

dwsi died without surviving male issue, also dwsmi

dwt pennyweight(s)

DX Dixie

dy died young

DY (1) Dakota Territory (2) Dorothy

dyet food, meals, as in a prisoner's dyet

dyg died young

E

E/e (1) Earl (2) East (3) ein-, a(n) (4) eldest (5) elected, appointed, or ran for office during the year (6) endowed previously (LDS) (7) endowment (LDS) (8) Estate (9) evening (newspaper) (10) Exchequer, Public Record Office, Kew, England

ea each

ead *eadem* (in the same way)

EAD Encoded Archival Description

EAN (1) European Academic Network (2) European Article Number

EAP Electronic Access Project (National Archives and Records Administration)

EaTU East Tennessee State University, Johnson City, TN 37614-0717

EB *Encyclopedia Britannica*

EBA Emerald Beneficial Association

EBB Electronic Bulletin Board

EBC Electronic Business Cards

Eben^r Ebenezer

EBSEES European Bibliography of Slavic and East European Studies

EC (1) East Central (2) European Community (3) Executive Committee

ECAT Everybody's Catalog

eccl/eccles ecclesiastical

Eccles Ecclesiastical Society

Ecc^{lia} church

ECDIS Electronic Chart Display and Information System

ECGS Eaton County Genealogical Society, P.O. Box 337, Charlotte, MI 48813-0337

ECHO Exporting Cultural Heritage Overseas, 1500 Broadway, Suite 1010, New York, NY 10036

ECHO Exploring Cultural Heritage Online

ECIF *Early Church Information File* (alphabetical card index to LDS Church and other records, microfilmed)

Eck/Eckie Hector

Ecl East Coast of Ireland

Ecol Ecological, Ecology

econ (1) economics (2) economy

Econ Economic, Economics

ECP Extended Capabilities Port

ECPA Electronic Communications Privacy Act

ECU/ECUA Ecuador

ecux a female executor (of probate)

ed(s)/Ed/ED (1) edited by, edited, editor(s) (2) edition(s) (3) *eodem die* (old date, to the same place or same point, the same day) (4) estate docket

ED (1) Efficiency Decoration (2) Enumeration District, a term used with U.S. census population schedules (a geographic area assigned to a census taker)

Ed/Eddie/Eddy Edgar, Edmond, Edmund, Edward, Edwin

EdB Bachelor of Education

ed cit *editio citata* (edition cited)

edcn education

edcnalist educationalist

EdD Doctor of Education

EDI electronic data interchange

Edie Edith

Edin Edinburgh, Scotland

edit editorial

EdM Master of Education

Edmn Edmonton

edn edition

EDN Edinburgh/Midlothian, Scotland

Edon Edon Public Library, Edon, OH

eds editors

educ (1) educated (2) educated at (3) education (4) educational

Educ Education, Educational

Edw/Edʷᵈ Edward

EE (1) Early English (2) Electrical Engineer

EECI *European Emigration Card Index* (Mormon immigrants to America)

EEI Essential Elements of Instruction

EEO Equal Employment Opportunity

e et OR *errore et omissione reservata* (error and omission reserved)

EF East Florida

EFA Evangelical Friends International

EFC Evangelical Friends Church, Eastern Region (Ohio)

EFIC Early Families in Cleveland (Ohio), Genealogical Committee of the Western Reserve Historical Society, 10825 East Blvd., Cleveland, OH 44106-1777

EFOIA Electronic Freedom of Information Act

EFTA European Free Trade Association

e.g. *exempli gratia* (for example)

EG/Eg (1) Egypt (2) Egyptian

EGA Enhanced Graphics Adapter

EGH *Everton's Genealogical Helper*

EgnW engineer's wife

EGS Elgin Genealogical Society, P.O. Box 1418, Elgin, IL 60121-1418

EGY/EGYP Egypt

EH Endowment House (LDS)

EH101 European Helicopter 101

Ehefr Ehefrau, wife

ehel/ehl *ehelich* (legitimate)

Ehl Eheleute, a married couple

E. Hmptn East Hampton, NY

EHOUS Endowment House (LDS)

EHR *Economic History Review*

ei early incident

Ei/EI/EIn/EIND East Indies

EI Essex Institute, Salem, Massachusetts

EIA Energy Information Administration

EIC East India Company

EIDB Ellis Island Database (American Family Immigration History Center)

1812 vet War of 1812 veteran

EIN/EIND East Indies

ej *ejus* (his, hers, of him)

ejournal electronic journal

ejusd *ejusdem* (in the same month or year), of the same (month)

El Elisabeth, Elizabeth

EL Election

ELCA Evangelical Lutheran Church in America

eld (1) elder (2) eldest

elec/elect electrical or electric

Elec Electrical

Elec Mail Electronic Mail

electn electrician

Electr Electronic, Electonics

electro electrotyper

Elem Elementary

elev elevator

ELEV Elevation

ELG Elgin/Morayshire, Scotland

Eli Elijah, Elisha

Elis/Eliz/Eliza Elisabeth, Elizabeth

Eliz/Elizᵗʰ Elizabeth

Ell Ellen

Ella Eleanor, Elinor, Isabella

Ellie Allice

ELN/E. Loth East Lothian, Scotland (*see* Haddington)

Elnr Eleanor

ELo/ELOT East Lothian, Scotland

Elr Eleanor

Els/ElsP Elsace, Prussia

ELS El Salvador

Elsac Elsac/Elsase

Elsb Elsbeth

Elsba Elsbetha, Elisabetha

ElSG Elsah, Germany

Elsie Alice, Elisabeth, Elisa, Elizabeth

ElsL Elsace, Lorraine

e-mail electronic mail

em (1) emigrate(d) (2) emigrant

em/emp/empl employed, employee, employing

Em (1) embarked (2) employee

EM Efficiency Medal

E-mail electronic mail (communication using the Internet)

embk embankment

EMC Episcopal Methodist Church

emig (1) emigrant (2) emigrated (3) emigration

Emig Emigration

emigr emigrate from

Emˡ Emaline, Emeline

Em'ly Emily

Emmie Emma

Emp Employee

empd employed

empl employees

EMS Expanded Memory Specification

emyr employer

en/En (1) and (2) engineer (3) English

En England

En/Ens Ensign

EN/ENG/Eng/ENGL England

ency/encyc encyclopedia

end endorsed

end/END (1) endowed (2) endowment (LDS)

Endl Endowment (LDS)

Endocrinol Endocrinology

ENE East Northeast

enfeoff to invest with a fee

eng engineer

Eng (1) Engineering (2) England (3) English

Enga Engagement

EngD (1) Doctor of Engineering (2) engineer/engine driver

engg/engrg engineering

Eng. Hist. Rev. *English Historical Review*

Engl English

Engn/engr/eng'r engineer(s)

Engrg Engineering

E. Nian East Niantic dialect

enl (1) enlarged (2) enlisted, drafted, volunteered, etc.

Enl enlisted

Enlg Bowels Enlargement of the Bowels

eno enough

Enriqᵉ Enrique

Enrl Enrollment

Ens Ensign

Ensign *The Ensign* (LDS periodical)

Ent Entrance

entd entered

entg entering

Entomol Entomology

Env/Environ Environmental

eo elected official

EO Executive Officer

Eod/eod *eodem* (on the same date)

EOD Explosive Ordnance Disposal

eodem die in court records, same place, same day

eoe errors and omissions excepted

EOTR End of the Trail Researchers, 145 24th Avenue, SE, Salem, OR 97301

ep ecclesiastical parish (British)

Ep Epiphania, Epiphany

EPC Episcopal Protestant Church

Epi (1) bishop's (2) epileptic

Epis/Episc Episcopal

Epit. Epitaph

EPNS English Place-Name Society

EPPP Electronic Publications Pilot Project

EPRU East Prussia (Ostpreussen)

EPS Encapsulated Post Script

EPW Camps Enemy Prisoner of War Camps

eq (1) equation (pl. eqq. or eqs.) (2) for example

EQC *Records and Files of the Quarterly Court of Essex County, Massachusetts*

equip equipment

Equip Equipment

e.r. *errore reservata* (error reserved)

ER (1) East Riding (2) Examination of Removal Order (*see also* E II R)

ER Ecclesiastical Review

E&R Evangelical and Reformed Church

Era *The Improvement Era* (LDS periodical)

ERDA Energy Research & Development Administration

Eres Electronic Reserves

ERIC Educational Resources Information Center

ERISA Employee Retirement Income Security Act

Erlle Erllebrun

Ernd errand boy, errand girl

ERP *The Early Records of the Town of Providence*

Erptn Vssl Eruption of Vessel

ERR Editorial Research Reports

ERS Economic Research Service

ERY East Riding of Yorkshire, England

es (1) east side (2) estate or pertaining to an estate

ES Bureau of Land Management, Eastern States Office, Springfield, VA (*see* BLM)

ESA Economics and Statistics Administration

Escot Edinburgh, Scotland

ESDC Empire State Development Corporation

ESE East Southeast

E II R Elizabeth II Regina (Queen Elizabeth)

ESF extra surveillance, folio, large

ESOG Essex Society of Genealogists, P.O. Box 313, Lynnfield, MA 01940-0313

esp (1) especially (2) esplanade (3) extrasensory perception

ESP Espagne/España (Spain)

esq/esqr/Esq esquire

Esq Esquire

ESQ extra surveillance, large

ESRC Economic and Social Research Council (Scotland)

ESS Experimental Search System (Library of Congress)

Ess/ESS/ESSX Essex, Great Britain

Est/Est (1) established (2) estate (3) estimate, estimation

EST (1) Eastern Standard Time (2) Estonia

Estab Established

estd estimated

est div estate division

Estn Eastern

et (1) also (2) and (3) yet

ét *étage*

et al. (1) *et alii* (and others), in a deed, the names of at least two others besides the grantor and grantee. An *et al.* deed is often, but not always, a deed of settlement of an estate and contains the names of heirs.

etc. *et cetera* (and so forth, and the rest)

ETH Ethiopia/Abyssinia

ETHS East Tennessee Historical Society, P.O. Box 1629, Knoxville, TN 37901

ETO European Theater of Operations

et passim (and) here and there

ETS Encoded Text Services

et seq. *et sequentes* (and the following)

et ux. (1) and wife (2) one other, this type of deed contains the name of one other person besides the grantor or grantee

et uxor and wife

EU/EUR/Euro/EURO/Europ (1) Europe (2) European (3) European Union (4) Euro currency

EUB Evangelical United Brethren Church

Eucl Euclid, OH

EUCLID European Co-operation for the Long Term in Defence

Eug Eugene

Eur European

EV entries have been evaluated by the Family History Department, Salt Lake City, UT

EV/Evan/Evang Evangelical

E Va/EVA East Virginia

evang evangelisch

Evang Evangelical

eve evening

Even Event

Everton Everton Publishers, P.O. Box 708130, Sandy, UT 84070-8130

EWGS Eastern Washington Genealogical Society, P.O. Box 2566, Spokane, WA 88220-2566

ex/exec/exc'r/exec^r/ex^r/ex^or executor

ex/Ex (1) example (pl. exx.) (2) excommunication (3) from

exam examination, examiner

exec (1) executed (2) executive

exec^x/ex^x/ex^ix/exc'x/extx executrix

exc (1) except (2) excepted (3) exclusive (4) exchange

Exc/Excelly Excellancy

exch (1) exchange (2) Exchequer, Court of

Excl Excluding

Exec/exec executive(s)

EXEC Executive Services

exh exhibit

exit it goes forth, the issuance of a process, writ, etc., by a court

exit. atta attachment was signed and issued by the court

exon/excn/exec/execn execution, as in law suits

Exon Exeter

exor executor (probate)

exp (1) expanded (2) express

Exp Expenditure

expd expired

expdn expedition

expdny expeditionary

Expy Expressway

exr executor

ex rul *ex relatione* (at the instance of)

ext (1) extended (2) extension (3) extra (4) extraordinary

Ext extention (of telephone)

Exten Extension

extr executor

extraord extraordinary

extrix/exrx/exx *executrix* (probate)

EYC Charles Travis Clay, *Early Yorkshire Charters*

EZ easy

Ez/Ezr Ezra

Ezek Ezekiel

F

f (1) father (2) feminine, female (3) flourished (4) and following

f/ff following page or pages

F (1) and following (pl. ff.) (2) Fahrenheit (3) farm and ranch censuses (4) Father (5) fellow (6) female (7) female form (8) Female Sealing List (LDS) (9) feminine (10) file/docket (11) filius (son) (12) film (microfilm) (13) folder (14) folio (15) former widow

F/fa/fr father

F/O flight officer

f/o or fa/o father of

F/Feb/FebR/Febr February

F/Fri Friday

fa filled alphabetically

FA (1) Father (2) Field of Artillery (3) French America

FAA Fleet Air Arm

FAA Free and Accepted Americans

Faamer Acad Opt Fellow of the American Academy of Opticians

FAAP Family Album Archive Project

fac factory

Fac Facilities, Faculty

FAC Federal Advisory Committee

facs (facsim) facsimile

FACS Fellow American College of Surgeons

Faer Faeroerne, Denmark

FAGS Fellow, American Geographical Society

FaH farm hand

fai faithful

FaL farm laborer

FAL Falkland Islands

FalD father-in-law's daughter

FaLS father-in-law's son

FaLW father-in-law's wife

fam family, families

F & AM or FAM Free and Accepted Masons

Fam Family

fam bible/fb family Bible

Famc Family child

fam. hist. family history, -ies

FaMo farmer's mother

fam rec family records

fam rep family representative

Fams Family spouse

fa/o father of

FAO Food and Agriculture Organization

FAQ frequently asked question(s)

Far Farleben

FARC Federal Archives and Records Centers (branches of the National Archives in Washington, DC)

FarD farmer's daughter

FarF farmer's father

farm farmer

Farmer John Farmer, *A Genealogical Register of the First Settlers of New England*

farmer rtr farmer renter

farr farrier

FarS farmer's son

FarW farmer's wife

FAS Free African Society

fasc fascicle

FASG Fellow of the American Society of Genealogists (P.O. Box 1515, Derry, NH 03038-1515). Fellowship in ASG is limited to fifty living inductees elected on the basis of their genealogical scholarship, as evidenced by the quality and extent of their scholarly publications. A person is voted on without prior knowledge of his or her consideration as a candidate for the honor.

FAST Foundation for Academic Standards and Tradition

FatB father's brother

fath father

Fath Father

father-i-l/F-in-l father-in-law

FatL father-in-law

FatS father's sister

FatW father's wife

FAY Fayal

FaW farm worker

FAZA Friends of the Arizona Archives

fb (1) family Bible (2) file (3) file box

FB (1) foreign born (2) foster brother (3) free black, a person of negro descent that was not a slave

FBA Fellow of the British Academy

Fbai farm bailiff

FBB Federal Bulletin Board

FBG Friends burial grounds (Society of Friends, Quaker)

FBH Friends of the Blue Hills Trust, 1894 Canton Avenue, Milton, MA 02186

FBI Federal Bureau of Investigation

FBIS Foreign Broadcast Information Service

Fboy farm boy

FBro foster brother

FBVCA Foreign-Born Voters of California

fc federal census

Fc/Fchd foster child

FC *Family Chronicle* (periodical)

FC Free Church (Presbyterian)

FC&AGR *French Canadian and Acadian Genealogical Review*

FCC Federal Communications Commission

FCHQ *Filson Club Historical Quarterly*

Fcom First communion

FCP Free Person of Color

fctry labr laborer in factory

fcty factory

fcy faculty

fd (1) fiduciary docket (2) file drawer(s)

FDau foster daughter

FDD floppy disk drive

FDDI Fiber Distributed Data Interface

FDLP Federal Depository Library Program

fdr founder

FDRL Franklin D. Roosevelt Library, Hyde Park, New York, NY

fdry foundry

fe for example

Feb February

fed federal, federation

Fed Federal, Federated

Fed/Fedn Federation

FED Field Emission Display

FEDIX Federal Information Exchange, Inc.

Fedl Federal

Fedn Federation

FEEFHS Federation of Eastern European Family History Societies, P.O. Box 510898, Salt Lake City, UT 84151-0898

Fel Fellowship

fell fellow

felw fellow

fem feminine, female

fem/feml female

Fema Female

Fem. Dis Female Disease

FER Fermanagh, Ireland

FERA Federal Emergency Relief Administration

Ferd Ferdinand

Ferdo Fernando

Ferman Fermanagh, Ireland

FERPA Family Educational Rights and Privacy Act

FesB Feshbag

feu late (deceased)

Fev (1) February (2) Fever

ff (1) and the following, and following pages (2) Fifer (3) family from (4) more than one microfilm or microfiche number in a series

FF First Families of Ohio, Ohio Genealogical Society, 713 South Main Street, Mansfield, OH 44907-1644

FF (1) foster father (2) frates: brothers

FFA Fellow, Faculty of Actuaries (in Scotland)

FFHS Federation of Family History Societies, c/o Benson Room, Birmingham and Midland Institute, Margaret Street, Birmingham, England B3 3BS

FFI *Family Finder Index*, Broderbund, P.O. Box 6125, Novato, CA 94948-6125

FFO First Families of Ohio, Ohio Genealogical Society, 713 South Main Street, Mansfield, OH 44907-1644

FFs First Families

FFT First Families of Tennessee

FFTT First Families of the Twin Territories (Oklahoma Genealogical Society), P.O. Box 12986, Oklahoma City, OK 73157-2986

FFV Order of First Families of Virginia, 1607-1624/25

FG French Grants

FGBS Fellow, the New York Genealogical and Biographical Society

FGCU Florida Gulf Coast University

FGR/fgr family group record

FGRA Family Group Records Archives at the Family History Library, Salt Lake City, UT (microfilmed)

FGRC Family Group Records Collection at the Family History Library, Salt Lake City, UT (microfilmed)

fgs family group sheet

FGS Federation of Genealogical Societies, P.O. Box 200940, Austin, TX 78720-0940

FGS/OGS Federation of Genealogical Societies/Ohio Genealogical Society

FGSP Fellow of the Genealogical Society of Pennsylvania

FH (1) family histories (2) family history (3) funeral home

FHA Family History Alliance

FHAF Family History Alliance Foundation, Brea, CA

FHC Family History Center of The Church of Jesus Christ of Latter-day Saints (local branch genealogical library)

FHCs Family History Centers

FHCIM Family History Center Inventory Manager

FHD Family History Department, 50 East North Temple, Salt Lake City, UT 84150 (the Family History Library is part of the Family and Church History Department)

FHG Fellow of the Institute of Heraldic and Genealogical Studies

FHH Family History Hero (Treasure Maps How-to Genealogy Internet Web Site)

FHiTL Family History Technology Laboratory, Brigham Young University, Provo, UT 84602

FHL Family History Library, 35 North West Temple Street, Salt Lake City, UT 84150

FHLC Family History Library Catalog, Family History Library, Salt Lake City, UT

FHND *Family History News & Digest*

FHQ *Florida Historical Quarterly*

FHS Family History Society

FHS Fellow, Heraldry Society

FHSA Family History Society of Arizona, P.O. Box 63094, Phoenix, AZ 85082-3094

Fi/fi (1) fireman (2) for instance

FI/FIN/FINL Finland

FIAG Fellow of the Institute of American Genealogy (defunct)

F&IW French and Indian War

fiche microfiche (e.g., frequently used as a Family History Library microfiche number)

fid (1) fidelity (2) fiduciary, held in trust

FID International Federation for Information and Documentation

FIELD Field News Service (formerly *Chicago Daily News-Sun Times*)

Fif/FIF Fife, Fifer, Fifeshire, Scotland

fi fa *writ of fieri facias* (commands a sheriff to take and sell property)

FifMaj/FM Fife Major

fig (1) figuratively (2) figure

FIGRS Fellow of the Irish Genealogical Research Society (Ireland), an honor awarded in recognition of outstanding service to the society and/or outstanding contributions to Irish genealogy.

FIGS Family Search™ Internet Genealogy Service

FIIC Fellow, International Institute for Conservation of Historic and Artistic Works

FIJ Fiji Islands

FIL/Fil/f-i-l/f.i.l. father-in-law

Filby P. William Filby's *Passenger and Immigration Lists Index* (Detroit: Gale Group)

FilCK Filson Club, Louisville, KY

FilDr Doctor of Philosophy

filia daughter

filius son

fille daughter

film film number, microfilm number (e.g., Family History Library microfilm number)

fils son

fin finance, financial

Fin Finance, Financial

FIN/Finn/FINL Finland

Finla Finland

FIOP Foreign and International Official Publications

first C/First C first cousin

First Fam of Miss Order of the First Families of Mississippi

First Fam of Ohio *First Families of Ohio*, Ohio Genealogical Society, 713 South Main Street, Mansfield, OH 44907-1644

FIS Faculty of Information Studies

FI SG Fellow of the Institute of American Genealogy

FIWBC French and Indian War Bounty Certificates (Virginia State Library)

Fk Frank

Fk fork, as in the Salt Fork of the river

FKC Fellow, King's College London

Fkn Franklin

FKW Frame knit worker

fl/FL (1) fall (2) father-in-law (3) floor (4) flore-at (5) floruit (flourished)

FL Family Line Publications, Rear 63 E Main Street, Westminster, MD 21157

FL/Fla Florida

FLA Fellow, Library Association

FLA Future Large Aircraft

Flab farm laborer

Flagon & Trencher Flagon and Trencher (Descendants of Colonial Tavern Keepers)

FLAI Fellow, Library Association of Ireland

fld/flds field(s)

Flem Flemish

FLHS Fellow, London Historical Society

FLIN Flint, Great Britain

Flint/FLN Flintshire

FLIR Forward-Looking Infra-Red

Flm Films

FLOW Franconia, Lower (Unterfranken), Bavaria, Germany

flr floor

flr pkr flower packer

fls falls

FlSU Florida State University, Tallahassee, FL

flt (1) flats (2) flight

Flt Flintshire, Wales

F/Lt Flight Lieutenant

FLT an inscription of the cemetery stone of an I00F member, meaning "Friendship, Love, and Truth"

fm from

FM/fm (1) Field-Marshal (2) foster mother (3) free mulatto (4) funeral marker

FMA Fellow, Museums Association

Fmag farm manager

FMID Franconia, Middle (Mittelfranken), Bavaria, Germany

Fmn Fermanagh, Northern Ireland

Fmot foster mother

FMRAAM Future Medium-Range Air-to-Air Missile

Fmt Date format

fn (1) footnote (2) free negro

FN (1) field-name(s) (2) Finland (3) First Name (4) free Negro(es) (5) Register of births, deaths, and marriages in foreign countries

fndl foundling

fndry clk foundery clerk

fndry fnsh finisher in foundery

fndry frmn foundery foreman

fndry mldr moulder in foundery

fndry tnshr tinesher in foundery

FNGS Fellow of the National Genealogical Society (4527 17th Street North, Arlington, VA 22207-2399). An honor accorded in recognition of outstanding service to NGS and/or worthy contributions to American genealogy.

FNS Family Name System (Family History Department, Salt Lake City, UT)

FNSH Federation of Nova Scotian Heritage (Halifax, NS)

fnshr finisher

fnshr mshp finisher in machine shop

FNYGBS Fellow, New York Genealogical and Biographical Society, 122 East 58th Street, New York, NY 10022-1939

fo folio

f/o, fa/o father of

f/o formerly of

FO *Family Origins* (genealogy software program)

FO (1) Fidelity Oath (2) Field Officer (3) Foreign Office (4) Foreign Officer

F/O Flying Officer

fob free on board

FoB (1) foreign birth (2) foster brother

FOE Fraternal Order of Eagles

Fof F Feet of Fines

FOG Friends of Genealogy

FOIA Freedom of Information Act

fol (1) folder (2) folio (3) following

FOLDOC Free On-Line Dictionary of Computing

Folle Follenze

for (1) foreign (2) foreigner

FOR (1) Forest (2) Forfar/Angus

Forest Forestry

forf forfeiture

form formerly

formn foreman

fortn fortnightly

FORUM *Federation of Genealogical Societies Forum*, P.O. Box 200940, Austin, TX 78720-0940

forwn forewoman

FoS foster son

FoSi foster sister

Fost Foster

FOTW Flags of the World

found foundation

Found Foundation

Founders of Norwich, Conn Society of the Founders of Norwich, Connecticut

Founders & Patriots of Amer Order of the Founders and Patriots of America

Four-H (4-H) Four-H (head, hands, heart, and health)

FOW *Family Origins* (genealogy software program)

fower four

fp Slave Freedom papers

FP/f.p. (1) foreign parts (2) Free Polls

F & PA The Order of the Founders and Patriots of America

FPC Free Persons of Color

FPD Flat Panel Display

FPDA Five Power Defence Arrangement

FPJMC Four Party Joint Military Commission

FPhS Fellow, Philosophical Society of England

FPO Fleet Post Office

FPR Fairview Park Regional, Cuyahoga County Public Library, 21255 Lorain Road, Fairview Park, OH 44126-2120

Fpup farm pupil

fr (1) family records (2) farmer (3) father (4) final record (5) friend (6) from

Fr friend

Fr/FR (1) France, French (2) Frau, wife

FR (1) Family Records program within *Personal Ancestral File* (2) Family Registry (3) Family Representative (4) Father (Roman Catholic Priest) (5) France (6) *see* FRA

FR Frame reference of an entry on a microfilm copy (especially Scottish parish registers or microfilm at the Family History Library)

Fra Francis

FrA French Army

FRA Fellow, Royal Academy (British)

FRA/Fran France

frac fractional

FraF Frankfurt, Germany

FRAHS Fellow, Royal Australian Historical Society

FraM Frankfort on the Maine

Fran Francis

Franc/FRAN France

Fran^{ca}/Fran^{co} Francisca/Francisco

Franklⁿ/Frank/Frankⁿ Franklin

frat fraternity

Frbg Frederiksborg, Denmark

FRC Family Records Centre, 1 Myddelton Street, London, England EC1R 1UW

FrCty Franklin County, Ohio

frd (1) ford (2) friend

Frds Friends (Society of Friends, Quakers)

Fre Freiburg

FRE family record extraction (LDS)

Fred Frederic, Frederick, Fredrick

Fred^ck/Fredk/Fred^k/Fredr^k Frederick

FreeBMD free births, marriages, and deaths

freem/frm oath of freeman

Frei Freisland, WI

Freibg Freiburg, Baden

freq (1) frequent (2) frequently

FRF France Francs

frg forge

FRG Federal Republic of Germany

Frgn Foreign

F.R.Hist.S. Fellow of the Royal Historical Society

Fri (1) Friday (2) Frieberberg (3) Frieburg

FRI Friesland, Holland

Fried Friedrich

frir friar

frk/frks fork(s)

Frk Frankfort, KY

frk(s) fork(s)

frm Freeman (a voter in a colony)

frm former

Frm/Hnd Farm Hand

frmn foreman, forewoman

frms farms

Frm/Wife Farmer's Wife

FrN French Navy

FRN France

FRNC Franconia

frnd friend

FRNH Frankenhausen

FRNK Frankfurt, Germany

fro from

frs francs (French or Swiss money)

FRS Fellow of the Royal Society (British)

FRSA Fellow of the Royal Society of Arts

FRSAI Fellow of the Royal Society of Antiquaries of Ireland

FRSC Fellow of the Royal Society of Canada

FRSE Fellow of the Royal Society of Edinburgh

FRSL Fellow of the Royal Society, London

FRSNZ Fellow of the Royal Society of New Zealand

frst forest

frt/fr't freight

FRU *Family Records Utilities* (a genealogy software utility for use with *Personal Ancestral File* 2.31)

fry ferry

fs (1) facsimile (2) footstone

Fs Filmstrips

FS female servant

FS FamilySearch™

FSA (1) Farm Security Administration (2) Fellow of the Society of Antiquaries (3) Field Services Alliance

FSC Field Standard C (Rapier)

FSAG Fellow of the Society of Australian Genealogists

FSAI Fellow of the Society of Antiquaries of Ireland

FSAL Fellow of the Society of Antiquaries of London

FSAS/FSA Scot Fellow of the Society of Antiquaries of Scotland

FSC Fitchburg State College

FSCK filesystem check (computer)

Fser farm servant

FSG Fellow of the Society of Genealogists (London), Society of Genealogists, 14 Charterhouse Buildings, Goswell Road, London, England EC1M 7BA. An honor accorded in recognition of outstanding service to the society and/or worthy contributions to British genealogy.

FSGs foster step grandson

FSGS Florida State Genealogical Society, P.O. Box 10249, Tallahassee, FL 32302-2249

FSgt Flight Sergeant

FSHSW Friends of the State Historical Society of Wisconsin

FSI FamilySearch™ Internet

Fsi Foster sister

Fsis foster sister

FSon foster son

Fsta Kaubisch Memorial Public Library, Fostoria

Fstw farm steward

ft (1) feet, foot (2) fort

Ft Fort

ft. linear feet (used for large quantities of loose papers)

FT Full Time

FTB Franchise Tax Board

FTC Federal Trade Commission

FTE Full Time Equivalent

fteen fifteen

FTG *Form Tool Gold* (computer software program)

FTJP Family Tree of the Jewish People

FTM *Family Tree Magazine*, 1507 Dana Avenue, Cincinnati, OH 45207

FTM *Family Tree Maker™* (Brøderbund Software, Banner Blue Division, P.O. Box 6125, Norato, CA 94948-6125); genealogy software program

FTML Fort Ticonderoga Museum Library, Ticonderoga, NY

Ftmn footman

ftn fountain

FTP *Family Tree Print* (a genealogy software utility)

FTP File Transfer Protocol (a method of transferring files from one computer to another via the Internet)

ftr fitter

FTSGS Fellow, Texas State Genealogical Society

FUGA Fellow of the Utah Genealogical Association (P.O. Box 1144, Salt Lake City, UT 84110). Honor accorded in recognition of outstanding service to the society and/or worthy contributions to genealogy at large.

funrl/mort funeral and mortuary records

FUPP Franconia, Upper (Oberfranken), Bavaria, Germany

furn (1) furnace (2) furniture

furngs furnishings

furntr dlr furniture dealer

furntr mct furniture merchant

furntr str furniture store

Fus Fusiliers

fut future

fv *folio verso* (on the back of the page)

F-v Catherine Fedorchak's Monroe County Records

FVGS Fellow of the Virginia Genealogical Society

FVGS Flathead Valley Genealogical Society, P.O. Box 584, Kalispell, MT 59903-0584

FVGS Fox Valley Genealogical Society, P.O Box 5435, Naperville, IL 60567-5435

FVSA Friends of the Virginia State Archives

FW father's will

FW Allen County Public Library, 900 Webster Street, Fort Wayne, IN 46802

fwd (1) forward (2) forwarded

FWGS Fort Worth Genealogical Society, Fort Worth, TX

FWif friend's wife

FWIW for what it's worth

FWK framework knitter (may be found in British census)

Fwy Freeway

FYI for your information

FxGS Fairfax Genealogical Society, P.O. Box 2290, Merrifield, VA 22116-2290

G

g groom

g/gr (1) grand (2) great

G (1) corresponding record is in computer file (LDS) (2) Gaelic (3) German (4) guardianship record (5) gulf

G/GER German, Germany

GA Great aunt

GA/Ga Georgia

GAB *Gene/Logical Aids Bulletin*, Miami Valley Genealogical Society quarterly

Gabby Gabriel, Gabrielle

Gab⁰ Gabriel

Gabˡ Gabriel

Gabr/Gabʳ Gabriel, Gabrielle

GACP Great American Census Program

Gael Gaelic

GAESRE Genealogical Association of English Speaking Researchers in Europe

GAGP Generally Accepted Genealogical Principles

GAHA German American Heritage Association of Oklahoma, Modern Language Department, Oklahoma City University, 2501 North Blackwelder, Oklahoma City, OK 73106

Garil Abigail

gal/gall gallon

Gal Galway, Republic of Ireland

GALI Galicia

galr gaoler

GALSTPTR German American Legion of St. Peter

GAM (1) Gambia (2) Guam

GamK game keeper

Gang Dipth Gangrenous Diphtheria

GAR Grand Army of the Republic (veteran's group of Union soldiers)

gardnr&frm gardener & farmer

GasAR Georgia State Department of Archives and History, Atlanta, GA

GAT Guatemala

GATE *Gateway to the West: Ohio*, genealogical periodical (defunct)

gatertendr gater tender

GaU Georgia University, Athens, GA

Gaun (1) grand aunt (2) great-aunt

Gavlbg Gavleborg, Sweden

Gaz Gazetteer

gb Guardian bond

GB (1) gigabytes (2) Great Britain

GB *Genealogical Bulletin* or *Genealogy Bulletin*

G&B *The New York Genealogical and Biographical Record. See* NYGBR

GBBS Genealogy Bulletin Board System(s)

GBE Knight (or Dame) Grand Cross of the Order of the British Empire

Gboy garden boy

GBP United Kingdom pounds

GBR/GBRI Great Britain

GbSC Glassboro State College, NJ

GC (1) *Genealogical Computing* (2) General Code (3) George Cross (4) grandchild (5) Greece

GCAH General Commission on Archives and History, United Methodist Church

G/Capt Group Captain

GCB Knight Grand Cross of the Order of the Bath

GCC Genealogical Coordination Committee

g. ch/gch/g chn grandchildren

GChd/Gcl grandchild

GCMG Knight or Dame Grand Cross, Order of St. Michael and St. George

GCO Genealogical Council of Oregon, P.O. Box 628, Ashland, OR 95420-0021

GCP genealogy computer program(s) (such as *Personal Ancestral File*)

gct granted a certificate to

GCV Great Central Valley (California)

GCVO Knight (or Dame) Grand Cross of the Royal Victorian Order

gd (1) grand (2) granddaughter (3) guard (4) guardian

GD (1) Genealogical Department (now Family History Department, Salt Lake City) (2) German Documents (3) gifts and deposits (manuscripts, British term) (4) Granddaughter

GDaH granddaughter's husband

GDaL granddaughter-in-law

GDau granddaughter

GDB Grand Duchy Badan

GdGS God-grandson

GDL Granddaughter-in-law

GDM Genealogical Data Model

GDMNH Noyes, Libby, and Davis, *Genealogical Dictionary of Maine and New Hampshire*

gdn(s) (1) garden(s) (2) guardian

GdnC gardener's child

GdnD gardener's daughter

gdn guardian

gdn/o guardian of

gdnr gardener

gdnship/gdnshp guardianship

GdnW gardener's wife

Gd/o granddaughter of

gdp grandparent

GDP Gross Domestic Product

GDPBM *Gale Directory of Publications and Broadcast Media*, 2 vols. (Detroit: Gale Research)

GDR German Democratic Republic (Soviet Germany; East Germany)

gds (1) goods (2) guards

GE Greece

GE/ge (1) German (2) Germany

geb *geboren* (born, maiden name)

GED (1) Genealogical Event Database (2) General Education Development

Gedc GEDCOM

GeDC Georgetown, DC

GEDCOM GEnealogical Data COMmunications. A format for genealogical data developed by the Family History Department, Salt Lake City, Utah, for transferring data from one type of genealogical software to another. It is a specification for a computer file of genealogy information. As an example, data may be downloaded (copied) from the *Ancestral File* into the *Personal Ancestral File*.

GED4WEB GEDCOM file conversion software

GEDISS Genealogical Data Interchange and Storage Standard

GEG Genealogical Educators Group of Greater Monroe County, NY

GEI Geiselsberg, Bavaria, Germany

Gem/GeM Gemeindsmann

gen (1) genealogy/genealogical (2) general (3) generation (4) genitive case (5) genus

Gen Geneva

Gen Genesee

Gen (1) General (2) Generated

GEN *Generations* (genealogy software program)

gén général(e)

Gen/Genl/Gen'l General (military rank)

GENCAP Genealogical Computing Association of Pennsylvania

GeNCount an e-mail report

Gen. Dept. Genealogical Department; now the Family History Department, Salt Lake City, UT 84150

Gen/Dipth General Debility

GENDIS Genealogical Death Indexing System (Michigan Division of Vital Records and Health Statistics)

GENE (1) genealogy (2) genealogical

geneal (1) genealogical (2) genealogist (3) genealogy

GeneaNet Genealogical Database Network

GENEVA Genealogical Events and Activities

GenH general help

gen'l/genl general

GENLOC Genealogy and Local History Discussion Group

Gen. Mag. *The Genealogists' Magazine* (Society of Genealogists, London, England)

GENO Genoa, Italy

genr generation

GENRT Genealogy Roundtable

Gen Soc Genealogical Society of Utah (see Family History Library), 35 North West Temple, Salt Lake City, UT 84150

GEN SOURCE GENealogy Source (Advanced Resources, Inc.)

GENSUP Genealogical Support Forum

gent/gentl^n/gen^t (1) gentleman/gentlewoman (2) gentlemen/gentle-women

Gent (1) Gentleman (a title, not an adjective) (2) Gentlemen

GENTECH Genealogy Technology. Chartered in Texas to educate genealogists in the use of technology. Now a division of the National Genealogical Society.

GENUKI (1) Genealogy United Kingdom and Ireland (2) UK and Ireland Genealogical Information Service

Geo/G° George

Geochem Geochemistry

Geof/Geoff Geoffrey, Jeffray, Jeffrey

GeoRef American Geological Institute's Geoscience database

geog (1) geographer (2) geographic (3) geographical (4) geography

Geog Geographical, Geography

geol (1) geological (2) geologist (3) geology

Geol Geological, Geology

geom (1) geometrical (2) geometry

Geophys Geophysics

Geor Georgian

Geordie/Georgie/Georgy George

Geosci Geosciences

ger gerund

GER/Ger/Germ (1) German (2) German Old Empire (3) Germanic (4) Germany

Gert/Gertie Gertrude

gest (1) *gestorben* (died) (2) guest

get *getauft* (baptized, christened)

getr *getraut* (married)

Gev/Gevat Gevatter(n), sponsor(s)

gf/gfa/GFat/grf/g fr/gff/GF grandfather

GF Genealogical Forum of Oregon (Portland, OR)

G & F Georgia & Florida Railroad

GFaL grandfather-in-law

GFO Genealogical Forum of Oregon, P.O. Box 42567, Portland, OR 97242-0567

GFOA Government Finance Officers Association

GFR German Federal Republic (West Germany)

GFWC General Federation of Women's Clubs

gg/gtgr greatgrand-

Gg Georg

GGCd great-grandchild

ggch great-grandchild

ggd/GGD/ggda great-granddaughter

GGD *Genealogical Research Directory* (surname queries listing)

GGD *German Genealogical Digest*

ggf/ggfa/GGF great-grandfather

ggg great, great grand

gggch great-great-grandchild

g-g-gfr/gggf/GGGF great-great-grandfather

g-g-gmor/gggm/GGGM great-great-grandmother

g-g-gp great-great-grandparent

ggm/GGM great-grandmother

GGMo great-grandmother

GGNe great-grandnephew

GGNi great-grandniece

GGS/GGSn great-grandson

GGSA German Genealogical Society of America, P.O. Box 291818, Los Angeles, CA 90029

GH *Genealogical Helper* (Everton Publishers, Logan, UT)

GHMA *Genealogical and Historical Magazine of the Arizona Temple District*

GHQ General Headquarters

GI General (or Government) Issue, a private soldier

GIA Genealogical Indexing Associates

GIB/GIBR Gibraltar

Gib/Gibbie Gilbert

GICS Geographic Information Coding Scheme (US Census)

GIE Genealogical Information Exchange (a program in *Personal Ancestral File* 2.31 and older versions). This program is not available in *PAF* 3.0 or later versions.

GIF Graphics Interchange Format (computer format). A graphics file format, used to compress digital images

GIG German Interest Group, P.O. Box 2185, Janesville, WI 53547-2185

GIGO garbage in garbage out

Gil/Gilb'/Gil'' Gilbert

GIL Government Information Locator

GIL *General Information Leaflet* (National Archives and Records Administration, Washington, DC)

GIL(s) *General Information Leaflet(s)* (National Archives and Records Administration, Washington, DC)

Gilb Gilbert

GILS Government Information Locator Service

GIM Genealogical Institute of the Maritimes

GIM/GIMA Genealogical Institute of Mid-America, Continuing Education, University of Illinois at Springfield, Springfield, IL 62794-9243

GIMP GNU Image Manipulation Program

GIPSI *Genealogical Index Processing System and Interpreter* (genealogy software utility)

GIS Geographic Information Systems

GISA Genealogical Institute of South Africa

GIT Genealogical Institute of Texas (now Institute of Genealogical Studies), P.O. Box 25556, Dallas, TX 75225-5556

giv (1) given (2) giving

GIX Government Information Exchange

GJ *Genealogical Journal*, Utah Genealogical Association, P.O. Box 1144, Salt Lake City, UT 84110

Gk Greek

GKpr gatekeeper

gl granted letter

Gl Gloucestershire, England

GL (1) Grand Lodge (2) Greater London, England (3) Guildhall Library, Aldermanbury, London, England EC2

GL Graduate in Law

GLA/Glam Glamorganshire, Wales

GLaB General laborer

GLAM/Glams Glamorgan, Wales

GLAN Greater London Archives Network

Glas Glasgow, Scotland

GlaS Glaris, Switzerland

GLAUM Grand Lodge Ancient Order of Mysteries-Masonic Order

GLC Greater London Council

gld guild

G&LH Genealogy and Local History Collection on microfiche (published by GLH University Microfilms). Includes compiled genealogies, local histories, genealogical serials, printed vital records, biographies, and other sources.

G&LHBIP *Genealogical and Local History Books in Print* (Baltimore: Genealogical Publishing Company)

GLHD Genealogy & Local History Department, Mid-Continent Public Library, Independence, MO

GLIN Global Legal Information Network (Library of Congress)

GLLDS Genealogical Library, The Church of Jesus Christ of Latter-day Saints. *See* FHL

Glm Glamorgan, Wales

GLMC *Genealogical Library Master Catalog* (bibliographical references)

gln glen

GLO General Land Office (*see also* BLM, Bureau of Land Management)

Glocs/Glos/GLOU/Glouc Gloucestershire (England)

Gloucs Gloucester, England

GLRO Greater London Record Office, 40 Northampton Road, Clerkenwell, London, England EC1R OAB

GLS Gloucestershire, England

Gls/Blo Glass Blower

glt granted letter to

gm (1) gram(s) (2) Grist Mill

gm/gma/grm/g mr/GM grandmother

GM Great Migration (Great Migration Study Project, 101 Newbury Street, Boston, MA 02116-3007)

GM *The Gentleman's Magazine*

GM (1) Glass Marker (gravestone) (2) grandmother

Gmc. Germanic

GMD Georgia Military District

GML/Gml Grandmother-in-law

GML Godfrey Memorial Library, 134 Newfield Street, Middleton, CT 06457

GMN *Great Migration Newsletter*, Great Migration Study Project, 101 Newbury St., Boston, MA 02116

GMNJ *The Genealogical Magazine of New Jersey*

gmo grandmother

GmoL grandmother-in-law

gmor grandmother

GMot grandmother

GMP Great Migration Project of the New England Historic Genealogical Society, Boston, MA

GMRV Granite Mountain Records Vault, Salt Lake City, UT

GMSP Great Migration Study Project, New England Historic Genealogical Society, 101 Newbury Street, Boston, MA 02116-3007

GMT Greenwich Mean Time

GMW Genealogy's Most Wanted

Gn/GN (1) General (2) great or grand nephew

GNA *Guide to the National Archives of the United States* (1974, repr. 1987)

GNE Grandnephew

GneL grandnephew-in-law

GNep grandnephew, Great-nephew

GNI/GNie grandniece, Great-niece

G94 deceased member file (LDS)

GNiL grandniece-in-law

GNIS Geographic Names Information System (USGS)

Gnr Gunner

GNS Gannett News Service

Gn/s Guineas-21 shillings

GNTP Genealogy Network Transfer Protocol

Go governess

GO (1) General Office (2) general order(s)

GOA Goa, East Indies

GOC General Officer Commanding

GOC-in-C General Officer Commanding-in-Chief

GodC/God C1 Godchild

GodD Goddaughter

godf Godfather

Godf Godfrey

godm/GodM Godmother

God'r Godmanchester

GodS Godson

GOONS Guild of One Name Studies

GOP Grand Old Party

Got & B Goteborg & Bohus

Gotld Gotland, Sweden

Gottf Gottfried

Gottl Gottlieb

gov (1) governing (2) governor

gov/govt government

Gov/Govr (1) governor (2) Royal Governor

Gov-Gen/Gov. Gen Governor General

gov^n governor

govt government

Govt Government, Governmental

govtl governmental

gp grandparent(s)

GP General Practitioner

GPAI *Genealogical Periodical Annual Index* Heritage Books, 1540-E Pointer Ridge Place, Bowie, MD 20716

GPC Genealogical Publishing Company, 1001 North Calvert Street, Baltimore, MD 21202

GPO general post office

GPO Government Printing Office

GPO Access Government Printing Office national bibliographic database

GPR Genealogical Projects Registry

GPrt gate porter

GPS Genealogical Proof Standard (a genealogical term to replace the term "preponderance of the evidence")

GPS Genealogy Publishing Service

GPS (1) Geo Positioning System (2) Geo Positional Satellite

GPS Global Positioning System

GPT GreenVille peace treaty of 1795

gr (1) grain (2) grand (3) grant or granted, grantor or grantee (4) grave (5) great (6) gross (7) grove

gr grandfather

gr-gr great-grandfather

GR general requirement (Board for Certification of Genealogists)

GR (1) Germany (2) gravestone record (3) Greece (4) Greek (5) microfilm catalog number at Ohio Historical Society, Columbus, OH

gra grange

GRA Genealogy Research Associates, Inc., 2600 Garden Rd., Suite 224, Monterey, CA 93940-5322; and Salt Lake City, UT

GRA German Research Association, P.O. Box 711600, San Diego, CA 92171-1600

GRA Grand Army of the Republic

grad (1) graduate(s) (2) graduated

Grad (1) Graduate (2) Graduation

gram grammar

grand jr/grand jur grand jury

grat great

GRB Genealogical Research Bureau (Genealogical Society, Salt Lake City, UT)

GRB Great Britain

GRBN *Genealogical Reference Builders Newsletter*

Gr Br/Gr Brit Great Britain

GRC Gravestone Records Committee

GRC Greece

GR(C) Certified Record Searcher (Canada)

grch/grchn/grchildn grandchildren

grchild grandchild

grd (1) ground (2) guard

grd/grdn guardian

GRD *Genealogical Research Directory* (research queries). Available in printed form and on compact disc, 737 Calle Pensamiento, Thousand Oaks, CA 91360-4839.

gr/dau/grdau granddaughter

grd/o or gr/d/o granddaughter of

grd(s) guard(s)

grdshp est guardianship and estate records

grdsn grandson

GRE/GREE Greece

Greg Gregory

Gren Grenadier

GREN Grenada

grf grandfather

gr-father grandfather

grgrch great-grandchild

GrHM Greensboro Historical Museum, North Carolina

GRHS Germans from Russia Heritage Society, 1008 East Central Avenue, Bismarck, ND 58501

GRINZ Genealogical Research Institute of New Zealand

GRIVA Genealogical Research Institute of Virginia, Richmond, VA

Grl Guerilla

grm grammar (school)

grn green

grnd grand

Grnpt Greenport

gro (1) gross (2) grove

GRO General Register Office, Dublin, Ireland

GRO General Register Office England (*see also* ONS, Office for National Statistics)

GRO General Register Office of Scotland

groc grocer/grocery

gro clk clerk in grocer store

gro kpr grocery keeper

grom groom

GROS/GRO(S) General Register Office for Scotland, New Register House, Edinburgh, Scotland EH1 34T

GROUP Genealogical Reference of Upcoming Publications

GRS Graves Registration Service

grs/o or gr/s/o grandson of

gr/son/grs/grson/gson grandson

grtd. granted

grv grove

Gr Yd graveyard

gs/GS (1) grandson (2) gravestone

Gs grandson

GS genealogical serials

GS (1) Genealogical Society (Family History Library, Salt Lake City, UT) (2) General Staff (3) genealogical society

GSA (1) General Services Administration (2) Girl Scouts of America

GSC General Staff Corps

GS call no. Genealogical Society call number (Family History Library, Salt Lake City, UT)

GSCW General Society of Colonial Wars

GSDa grandstepdaughter

GSDS Genealogical Software Distribution System

Gser general servant

GSF Genealogical Society (Family History Library) film number

GSG Genealogical Speakers Guild, P.O. Box 2818 Pennsylvania Avenue NW, Suite 159, Washington, DC 20007

GSHA-SC Genealogical Society of Hispanic American-Southern California

Gsl/GsL/GSL grand son-in-law

GSL Great Salt Lake (Salt Lake City, UT)

GSMD General Society of Mayflower Descendants

GSnD grandson's daughter

GSNJ Genealogical Society of New Jersey, P.O. Box 1291, New Brunswick, NJ 08903-1291

GSnL grandson-in-law

GSNOCC Genealogical Society of North Orange County California

GSnS grandson's son

GSnU grandson's uncle

GSnW grandson's wife

Gs/o grandson of

GSO General Staff Officer

g son grandson

GSP Genealogical Society of Pennsylvania, 1305 Locust Street, Philadelphia, PA 19107-5405

GSP Genealogical Standard of Proof

GSS Grand-stepson

GSS Genealogical Search Services

GS ser no. Genealogical Society serial number (Family History Library, Salt Lake City, UT)

GSSI Genealogy Society of Southern Illinois

GSU Genealogical Society of Utah, 35 North West Temple Street, Salt Lake City, UT 84150. See FHL, Family History Library.

g.s.w. gunshot wound (military)

GSW 1812 General Society of the War of 1812

GSY Guernsey

gt great

GT GENTECH

GT (1) Germany (2) Grant

GTA *Germans to America* (Genealogical Publishing Co., Baltimore, MD)

GTA Greater Toronto Area (Canada)

Gt Br Great Britain

GTI GENTECH, Inc. *see* GENTECH

Gtlm gentleman

GTT Gone to Texas

GTTW *Gateway to the West*

gtwy gateway

gu guardian

Gu/gu gules, red (heraldry term)

GU (1) Great Uncle (2) Guinea, Africa

gua/guard/Gua (1) guardian (2) guardianship

GUA/GU/GUAM Guam

GUAD Guadaloupe

guar (1) guarantee (2) guardianship

Guat/GUE Guatemala

Gue Isd of Guenesey

Guern Guernsey, Channel Islands

Guest Guest

GUI graphical user interface

Guid Guidance

Guliel/Gul William

Gunc (1) granduncle (2) great-uncle

gunr gunner

GUOOF Grand United Order of Odd Fellows

gurd guard

Gus (1) Augustus (2) Gustave

GUTT Guttenburg

GUY Guiana

GUYA Guyana

GvnD governess's daughter

gvnr governor

gvns/go governess

GvrD governor's daughter

GvrS governor's son

GvSt gravestone

GW (1) *Gateway to the West* (2) George Washington

GWPDA Great War Primary Document Archive

GWR Great Western Railway

GWU George Washington University

GWSC Genealogical Websites of Societies and CIG's

gz gazetteer

H

h (1) heir/heiress (2) hot (3) hour (4) house (5) householder (6) husband (of)

H (1) Herr, a title of respect, often stylized (2) Historical Dept. (PBO deaths) (3) head of household (in the U. S. census)

1/h, 2/y First husband, second husband, etc.

1.h. first husband

Ha (1) Haiti (2) Hampshire, England (3) Hawaii

HA Historical Association

HAC Honourable Artillery Company (British) Armoury House, City Road, London, ECIY23Q

HACW Home for Aged Colored Women

HAD Haddington/East Lothian

Hag Haggai

HAGA Houston Area Genealogical Association, 2507 Tannehill, Houston, TX 77008-3052

HAI/HAIT Haiti

hairdrsr hairdresser

Halafax *see* Nova Scotia

HalB hall boy

HalF/HalX Halifax

Half a person who shares only one parent (half-brother or half-sister)

half bro half brother

half sis half sister

HALIF Halifax, Nova Scotia, Canada

Hall Halland, Sweden

Ham/Hambg/Hambu/HAMB Hamburg, Germany

HAM Hampshire/Hants/Southampton, England

Hamil Hamilton

Hammon Hammonassett dialect

HAMP/Hamps Hampshire (England)

Han/Hanah Hannah

Han/HANO Hanover

handks/hk/hhk handkerchief or handkerchiefs

Hank Henry

Hann Hannover, Prussia

Hans Johann, John (German)

Hants Hampshire, England

HAPAG Hamburg Amerika Line (steamship)

HAPI *Hispanic American Periodical Index* (available on Local Area Networks)

Har Harold

Harl mss Harleian Manuscripts (British Library, London)

Harl. Soc. Pub. Harleian Society Publications

Harv. Harvard

HAT Haiti

Hattie Harriet

hawk hawker

Hb/HB half brother

HB Hamburg, Germany

HB Heritage Books, 1540-E Pointer Ridge Place, Bowie, MD 20716

HBC The Hudson's Bay Company Archives, Provincial Archives of Manitoba, 200 Vaughan St., Winnipeg, Manitoba Canada, R3C 1T5

Hbl half brother-in-law

HBM His or Her Britannic Majesty

Hb/o half brother of

Hboy house boy

hbr harbor

Hbro half brother

hc (1) Habeas Corpus (2) *honoris causa* (honorary)

HC (1) Havana, Cuba (2) Harvard College (3) Haut-Canada (i.e., Upper Canada or Ontario) (4) heads of cattle (5) Holy Cross

HCA High Court of Admiralty

HCAS Hesse Cassel (Kurheessen)

HCC Historical Chattahoockee Commission, P.O. Box 33, Eufawla, AL 36072-0033

HCGL Historical Collections of the Great Lakes, Bowling Green State University, Jerome Library, Bowling Green, OH 43403

HCL Haverford College Library, 370 Lancaster Ave., Haverford, PA 19041-1392

HCL Hebrew College Library, 43 Haves St., Brookline, MA 02446

HCou half cousin

HCPL Hamilton County (Ohio) Public Library

Hd Hundred

Hd/HDAR Hesse Darmstadt Germany

HD (1) hard disk/ hard drive (2) high density (3) House Document

HD Holland

HDAR Hesse Darmstadt, Germany

Hdau half daughter

HDC Historical Department of The Church of Jesus Christ of Latter-day Saints, Salt Lake City, UT 84150

HDD hard disk drive (computer term)

HDFA Higher Diploma in Fine Art

HDipEd Higher Diploma in Education

Hdlbg Heidelberg, Baden, Württemberg, Germany

HDoc house doctor

H'don Huntingdon

hdqrs headquarters

Hdqrs Headquarters (*see also* HQ)

hds hands

HDS Harvard Divinity School

Hdsl Haderslev, Denmark

hdw (1) handwritten (2) hardware

he/He herder

He Herefordshire, England

HE His (or Her) Excellency, His Eminence

head head

Head Header

HeaM headmaster, headmistress

Heart Comp Heart Complaint

HED House Executive Document

Hedm Hedmark, Norway

HEF/HERE/Heref Herefordshire, England

HEG Heligoland (Helgoland), Northwestern Germany

HEH Henry E. Huntington Library, 1151 Oxford Rd., San Marino, CA 91108

HEH His (or Her) Exalted Highness

HEIC Honourable East India Company

HEICS Honourable East India Company Service

Heini Heinrich

heir-app heir-apparent

Hel Helle/Hellen

HEL Helingrad

help/Help help, helper

HELPER *Everton's Genealogical Helper*, P.O. Box 708130, Sandy, UT 84070-8130

Hema Hematology

Hen/Hen' Henry

HEQ *History of Education Quarterly*

her heraldry

Her Hersotom

Her/Herds/HERE Herefordshire, England

Herefs Hereford, England

Her & Gen *The Herald and Genealogist*

Hernand² Hernandez

hers herself

HERT/Herts (1) Hertford, England (2) Hertfordshire, England

Hes/HESS Hesse/Hessen/Hessian/Hissin

HES Hamlet Evaluation System

HES Hesse-Darmstadt

HESA Higher Education Statistics Agency (British)

HesC Hesse Castle

HesD Hesse Darmstadt/Hessendame

HesM Hessendame

HesN Hesse Nausau

HESS Hess Darne/Darm

Hess/HessD Hesse-Darmstadt

HessC Hesse Cassel

Hesse Hessen/Hesse

HesseH Hesse Holstein

Hessna Hessen-Nassau, Purssia

HFRA Honorary Foreign Member of the Royal Academy

HFT *Heirloom Family Tree* (genealogy software program)

HG (1) Hagley Museum and Library, P.O. Box 3630, Wilmington, DE 19807-0630 (2) *Harvard Guide to American History* (3) High German (4) Home Guard (5) Hungary

HGC Heritage Genealogy College, Salt Lake City, Utah

HGF Houston Genealogical Forum, P.O. Box 271466, Houston, TX 77277-1466

hgi/H.Gi hired girl

hglds highlands

HGR Hungary

HGS Heartland Genealogy Society

HGSNY Hispanic Genealogical Society of New York, P.O. Box 818, New York, NY 10156-0602

Hgts/Hgts heights

hh/Hh hired hand

HH Hempstead House, New London, Connecticut

HH His or Her Highness (Holiness)

hhd/hd hogshead

HHD Doctor of Humanities (US)

HHEC Hohenzollern Hechingen

HHOM Hesse Homberg

HHS Hearst Headline Service, 1701 Pennsylvania Ave. N.W., Washington, DC 20006

hi high

HI (1) Hawaii (2) Hawaiian Islands

HI and RH His or Her Imperial and Royal Highness

HIAS Hebrew Immigration Aid Society, 333 Seventh Avenue, New York, NY 10001

hic jacet here lies

hic sit here is buried

Highrs Highlanders

HIH His or Her Imperial Highness

HIM His or Her Imperial Majesty

hims himself

hind hind

hird hired

hist (1) historian (2) historical (3) history

Hist Historical, History

Hist Coll Charles A. Hanna, Historical Collections of Harrison County, OH

HISTGEN New England Historic Genealogical Society, 101 Newbury Street, Boston, MA 02116-3007

histl historical

Hist MSS Comm Royal Commission on Historical Manuscripts

histn historian

hist soc historical society

Hist. Soc. Historical Society

HJ (1) Here lies (2) *Historical Journal* (British)

Hjor Hjorring, Denmark

HJS *Hic Jacet Sepultus* (here lies buried)

hk/Hk housekeeper

hk(s) hank(s)

hl/hls hill(s)

HL Hayes Library, Edenton, NC

HL/HLD Holland

HLA human leukocyte antigens

HLD Doctor of Humane Letters

hldr householder

hlg/Hlg hireling

HLI Highland Light Infantry

HlpM helpmate

hlpr helper

HLQ *Huntington Library Quarterly*

hls hills

Hls Holistine

HLS *Hoc Loco Situs* (laid in this place)

HLS Holstein

HLSMCa Henry Huntington Library, San Marino, CA

Hlth Health

HLW hand loom weaver

hm *hoc mense* (in this month)

Hm Hired man

HM (1) His Majesty or Her Majesty (2) Honorable Mention (3) horses and mules

HM *Historical Methods*

HMaid housemaid

HMan headman

HMC/H.M.C. Historical Manuscripts Commission, London

HMCS His or Her Majesty's Canadian Ship

HMD House Miscellaneous Document

Hmgr hotel manager

Hmls homeless

HMN *Historical Methods Newsletter*

HMS His or Her Majesty's Service or Ship

HMS Her Majesty's Ship

HMSO Her Majesty's Stationery Office, Publications Centre, P.O. Box 276, London, England SW8 5DT

Hmst housemaster

HMth housemother

HMY Her Majesty's Yacht

HN (1) Hanover (2) Holstein, Germany (3) HotNotes! (Silicon Roots! Associates, P.O. Box 20541, San Jose, CA 95160-0541)

hnd hundred

HND Honduras

hndlr handler

HNG/Hngr/HUN/HU Hungary

HNie half niece

HNK Hong Kong

Hnur house nurse

ho house

h/o husband of

HO (1) Historian's Office, The Church of Jesus Christ of Latter-day Saints, Salt Lake City, UT (2) Holland (3) Home Office, Public Record Office, Kew, Richmond, Surrey, England TW9 4DU

Hoanz Hoanzoller

H of C House of Commons

H of L House of Lords

HOHE Hohenzollern

Hohenz Hohenzollern, Prussia

Hol (1) Holiday (2) Hollow

Hol/HOL/Holl Holland

Holb Holbaek, Denmark

Holbrook Jay Mack Holbrook, microfiche edition of Massachusetts town records

HOLD Hesse Olddorf

HOLL Holland

Holland Soc Holland Society of New York, 122 East 58th Street, New York, NY 10022

Holman Mary Lovering Holman and Winnifred Lovering Holman, manuscript papers, New England Historic Genealogical Society, Boston, MA 02116-3007

Hols/Holst Holstein

holw hollow

hon (1) honor (2) honorable (3) honorary

hon/honble/hon^ble honorable

Hon (The) Honourable

HON/Hond Honduras

Hono Honolulu

hons/Hons. Honors

Hoop Cgh Hooping Cough

HorS horseler

horse dr horse doctor

horse farr horse farrier

hort horticulture

Hort Horticultural, Horticulture

hortcltist horticulturist

hosp hospital

Hosp Hospital

Host hostler

Hous Housing

Hotten's Lists John Campden Hotten, *The Original Lists of Persons of Quality*

hou/hous house, houses

housecarpt house carpenter

house devel house development

house kpr house keeper

HP/hp (1) Hewlett-Packard (2) horsepower

HPNS Heirs Pensioned

Hprt house porter

Hprus Hesse Prussia

HPSO Historical and Philosophical Society of Ohio

HPSOB *Historical & Philosophical Society of Ohio Bulletin*

hq headquarters

Hq Headquarters

HQ *Heritage Quest Magazine*, P.O. Box 329, Bountiful, UT 84011-0329

HQRL Heritage Quest Research Library

hr (1) heir (2) hour(s)

HR (1) House Report (2) House of Representatives (3) Human Resources

HRC Historical Research Center, Deerfield Beach, FL

Hrdl Hordaland, Norway

HrdM herdsman

hrdwa mct hardware merchant

H.R.H. His or Her Royal Highness

HRIP *Hic Requiescit Pace* (here rests in peace)

HrnM harnessmaker

hrnss mkr harness maker

hrs hours

HRS Historical Records Survey (WPA)

HRSA Honorary Member, Royal Scottish Academy

HrsD horse dealer

Hrshp heirship

Hrt/HRT Hertfordshire, England

hs (1) half sister (2) *hic sepultus* (here is buried) (3) house

Hs Hans

HS (1) Half Sister (2) Hesse-Darmstadt, Germany (3) High School (4) Holland Society (5) Historical Society)

HS *Hocking Sentinel*, Logan, Hocking County, OH

HS Home Service

HSA Hereditary Society Lineages (Board for Certification of Genealogists)

HSA Historical Society of Alberta (Calgary, Alberta)

HSA Huguenot Society of America, 122 East, 58th Street, New York, NY 10022

HsBr husband's brother

HsConr Hans Konrad, Hans Conrad

HSD Historical Society of Delaware, 505 Market Street, Wilmington, DE 19801

hse house

HSH His or Her Serene Highness

HSi/HSis half sister

HSIG Hohenzollern Sigmaringen

Hsil half sister-in-law

Hs Jb Hans Jakob, Hans Jacob

HskC housekeeper's child

HskD housekeeper's daughter

HskF housekeeper's father

HskH housekeeper's husband

HskN housekeeper's nephew or niece

Hskp/HsKpr housekeeper

HskS housekeeper's son

HsMd housemaid

Hs/o half sister of

HSon half son

HSP Historical Society of Pennsylvania, 1300 Locust Street, Philadelphia, PA 19107-5699

Hs/Pntr House Painter

Hsrg house surgeon

Hs Rud Hans Rudolf

HSrv house servant

Hss/Ger Hesse, Germany

.hst history file(s) extension

Hst (1) Holstein (2) name is listed in the index of a history book

Hstw house steward

Hs Uli Hans Ulrich

Hs Wilh Hans Wilhelm

ht (1) height (2) *hoc tempore* (at this time)

HT (1) Haiti (2) Hearth Tax

htg heating

HTI Humanities Text Initiative, University of Michigan

HtlG hotel guest

HTML Hyper Text Markup Language (Internet web pages are written in HTML language; a set of computer instructions)

Hts heights

HTTP Hyper Text Transfer (Transport) Protocol

Htz Holtenzen

Hu Huntingdonshire, England

HU (1) Harvard University Library, Cambridge, Massachusetts (2) Hungary (3) Husband

HubD husband's daughter

HUD Hudson Tombstone Collection

HuGM husband's grandmother

Huguenot Soc, Founders of Huguenot Society of the Founders of Manakin in the Colony of Virginia

Huguenot Soc of SC Huguenot Society of South Carolina, 138 Logan Street, Charleston, SC 29401

HUL Huntington Library, 1151 Oxford Road, San Marino, CA 91108

Hum Human, Humanistic, Humanities

Hum Humphrey

hun/hds/hund hundred(s)

HUN (1) Hungary (2) Huntingdonshire

HUNG Hungary

HUNT/Hunts Huntingdonshire, England

hus/husb/husbn husband

Hus Hussars

Husb Husband

husbm husbandman

HusF husband's father

HusM husband's mother

HusN husband's nephew or niece

HusS husband's sister

HusU husband's uncle

HV Hannover, Germany

hvn haven

HVR *Hocking Valley Republican*, Logan, Hocking County, OH

Hvy Art Heavy Artillery (military regiment)

hw his wife

hw/Hw houseworker

HW husband's will

Hwy Highway

hy heavy

Hy Henry, Hyrum

Hyg Hygiene

Hz hertz

Hzk Hezekiah

I

i (1) instant (2) inventory (3) island (4) isle (5) issue

I Invalid

I (1) Immigrant (2) independent (newspaper) (3) inmate (4) Instance Books (5) inventory (6) Ireland (7) Irish

I- institution

ia person was in the area during the year mentioned

i.a. *in absentia*

Ia (1) Iowa (2) old abbreviation for Indiana

IA (1) Indian Army (2) Invalid's Application (3) Iowa (4) used for Indiana in 1850

IACI The Irish American Cultural Institute, University of Saint Thomas, 2115 Summit Avenue, Mail #5026, Saint Paul, MN 55105-1096

IAF Internet Address Finder

IAJGS International Association of Jewish Genealogical Societies

IaHS Iowa Historical Society, Iowa City, IA

IASS International Association for Scandinavian Studies

IaU University, Iowa City

Ib/IB (1) International Standard Book Number (2) inventory book

ib/ibid/Ibid/ibm *ibidem* (in the same place, the same)

IBA International Bar Association

IBC inside back cover (of a book)

ibid *ibidem* (in the same place, the same)

IBSSG International Blacksheep Society of Genealogists

i/c in charge of

IC (1) Iceland (2) Invalid's Certificate

ICA International Council of Archives

ICAPGen International Commission for the Accreditation of Professional Genealogists, P.O. Box 970204, Orem, UT 84097-0204

ICBM Intercontinental Ballistic Missile

ICC Interstate Commerce Commission

ICCS International Council for Canadian Studies

ICE Iceland

ICEL Iceland, Icelandic

Ichg in charge

ICOMOS International Council on Monuments and Sites

ICPSR Inter-university Consortium for Political and Social Research, Ann Arbor, MI

ICQ I Seek You

id *idem* (the same)

id identity

ID (1) identification (2) *Independent Democratic* (newspaper)

ID/Ida Idaho

IDA/IDI India

IDC International Data Corporation

IDEA Individual Development and Educational Assessment

IDN *In Dei Nomie* (in the name of God)

Idno Identification number

IDRC International Development Research Centre

IdSHS Idaho State Historical Society, Genealogical Library, 450 North Fourth Street, Boise, ID 83702

i.e. *id est* (that is)

IE (1) *Improvement Era* (2) Indo-European (3) Internet Explorer (Microsoft's Web browser)

ien Indian masculine (feminist)

if *ipse fecit* (he did it himself)

IF Invalid's File

IFA Internet Family Archives (*Family Tree Maker*)

IFF Internet Family Finder (*Family Tree Maker*)

IFGSX Irish Family Group Sheet Exchange, P.O. Box 535, Farmington, MI 48332

IFHF Irish Family History Forum

IFLA International Federation of Library Associations and Institutions

IFOR Implementation Force

IG Inspector General

IGC Inter-Governmental Conference

IGCh illegitimate grandchild

Ig^{co} Ignacio

IGDa illegitimate granddaughter

IGG Italian Genealogical Group

IGHL Institute of Genealogy and History for Latin America

IGHR Institute of Genealogy and Historical Research, Samford University, Harwell G. Davis Library, 800 Lakeshore Drive, Birmingham, AL 35229-7008

IGI *International Genealogical Index* (database in FamilySearch™)

ign ignorant, ignotus

IGP Ireland Genealogy Projects

IGS Indiana Genealogical Society, P.O. Box 10507, Fort Wayne, IN 46852-0507

IGS Institute of Genealogical Studies, P.O. Box 25556, Dallas, TX 75225-5556 (formerly Genealogical Institute of Texas)

IGS Iowa Genealogical Society, P.O. Box 7735, Des Moines, IA 50322-7735

IGSI Irish Genealogical Society, International, P.O. Box 13585, St. Paul, MN 55116-0585

IGSn illegitimate grandson

IGV Indische Genealogische Vereniging (Dutch Indische Genealogical Association)

ih *iacet hic* (here lies)

IHAF Institut d'Histoire de l'Amérique Française

IHGR Institute of Heraldic and Genealogical Research

IHGS Institute of Heraldic and Genealogical Studies, 79-82, Northgate, Canterbury, Kent, England CT1 1BA

IHR Iowa Historical Record

IHRC Immigration History Research Center, University of Minnesota, 826 Berry Street, St. Paul, MN 55114

IHS first 3 letters of Greek name for Jesus Christ; a symbol of the Holy Name

IHS Indiana Historical Society, 315 West Ohio Street, Indianapolis, IN 46202-3299

IHSV Red Cross of Constantine

II India

IIGS International Internet Genealogical Society

IJF Island Juan Fernandas

IJGS Illiana Jewish Genealogical Society, P.O. Box 384, Flossmoor, IL 60422-0384

IJH *Iowa Journal of History*

IJHP *Iowa Journal of History and Politics*

Ikep innkeeper

il/i-l in-law

Il Illegitimate

IL Kaskaskia Campaign (Illinois)

IL/Ill Illinois

ILA International Law Association

IlHS Illinois State Historical Society, Old State Capitol, Springfield, IL 62701

ill illuminated (document)

ILL Interlibrary loan

IllC illegitimate child

IllD illegitimate daughter

Ille Illegitimate

illeg (1) illegible (2) illegitimate

illg/illeg/illegit/ille`gitime illegitimate

IllN illegitimate niece or nephew

ills/illus/ill illustrated

IllS illegitimate son

Illustr Illustrator

ILO International Labor Organization

IlSAr Illinois State Archives, Springfield, IL

i/m Indian male

im Intinerant Minister

IMAP Internet Message Access Protocol

IM, I/M Isle of Man

IM instant messaging

I. Man Isle of Man, Great Britain

IMAR Institue for Migration and Ancestral Research

IMH *Indiana Magazine of History*

IMHO In My Humble Opinion

IMLS Institute of Museum and Library Services

imm (1) immigrant(s) (2) emigrated (3) migrated (4) immigrated

Immi Immigration

immig/pass immigration and passenger lists

immigr immigrate to

imp/Imp' *imprimis* (in the first place)

Imp Imperial

imper imperative

impl implement

implts implements

importacon importation

impr impression

imprimis in the first place, first

improvem'/improv' improvement

imps *imprimis* (in the first place)

impts improvements

impv improver

IMSI International Microcomputer Software, Inc., San Rafael, CA

In (1) inch(es) (2) Indiana (3) Inmate

IN/Ind/IND Indiana (at Vincennes)

inc (1) inclosure (2) incomplete (3) incorporated (4) incorporée

Inc (1) Income (2) Incorporated (3) Incumbent

incl (1) include(s) (2) includes (3) including (4) inclusive

Incomp incompetent

inconm surname not known

incorp incorporated

ind (1) independent (2) Indian(s) (3) indictment (4) industrial

Ind (1) a person of independent means (2) Indian (3) Indiana

IND (1) India (2) Indonesia

I.N.D. *In Nomine Die* (in God's name)

indef indefinite

Indents small page, often found before an original will

IndHS Indiana Historical Society, 315 West Ohio Street, P.O. Box 88255, Indianapolis, IN 46202

INDI (1) India (2) individual

Indi Individual

indic indicative

indien Indian (masculine)

indiene Indian (feminine)

indl industrial

indpt independent

indr indenture

Inds Indians

IND. S.C. Indian Survivors' Certificates

IndSL Indiana State Library, Indianapolis, IN

Ind. S.O. used in pension files—Indian Wars Survivor's Original certificate

indt indictment

IndT/Ind T/Ind Ter/Indty Indian territory

Indust Industrial, Industry

Ind. W.C. Indian Wars Widow's Certificate

indy industry

ined ineditus (not made known, unpublished)

in esse in being, usually refers to an unborn child

inf/INF (1) infancy (2) infant (3) infinitive (4) informant (5) information (6) informed (7) infra, below

Inf. Infantry (military regiment)

Inf Bowels Infirmation or Inflamation of Bowels

Inf Brain Infirmation or Inflamation of Brain

Infect Infectious

infin infinitive

Inf/Lungs Infirmation or Inflamation of Lungs

info information

Info Information

infra below

infra dig *infra dignitatem* (undignified)

inft infant

inh inherited

inhab inhabitant

INHS Indiana State Historical Society, Indianapolis, IN 46202

Inlaw a person related through marriage (rather than blood relative)

in loco in place of

in loc citata in the place cited

inlt inlet

InLw in-law

InmD inmate's daughter

InmF inmate's father

InmM inmate's mother

InmR inmate of refuge

InmS inmate's son

Inmt inmate

InmW inmate's wife

INO Indonesia

INPCRP Indiana Pioneer Cemeteries Restoration Project

in poss of in possession of

in pr *in principio* (in the beginning)

inq Inquisition Post Mortem

inq/inqr inquiry

inqst inquest, as in coroner's inquest

INRI *Jesus Nazarene Rex Judaeorum* (Jesus of Nazareth, King of the Jews)

ins (1) insane (2) insert (3) insurance

Ins Insurance

INS Immigration and Naturalization Service, 425 I Street NW, Washington, DC 20536

INS International News Service

ins agt insurance agent

Inscr inscriptions

InsL intended son-in-law

INSL Indiana State Library, Indianapolis, IN

insp (1) inspection (2) inspector

inst (1) instant, this month, or within the same month (2) institute (3) institution (4) instructor

Inst Institute, Institutional

instn institution

instr (1) instructor (2) instrumental

Instr Instructor

Instrul Instructional

int (1) intention(s) (marriage) (2) interest(ed) (3) interred (4) intestate

Int International

int dec interior decorator

Inter Interior

interj interjection

internat international

InterNIC Internet Network Information Center

intest intestate

Int/Fever Intermittent Fever

Intl International

intrans intransitive

intrd introduced

int rev Internal Revenue

introd/intro introduction

INTSUMs Intelligence Summaries

inv (1) investment (2) inventory

inv/invd invalid

inv/invt/invent⁷ (1) inventory (of possessions) (2) inventoried (estate)

Inv/INV/INVE/Invern Inverness, Scotland

INVST International and National Voluntary Service Training Program

Io Iowa

IOAA Independent Offices Appropriation Act

IOF Isle of Flores

IOFC Isle of Corsica

IOFG Isle of Guernsey

IOFM/IOM Isle of Man

IOFW Isle of Wight

IOG Isle of Guernsey

Ioh John ("I" interchangeable for "J")

IOI Independent Order of Immaculates

IOJ Isle of Jersey

IOKP Independent Order of Knights of Pythias

IOLR India Office Library and Records

IOM Isle of Man (British Isles)

IOMFS Isle of Man Family History Society, 6 Selbourne Drive, Douglas, Isle of Man

ION Ionian Islands

IOOF Independent Order of Odd Fellows

IORM Improved Order of Redmen

IOS Isles of Sicilly

IOTHSA Illinois Orphan Train Heritage Society

IOU I Owe You

IOW Isle of Wight

IowC Iowa City, Iowa

IP Internet Protocol (computer term), i.e., IP address

IPA International Phonetic Alphabet

IPGS Imperial Polk Genealogical Society, Box 10, Kathleen, FL 33849

IPL Internet Public Library

IPM/ipm/inq pm *inquisition post mortem* (an inquest held to determine a deceased person's land holdings, usually dated by "regnal year", e.g., 3 Hen. 4, 3 Hen IV = third year of the reign of Henry IV)

IPR International Passenger Records

ipso facto by the act itself

IPX Internetwork Packet Exchange

IPX/SPX Internetwork Packet Exchange/ Sequenced Packet

iq *idem quod* (the same as)

IQ intelligence quotient

ir Invention Recorded

ir/irreg irregular

Ir Ireland, Irish

IR (1) *Independent Republican* (newspaper) (2) Irish

IR/IRE/IREL/IRL Ireland

IRA (1) Iraq (2) Persia

IRAD Illinois Regional Archives Depositories

IRC (1) Internet Relay Chat (2) International Reply Coupon

IRCM Infra-Red Countermeasures

IRE/IREL Ireland

IRIS Illinois Research Information Systems (Service), University of Illinois at Urbana-Champaign, 901 South Mathews Avenue, Urbana, IL 61801

IRL Ireland

irnr ironer

IRO International Refugee Organization

irreg irregular

IRS Internal Revenue Service

is (1) island(s) (2) isle

Is (1) Isabella (2) Isaiah (3) Islam (4) Israel

IS (1) Independent Study (2) International Standard Serial Number

IS In Slavery

ISA Illinois State Archives, Springfield, IL

Isa Is a kind of

Isa/Isab/Isb Isabel, Isabella

ISBG International Society for British Genealogy and Family History

ISBGFH International Society for British Genealogy and Family History, P.O. Box 3115, Salt Lake City, UT 84110-3115

ISBN International Standard Book Number

ISC Isle of St. Christopher, Isle of Wight

ISD In-Service Date

ISDN Integrated Services Digital Network

ISDSA International Society of Sons and Daughters of Slave Ancestry, P.O. Box 436937, Chicago, IL 60643-6937

ISFHWE International Society of Family History Writers and Editors

ISFL International Society of Family Law

ISGS Illinois State Genealogical Society, Illinois State Archives Building, P.O. Box 10195, Springfield, IL 62791-0195

ISH Independent Sons of Honor

IsJ Island of Jersey

Isl/isl/isld island

ISL Indiana State Library, Indianapolis, IN

IsMan Isle of Man

ISO International Standards Organization

ISOA In Search of Ancestors

ISP International Study Program(s)

ISP Internet Service Provider

ISPC International Statistical Programs Center

ISR Israel

ISRR International Soundex Reunion Registry, P.O. Box 2312, Carson City, NV 89702-2312

ISSA International Society Security Association

ISSN International Standard Serial Number

IsT Isle of Tenerife, Canary Islands

ISTG Immigrant Ships Transcribers Guild

IsTr Isle of Trinidad, West Indies

it. Item

It Italy, Italian

IT (1) Indian Territory (2) Indian Territory, Oklahoma (3) information technology

IT/ITA/ITL/ITAL (1) Italian (2) Italy

ital italic type

ite item

ITER Indian Territory

ITL Italy Lira

ITO International Trade Organization

ITT Invitation to Tender

ITV in this village

IU Indiana University Library, Bloomington, IN

IVC Ivory Coast

IWW International Workers of the World

IY (1) Idaho Yesterday (2) Italy, Italian

J

(2) journal (3) served on a jury dur-
[...] given year

[...]ahr(e), year(s) (2) Johann or Johannes (3)
journeyman

Ja James, Jane

Ja/JA/JAM/JAMA Jamaica

Jab Jabal, Jabalpur, Japez, Jabreel

Jac L. Jacobus, James

JAMA *The Journal of the American Medical Association*

Ja/Jan/Janry/JanRy January

JA (1) Japan (2) Judge Advocate

JAD Joint Application Development

JAG Judge Advocate General

JAH *Journal of American History*

JAM Jamaica

Jam/Jamie James

Jamtld Jamtland, Sweden

jan janitor

Janv January

JAOUW Junior Order-Ancient Order of United Workmen

JAP/JAPA (1) Japan (2) Japanese

jas joined another society

Jas/Ja' James

Jaser Jasper

jASF joined Anti-Slavery Friends

JAV Batavia (Java)

Jb (1) Jacob (2) Jakob

jC member joined a group of Conservative Friends (Quaker)

JC (1) June Court (2) Justiciary Court (British)

JCAL *Jewish Calendar* (genealogy software utility)

JCBL John Carter Brown Library, Providence, RI

jccp judge court of common pleas

JCD (1) Doctor of Canon Law (2) Doctor of Civil Law

JCGS Johnson County Genealogical Society, P.O. Box 12666, Shawnee Mission, KS 66382-2666

JCH *Journal of Contemporary History*

jcky jockey

J Conr Johann Konrad, Johann Conrad

JCRC Joint Casualty Resolution Center

JCS Joint Chiefs of Staff

JCSI Joint Command Systems Initiative

Jct. Junction

JD (1) Doctor of Jurisprudence (2) Judicial (probate) districts (Connecticut and Vermont) (3) *Juris Doctor* (Doctor of Law)

Jef Jeffrey

Jeff Geoffrey, Jeffray, Jeffrey

JEH *Journal of Economic History*

Jennie/Jenny Jane, Jean, Jennifer

JEPN *Journal of the English Place-Name Society*

Jer Jeremiah, Jeremy, Jerome

Jer/Jerᵃ/Jere/Jeremᵃ Jeremiah

Jersey Blues The Ancient and Honorable Order of the Jersey Blues

JERU Jerusalem

JFH *Journal of Family History*

Jfr. Jungfrau (maiden, virgin)

JG Junior Grade

JGFF JewishGen Family Finder

Jgfr/Jngfr Jungfrau, a girl never married

JGS Jefferson Genealogical Society, P.O. Box 961, Metairie, LA 70004-0961

JGS Jewish Genealogical Society, Inc., P.O. Box 6398, New York, NY 10128

JGSBCNJ Jewish Genealogical Society of Bergen County, New Jersey, 155 N. Washington Ave., Bergenfield, NJ

JGSG Jewish Genealogical Society of Georgia, Inc., 2700 Claridge Court, Atlanta, GA 30360

JGSGB Jewish Genealogical Society of Great Britain, P.O. Box 13288, London, England N3 3WD

JGSGB Jewish Genealogical Society of Greater Boston, P.O. Box 610366, Newton, MA 02461-0366

JGSGO Jewish Genealogical Society of Greater Orlando, P.O. Box 941332, Maitland, FL 32794-1332

JGSGW Jewish Genealogical Society of Greater Washington, D.C., P.O. Box 31122, Bethesada, MD 20824-1122

JGSLA Jewish Genealogical Society of Los Angeles, P.O. Box 55443, Sherman Oaks, CA 91413

JGSO Jewish Genealogical Society of Oregon

JGSP Jewish Genealogical Society of Philadelphia

JGSR Jewish Genealogical Society of Rochester, New York

JGSS Je...
Sacran...
CA 9582...

jH joined the H...

JHSCJ Jewish Histor... Jersey, 228 Livingst... NJ 08901

JHUL John Hopkins Univers... Baltimore, MD

JHVH Jehovah

JIC John Insley Coddington Collectio... England Historic Genealogical So... Boston, MA, 02116-3007

JIH *Journal of Interdisciplinary History*

Jill/Jilly Gillian, Jillian

Jim/Jimmie/Jimmy James

JISHS *Journal of the Illinois State Historical Society*

J./Jour journeyman

J Jb (1) Johann Jacob (2) Johann Jakob

jl(s) Journal(s)

Jla Julio

J Lud Johann Ludwig

Jmc Jamaica

JMC Joint Maritime Course

jMeth joined the Methodist Church (Quaker)

JMH *Journal of Mississippi History*

JMH *Journal of Modern History*

JMSIUS *Journal of the Military Service Institution of the United States*

JMU James Madison University, 800 South Main Street, Harrisonburg, VA 22807

jn (1) journeyman (2) journeymen

Jn John

JNH *Journal of Negro History*

jnl journal

Jno/Jn° (1) John (2) Jonathan

jnr junior

Jntn Johnstown Public Library, Johnstown, PA

Jo Johann, Johannes, John, Joseph, Josephine

Jocu joint occupant

Joe Joel, Joseph, Josephine

Joes Johannes

Joh Johann, Johannes

Joh/Jo/Ioh/Jno John

Joha Johanna

Johes Johannes

Johnnie/Johnny John, Johnathan

join joiner

Jois Johannis (of Johannes)

Jon/Jon'/Jon'/Jonath' Jonathan

Jonkpg Jonkoping, Sweden

Jos Joseph, Josephine, Josiah

Jos' Josiah

Josh Joshua

Josie/Josy Josephine

JOUAM Junior Order-Order of United American Mechanics

jour journal

Journ Journalism

JP (1) Japan, Japanese (2) Justice of the Peace

J-PCT Justice Precinct

JPEG (1) graphics file format (2) Joint Photographic Experts Group

JPG Compressed version of GIF

JPG Joint Photographic Experts Group (*see also* JPEG)

JPH *Journal of the Presbyterian History Society/Journal of Presbyterian History*

JPN Japan

JPRC Joint Personnel Recovery Center

JPRS Joint Publication Research Service

JPS Jewish Publication Society

Jr/Jr./Junr/Jun'/J' Junior

Jr Junior

Jr blksmth junior blacksmith

Jr hrnssmk junior harness maker

JRDF Joint Rapid Deployment Force

JRI Jewish Records Indexing

JRN Jordan

jrnl journal

jrnm journeyman

Jr° Jerome

J Rud Johann Rudolf

jr wagnmkr junior wagon maker

JSCSC Joint Service Command and Staff College

JSH (1) *Journal of Social History* (2) *Journal of Southern History*

JSMB Joseph Smith Memorial Building, Salt Lake City, UT 84150

JsoH *Journal of Southern History*

Jst/Pce Justice of the Peace

JSTOR Journal Storage (online journal database)

JSY Jersey

jt joint

JTF-FA Joint Task Force—Full Accounting

JTIDS Joint Tactical Information Distribution System

jtly jointly

j.u. *Jure uxoris* (right of wife)

Ju/Je June

jud (1) judge (county common court) (2) judicial

Jud Judith

JUD *Juris Utriusque Doctor* (Doctor of Laws)

judg judges

Judge Ad. Judge Advocate

judgmt/judgmnt judgement, as at law

judic judicious

JUH *Journal of Urban History*

Juin June

Juill July

Jul Julia, Julian, Juliet, Julius

Jul/Jl July

J Uli Johann Ulrich

Jun (1) June (2) junior

junc junction

jur (1) *juratum* (it has been sworn) (2) jurisprudence (3) jury or juror

Jur D *Juris Doctorate* (Doctor of Law)

JUSCA *Journal of the United States Calvary Association*

Just Justice

JUTL Jutland

juv juvenis (young)

Juv Juvenile

JWHA John Whitmer Historical Association

jwlr jeweler

Jer Jeremiah, Jeremy, Jerome

Jer/Jer'/Jere/Jerem' Jeremiah

Jersey Blues The Ancient and Honorable Order of the Jersey Blues

JERU Jerusalem

JFH *Journal of Family History*

Jfr. Jungfrau (maiden, virgin)

JG Junior Grade

JGFF JewishGen Family Finder

Jgfr/Jngfr Jungfrau, a girl never married

JGS Jefferson Genealogical Society, P.O. Box 961, Metairie, LA 70004-0961

JGS Jewish Genealogical Society, Inc., P.O. Box 6398, New York, NY 10128

JGSBCNJ Jewish Genealogical Society of Bergen County, New Jersey, 155 N. Washington Ave., Bergenfield, NJ

JGSG Jewish Genealogical Society of Georgia, Inc., 2700 Claridge Court, Atlanta, GA 30360

JGSGB Jewish Genealogical Society of Great Britain, P.O. Box 13288, London, England N3 3WD

JGSGB Jewish Genealogical Society of Greater Boston, P.O. Box 610366, Newton, MA 02461-0366

JGSGO Jewish Genealogical Society of Greater Orlando, P.O. Box 941332, Maitland, FL 32794-1332

JGSGW Jewish Genealogical Society of Greater Washington, D.C., P.O. Box 31122, Bethesada, MD 20824-1122

JGSLA Jewish Genealogical Society of Los Angeles, P.O. Box 55443, Sherman Oaks, CA 91413

JGSO Jewish Genealogical Society of Oregon

JGSP Jewish Genealogical Society of Philadelphia

JGSR Jewish Genealogical Society of Rochester, New York

JGSS Jewish Genealogical Society of Sacramento, 2351 Wyda Way, Sacramento, CA 95825

jH joined the Hicksite Friends (Quaker)

JHSCJ Jewish Historical Society of Central Jersey, 228 Livingston Ave., New Brunswick, NJ 08901

JHUL John Hopkins University Library, Baltimore, MD

JHVH Jehovah

JIC John Insley Coddington Collection, New England Historic Genealogical Society, Boston, MA, 02116-3007

JIH *Journal of Interdisciplinary History*

Jill/Jilly Gillian, Jillian

Jim/Jimmie/Jimmy James

JISHS *Journal of the Illinois State Historical Society*

J./Jour journeyman

J Jb (1) Johann Jacob (2) Johann Jakob

jl(s) Journal(s)

Jla Julio

J Lud Johann Ludwig

Jmc Jamaica

JMC Joint Maritime Course

jMeth joined the Methodist Church (Quaker)

JMH *Journal of Mississippi History*

JMH *Journal of Modern History*

JMSIUS *Journal of the Military Service Institution of the United States*

JMU James Madison University, 800 South Main Street, Harrisonburg, VA 22807

jn (1) journeyman (2) journeymen

Jn John

JNH *Journal of Negro History*

jnl journal

Jno/Jn° (1) John (2) Jonathan

jnr junior

Jntn Johnstown Public Library, Johnstown, PA

J

j (1) joined (2) journal (3) served on a jury during the given year

J (1) Jahr(e), year(s) (2) Johann or Johannes (3) journeyman

Ja James, Jane

Ja/JA/JAM/JAMA Jamaica

Jab Jabal, Jabalpur, Japez, Jabreel

Jac L. Jacobus, James

JAMA *The Journal of the American Medical Association*

Ja/Jan/Janry/JanRy January

JA (1) Japan (2) Judge Advocate

JAD Joint Application Development

JAG Judge Advocate General

JAH *Journal of American History*

JAM Jamaica

Jam/Jamie James

Jamtld Jamtland, Sweden

jan janitor

Janv January

JAOUW Junior Order-Ancient Order of United Workmen

JAP/JAPA (1) Japan (2) Japanese

jas joined another society

Jas/Ja' James

Jaser Jasper

jASF joined Anti-Slavery Friends

JAV Batavia (Java)

Jb (1) Jacob (2) Jakob

jC member joined a group of Conservative Friends (Quaker)

JC (1) June Court (2) Justiciary Court (British)

JCAL *Jewish Calendar* (genealogy software utility)

JCBL John Carter Brown Library, Providence, RI

jccp judge court of common pleas

JCD (1) Doctor of Canon Law (2) Doctor of Civil Law

JCGS Johnson County Genealogical Society, P.O. Box 12666, Shawnee Mission, KS 66382-2666

JCH *Journal of Contemporary History*

jcky jockey

J Conr Johann Konrad, Johann Conrad

JCRC Joint Casualty Resolution Center

JCS Joint Chiefs of Staff

JCSI Joint Command Systems Initiative

Jct. Junction

JD (1) Doctor of Jurisprudence (2) Judicial (probate) districts (Connecticut and Vermont) (3) *Juris Doctor* (Doctor of Law)

Jef Jeffrey

Jeff Geoffrey, Jeffray, Jeffrey

JEH *Journal of Economic History*

Jennie/Jenny Jane, Jean, Jennifer

JEPN *Journal of the English Place-Name Society*

K

k (1) killed (2) king

K (1) Kent, England (2) Kinder (children)

ka killed in action

Kan Kanada/Canada

Kan/Kans/KANS Kansas

KANA Kashubian Association of North America

KARA Kawartha Ancestral Research Association, P.O. Box 162, Peterborough, Ontario K9J 6Y8

Karls/Karlsr Karlsruhe, Baden

KaSHS Kansas State Historical Society, Reference Services, 120 West Tenth Street, Topeka, KS 66612

Kat Katham

Kath Katharine, Katherine, Kathryn

KB (1) kilobyte(s) (2) Kirchenbuch, parish register (3) Knight of the Bath (4) knowledge base

KBE Knight Commander of the Order of the British Empire

Kbl Kabul, Afghanistan

kc kilocycle(s)

KC Kansas City (Missouri, Kansas)

K.C. (1) King's Counsel (2) Knights of Columbus

Kcb Kirkcudbrightshire, Scotland

KCB Knight Commander of the Order of the Bath

KCD Kincardine, Kincardineshire, Scotland

KCGS Kansas Council of Genealogical Societies, P.O. Box 3858, Topeka, KS 66604-6858

KCL King's College London, England

KCPL Kansas City Public Library, Kansas City, MO

KCPL-KVSC Kansas City Public Library, Missouri Valley Special Collections

KCVO Knight Commander of the Royal Victorian Order

keep keeper

KeHS Kentucky Historical Society, P.O. Box H, Frankfort, KY 40602-2108

Kel Keller

Ken Kentucky

Ken/Kennie/Kenny Kenneth

KEN/KENT Kent

KepC keeper in charge

kept (1) keep (2) kept

Ker Kerry, Republic of Ireland

KeSCF Kentucky State College, Frankfort, KY

Kester Christopher

KFM Knights of Father Matthew

kg (1) keg(s) (2) kilogram(s)

KG (1) Knight of the Order of the Garter (2) Knights of St. George

KGE Knights of Golden Eagle

KGL Knight Grand Legion

KGS Kansas Genealogical Society, P.O. Box 103, Dodge City, KS 67801

kh Keeping house/housekeeper

KHC Knights of Holy Cross

KHess Kurhessen

KHQ *Kansas Historical Quarterly*

KHS Kansas State Historical Society, Reference Services, 120 West Tenth Street, Topeka, KS 66612

ki killed by Indians

KIA killed in action

KID Kildare

KIK Kilkenny

Kild Kildare, Ireland

Kilk Kilkenny, Ireland

kilo (1) kilogram (2) kilometer

kin blood relatives or in-laws

Kinc/KINC Kincardine, Scotland

kind kindred

Kinr/KINR Kinross, Scotland

kinsm kinsman

kinsw kinswoman

Kirk/KIRK Kirkcudbright, Scotland

Kit Catherine, Christopher, Katherine, Katharine

kith friends and relatives

KitM kitchen maid

KitP kitchen porter

KitS kitchen superintendent

Kittie/Kity Catherine, Katherine

KKD Kirkcudbright, Scotland

KKD Kirkcudbright, Scotland

KKK Ku Klux Klan

Kld Kildare, Republic of Ireland

kln kilderkin

km murdered

KM (1) Knights Militant (2) Knights of Malta (Masonic)

KMC Knights of the Mystic Chain

kn known

KN Kansas

Knc/KNC Kincardineshire, Scotland

knls knolls

Knr/KNR Kinrosshire, Scotland

knt/kt knight

Knxv Knoxville, TN

KO knockout

KO/KOA/KOR/Kor Korea

K. of C. Knights of Columbus

K of FM Knights of Father Matthew

K of H Knights of Honor

K of L Knights of Loyola

K of M Knights of Malta (Masonic)

K of P Knights of Pythias

K of SJ Knights of San Juan

K of STP Knights of St. Patrick

K of STW Knights of St. Wenceslas

K of T Knights of Tabor

Kol Kollans

Konstz Konstanz, Baden

Koppg Kopparberg, Sweden

KOR Korea

KOTM Knights of Macabees

KP Knights of Pythias

KPC Knights of Peter Claver

KPL Kansas Pioneers List

kpr keeper

Krist Kristianstad, Sweden

Kristy Christina, Christine

KRK Kircudbrightshire, Scotland

Kronbg Kronoberg, Sweden

KRS Kinross, Scotland

KRS Kinross-shire, Scotland

KS/Kans Kansas

KSC Knights of St. Columbkille

KSF Knights of Sherwood Forest

KSHS Kansas State Historical Society, Reference Services, 120 West Tenth Street, Topeka, KS 66612

KSL Knights of St. Lawrence

KST Kansas Territory

KSTG Knights of St. George

KSTI Knights of St. Ignatius

KSTJ Knights of St. Joseph

KSTM Knights of St. Martin

KSTP Knights of St. Paul

KSTP Knights of St. Peter

KSTT Knights of St. Thomas

KSU Kent State University Network Center, Kent, OH

kt knight

KT Knights of Tabor

KT (1) Knight of the Thistle (Scotland) (2) Knight Templar (masonic)

ktd knighted

KurH KurHessen/Kurkessen

Kuw Kuwait

KVGS Kalamazoo Valley Genealogical Society, P.O. Box 405, Comstock, MI 49041

kw killed in war

KWM Knights of Wise Men

ky key

KY/Ky Kentucky

L

l (1) law (2) leaf (leaves) (3) liber/libre, book or freespoken (4) license (5) line (6) lived (7) lodger

-l (word ending in l.) = root word + lichB or -lein; a similar scriptural notation means that the end of the word is missing

L (1) American Indian (2) Lake (3) Latin (4) Lawful (5) left (in stage directions) (6) Left the area shown. Migrated to another place (7) Liber (8) *Libra* (Pound) (9) Licentiate (10) living (less than 110 years) (11) Lodger (12) lot

L/Lieut Lieutenant

L1/1Lt First Lieutenant

L2/2Lt Second Lieutenant

L3 Third Lieutenant

la (1) laborer (2) lane (3) language (4) letters of administration

La (1) Laborer (2) Lancashire, England (3) Louisiana

La/Ln Lane

LA (1) Latin, academic (2) Letters of Administration (3) Library Association (4) Louisiana

LA/La Louisiana

L-An Lesser Antilles (Virgin Islands)

lab (1) laborer (2) Labrador

Lab Laboratories, Laboratory

Labl Label

LabM labor master

labr laborer

laby laboratory

Lac a resinous substance used in sealing wax, lacquer, etc.

La Colonials Louisiana Colonials

lad lad

Ladies of GAR Ladies of the Grand Army of the Republic

lady lady

LAE Lake Erie

LAESI Local Authority and Emergency Service Information

LAGS Livermore-Amador Genealogical Society, Pleasanton Library, 400 Old Bernal Avenue, Pleasanton, CA 94566

LAK Lanark, Scotland

LAm Latin America

LAN Local Area Network (computer term)

LAN/LANC/Lancs Lancashire, England

LANA Lanark, Great Britain

Lanc Lancelot

Landsc Landscape

lang language

Lang Language

Langs Languages

LAO Laos

LAOH Ladies Ancient Order of Hibernians

LAPL Los Angeles Public Library, History and Genealogy Department, 630 West Fifth Street, Los Angeles, CA 90071

LaSL Louisiana State Library, Baton Rouge, LA

Lat/L(at) Latin

LAT Latvia

LAT-WP *Los Angeles Times—Washington Post* News Service

lau laundry

Lau Launderer

LaU Louisiana State University, Baton Rouge, LA

LAUF London Archives Users Forum

LAUE Lauenburg

Laur Laurence

Laurie Lawrence

/law in-law, e.g. mother/in/law

LAW Letters of Administration with Will Annexed

LawP Lawrence, Pennsylvania

Lawr/Lawr Lawrence

Laz Lazarus

lb pound

LB (1) Bachelor of Letters (2) Brevet Lieutenant (3) Labrador, Canada (4) London Borough

LBC Letter Book Copy

LBL Land between the Lakes (Kentucky and Tennessee)

lbr lumber

l.c. lower case (type)

Lc local census

LC (1) Landing Craft (2) Lower Canada (i.e., Bas-Canada or Québec)

LC Library of Congress

L.C./l.c. legitimate child

LC/LtCol Lieutenant Colonel

LC/LOC Library of Congress, Local History and Genealogy Reading Room, Thomas Jefferson Building, 10 First Street SE, Washington, DC 20540-5554

LCA Lutheran Church in America

LCC London County Council

LCD Liquid Crystal Display

LCI landing craft, infantry

lcks locks

LCMA Missouri Synod Lutheran Church

Lcmp lady's companion

LCMS Lutheran Church – Missouri Synod

Lcn Lincoln

LCol Lieutenant Colonel

lcor Licking Co. Probate Records, Licking Co. Ohio Genealogical Society

LCP landing craft, personnel

LCSH Library of Congress Subject Headings

Lctr lecturer

ld (1) land (2) lawful daughter

Ld (1) land (2) Lodger (3) Lord

LD Doctor of Letters

LDAP Lightweight Directory Access Protocol

Ld B^p Lord Bishop

LDE *London Daily News*

LDET Lipp Detmold (Lippe Detmold)

ldg lodge

LdgB lodger's brother

LdgC lodger's child

LdgD lodger's daughter

LdgF lodger's father

LdgH lodger's husband

LdgK lodge keeper

LdgM lodger's mother

LdgN lodger's nephew or niece

LdgS lodger's son

LDGS Lower Delmarva Genealogical Society P.O. Box 3602, Salisbury, MD 21802-3602

LdgW lodger's wife

LdKs lodge keeper's son

LDMS London Domestic Mission Society (England)

ldr leader

lds lords

Lds LDS

LDS Latter-day Saint. Member of The Church of Jesus Christ of Latter-day Saints (sometimes known as the Mormon Church)

LDSCA LDS Church Archives

LDY Londonderry

LdyH lady helper

LdyM lady's maid, lady's matron

le local elder in a church

LE (1) Lake Erie (2) London, England

Learn Learning

LEB (1) Lebanon (2) Lebbe

LEC/Lei/LEIC/Leic Leicestershire, England

Lechford *Note-Book Kept by Thomas Lechford*

lect lecturer

Lectr Lecturer

led *ledig* (unmarried)

Lees of Va Society of the Lees of Virginia

leg legacy, legatee

Leg/legis Legislation, legislative

LEG *Legacy* (genealogy software program)

Legis Legislative, Legislature

legit/legt legitimate

legn legion

Leics/LEIC Leicester, Leicestershire (England)

Leipzg Leipzig, Saxony, Germany

Leisureman man of leisure

Leitr Leitrim, Ireland

Leix Leix, Ireland

Len (1) Lenan/Lennen (2) Leonard

Lena Helena, Magdelen, Magdelene

Len^d Leonard, Lenard

LenH Lenhosk

Leo Leonard, Leanora

Leon Leon, Leonard

Leon^d/Leon'd Leonard

Leonh Leonhard, Leonhart

Les Lesley, Leslie, Lester

LET Leitrim

LetC letter carrier

letters CTA letters cum testamento annexed

Lettie/Letty Letita

LEX Leix (Queens)

LEXIS/NEXIS computer full-text research and informational retrieval service containing current news information databases; legal research database of current federal and state appellate court decisions

lf loaf

Lfd Longford, Republic of Ireland

lg letters of guardianship

Lg lodge or club membership

LG Landed Gentry

LGAR Ladies of the Grand Army of the Republic

LGen Lieutenant General

LgGC lodger's grandchild

LgGD lodger's granddaughter

LgGS lodger's grandson

LGL large genealogical libraries

LgMD lodger's maid

LGO Land Grant Office

LGS Local Government Services

lgt light

Lgt. Art. Light Artillery (military regiment)

LgtM lighterman

LH (1) *Labor History* (2) local history

LH *Louisiana History*

LHD *Litterarum Humaniorum Doctor* (Doctor of Humanities, Doctor of Humane Letters)

LH & GL/LHGL Local History & Genealogy Librarian News Online

LHo Parts of Holland, Lincolnshire, England

lht light

LHQ *Louisiana Historical Quarterly*

li (1) abbreviation for pound (2) lines (3) lived, living

LI (1) Light Infantry (2) Long Island (New York)

lib liber (book)

LIB (1) Libeg/Liebig/Liberia (2) Libya

lib/libr library

Libby & Noyes Noyes, Libby, and Davis, *Genealogical Dictionary of Maine and New Hampshire*

Libl Liberal

libn/libr/librn librarian

Libr Library, Libraries

Librn Librarian

lic license

Lic Lichtenfels

Lie (1) Liebbo/Lebbe/Liennen (2) Liepsic

LIE/LIEC Liechtenstein

Lienh Lienhard, Lienhart

Lieut/Lt Lieutenant

Lif Livingston

LIHS Long Island Historical Society, Brooklyn, NY

LiIre Lisbon, Ireland

LIJGS Jewish Genealogical Society of Long Island, 37 Westcliff Dr., Dix Hills, NY 11746

Lim/Limer/LimI Limerick, Ireland

Lime brnr lime burner

Lin Linn/Linnen/Liennen/Lienen

LIN/LINC/Lincs Lincolnshire, England

Lincs Lincoln, England

Ling Linguitics

LinN Lincoln, Nebraska

lino linotype

LipD Lippe Detmold/Lippe Darmstadt, Germany

LipM Lippemold

Lippe Lippe-Detmold, Germany

Lis Elisabeth, Lisette

LIS Library Information Services

Lis/Lisbeth Elizabeth, Elisabeth, Eliza

ListProc mailing list software

ListServ mailing list software

lit (1) literally (2) literary (3) literature

Lit Literature

LIT/LITH Lithuania

Lit B/Litt B (1) *Literatura Bachelor* (Bachelor of Literature) (2) *Litterarum Bachelor* (Bachelor of Letters)

Lit D/Litt D (1) *Literatura Doctor* (Doctor of Literature) (2) *Litterarum Doctor* (Doctor of Letters)

LITH/Lith Lithuania

litho lithographer

liv livery

liv/li lived or living

Liv Liverpool, England

Liv. Livingston

liv.abt lived about

live/w lives with

LivT living together

Liz Elizabeth

lk/lke/lks lake(s)

Lk Luke

LK of a Loyal Knights of America

Lke Parts of Kesteven, Lincolnshire, England

LK of A Loyal Knights of America

LKS Lanarkshire or Lanark, Scotland

LkSm locksmith

ll (1) lines (2) local libraries

LLB *Legum Baccalaureus* (Bachelor of Laws)

LLC Logical Link Control

LLCGS Lincoln – Lancaster County Genealogical Society, Box 30055, Lincoln, NE 68503-0055

LLD *Legum Doctor* (Doctor of Laws)

LLD Lineage-linked databases

LLDB Linked Lineage Data Base

LLi Parts of Lindsey, Lincolnshire, England

LLM *Legum Magister* (Master of Laws)

Llrd landlord

LlrS landlord's son

LLUSI Lovejoy Library, University of Southern Illinois

LM lawful money

LMA London Metropolitan Archives

Lmat laundry matron

lmbr mct lumber merchant

LMC Library Management Committee

LMI Lake Michigan

ln lane

LN Last name

lnd land

Lnd Londonderry, Northern Ireland

LND/Lnd London (city)

LND Noyes, Libby, and Davis, *Genealogical Dictionary of Maine and New Hampshire*

Lnd/Lrd Land Lord

lndg landing

LndL landlady

Lndr laundress

lndrs laundress

lndry laundry

Lnk Lanarkshire, Scotland

LNL Linlithgow/West Lothian, Scotland

Lnm Landsman

LnMd laundrymaid

lo lodge

LO Lookout

l/o late of

loc (1) local (2) locative (3) location

Loc. location of original item

LOC Library of Congress, 10 First Street SE, Washington, DC 20540-5554

local hist local history

loc cit *loco citato* (in the place cited)

Lodg lodger

Loerr Loerrach, Baden

L of C Library of Congress, Washington, DC

LOG Longford

LOL Laughing Out Loud

Lom/LOMB Lombardy

LOM Loyal Order of M.O.O.S.E.

Lon Londonderry, Northern Ireland

Lond/LOND/LonE London, England

Longfd Longford, Ireland

L.O.O.M. Loyal Order of Moose

loq *loquitur* (he/she speaks)

Lor Lorraine

Lorai Loraine

Lord-Lieut Lord-Lieutenant

Lot Lottering

Lou Louis

LOU Louth

Louis Louise

LovC love child

Low Lower

LowH Lower Hesse/Hessen

lp local preacher

LPC likely public charge

LPH Landing Platform Helicopter

LPI/lpi lines per inch

lr Law Record

at liberty to marry

Ireland

s Massachusetts

Military Assistance Advisory Group

Massachusetts Archives

America

Germany

nd

l

nburg

ia Access Control

icarus

mplaint

bers' Ancestor Charts. A collection of
e charts maintained by the National
ogical Society, 4527 17th Street
Arlington, VA 22207-2399

tenberg

LUXE Luxembourg,

ry Airlift Command

achine (2) machinist (3)
nerie (Norman) masonry

inia

tary Aid to the Civil Power

tary Assistance Command, Vietnam

G MACV Studies and Observations

of Maderia (2) Madagascar

ablic Library, Las Vegas, NV

or Patent. Most often from the
antee.

e, Madison

gascar

orld Federation

ra

orking Group

ret

Madam

Madrid, Spain

ix), Republic of Ireland

g, Belgium

istrate

(5) measure (pl. mm) (6) meter (7) mile or miles (8) mill (9) mineur-minor (10) month(s), monthly (11) mother (12) noon (13) thousand

m/ma/marr (1) marriage (2) married

M (1) Controlled Extraction number (LDS) (2) indicates marriages extracted in the Controlled Extraction Program (LDS) (3) Magister or Meister, master (either by university degree or of a craft) (4) majeur-of age (5) Male Sealing List (LDS) (6) Manufactures censuses (7) Manuscript page (8) marker (gravestone) (9) Marquess (10) Marriage Register (11) married (12) masculine (13) Master (of) (14) *meridies* (noon) (15) Microfilm/microfiche (16) Middle (17) Minor (18) miscellaneous (19) Monat(e), month(s) (20) Monday (21) Monsieur (22) morning (newspaper) (23) Mother (24) National Archives microfilm series (25) thousand

M Marie

M/Mon Monday

m int marriage intentions

m1/m. 1 (1) married first (2) mother-in-law

m/1, m/2 first marriage, second marriage, etc.

m2/m. 2 married second

Ma (1) Malay (2) Mary

MA (1) Mary Ann (2) Massachusetts (3) Master of Arts degree (4) metropolitan area (6) Military Academy (7) Minor's Application

MAAG

MA Arch

M-A Mid

Ma Maria

Mab Mab

Mac Mac

MAC Mec

MAC Mer
  pedigr
  Geneal
  North,

MAC Milit

mach (1) m
  macher

MACP Mili

MACV Mili

MACV-SO
  Group

MAD (1) Isl

Mad Madelir

Madag Mada

MADE Made

Madge Marg

Madm/Mdm

Madr Madras,

mag magazi

mag/mag

Mag (1) Magazine (2) Magdalene, Magdalena (3) Magistrate (4) Magnate

Magd. (1) Magdalena (2) servant girl, maid

Mag^d Magdalena

MAGIC Midwest Afro-American Genealogical Interest Coalition, P.O. Box 300972, Kansas City, MO 64130-0972

MAGIC Mohican Area Genealogists Interested in Computers (Ohio)

magist magistrate

mag^la Magdalena

Magna Charta National Society Magna Charta Dames, P.O. Box 4222, Philadelphia, PA 19144

M Agr Master of Agriculture

MAGS Mid-Atlantic Germanic Society, 14710 Sherwood Drive, Greencastle, PA 17225-8403

Mah Mahican dialect

mah^y mahogany

mahog^y mahogany

Mai May

maid/Maid maid, maidservant

mail cntr mail contractor, rent contractor

Maisie Maria, Marie, Mary

maj/majr major

Maj/Mj Major (military rank)

Maj Gen/Major-Gen Major General

mak making

MAL/MALTA/MALT Malta

malls measles

Malmhs Malmohus, Sweden

malt maltster

Mamie Maria, Marie, Mary

MAN Metropolitan Area Network

man/Man (1) manager (2) manor

Man/MAN/MB Manitoba, Canada

Mana· Manuela

Manch Manchuria

Man Dir Managing Director

Man^l Manuel

Man. List State Register and Manual lists of villages, etc., without post offices

Mannh/Mannhm Mannheim, Baden

mannl. mannlich (masculine)

mans mansions

manu (1) manumission, the act of formally freeing a slave (2) mauscript

Manuel/Many Emmanuel

manuf'r manufacturer

manuf'y manufactory

MAPLIN Manitoba Public Library Information Network (Canada)

mar/MAR/marr/MARR (1) marriage (2) married

Mar (1) Maria (2) Marines

Mar/Mr/mRch March

MAR Marburg

MAR Microfilm Action Request(s)

MARA machine-readable accessions

Marb Marriage bann

MarbHS Marblehead Historical Society, 161 Washington Street, Marblehead, MA 01945

marble ctr marble cutter

Marc Marriage contract

MARC Machine-Readable Cataloging

MARCH Montague Association for the Restoration of Community History, 320 River Road, Montague, NJ 07827

MarD married daughter

marg (1) margin (2) marginal

Marg/Margie/Margot/Marg^t/Margt/Mrgt Margaret

Marg^ta Margarita

Margy Margaret, Margret, Margery

Marion Mary

Marl Marriage License

mar.lic marriage licence

marr marriage

Marr Marriage

Mars Marriage settlement

MarS married son

marsh marshall

Mart Martin

MaSAr Massachusetts Secretary of State, Archives Division, Boston, MA

masc masculine

MASc Master of Applied Science

Mass/Massa Massachusetts

Mass. Arch. Massachusetts Archives Collection (Massachusetts Archives), 220 Morrissey Boulevard, Boston, MA 02125

Mass. Archives Massachusetts State Archives, Columbia Point, Dorchester, Massachusetts

Mass. Bay Rec. Records of the Governor and Company of the Massachusetts Bay

Mass HS Massachusetts Historical Society, 1154 Boylston Street, Boston, MA 02215

Mass in the War James L. Bowen, *Massachusetts in the War, 1861-1865*

MASSOG *A Genealogical Magazine for the Commonwealth of Massachusetts*

Mass. Reports *Massachusetts Reports* (published reported decisions of the Massachusetts Supreme Judicial Court)

Mass soldiers (1) Massachusetts Soldiers, Sailors and Marines in the Civil War (2) Massachusetts Soldiers and Sailors of the Revolutionary War

mast master

mat/mater (1) maternal (2) matron

Mat (1) Martha, Matilda, Matthew (2) Materials (3) Matron

MAT Master of Arts in Teaching

mate (1) mate (2) spouse (3) consort

math (1) mathematical (2) mathematics

MATh Master of Arts in Theology

Math (1) Mathematical, Mathematics (2) Mathew

Maths Mathias

Mathw Mathew

Matie/Matys/Mats/majt Majesty's, as in "His Majesty's horse"

Matr Matross

matric matriculated (entered and recorded at a college or university)

Matt Matthew, Mathew

Matth Matthaeus

Matty Martha, Matilda, Matthew

MAU Mauritius

MaUA Massachusetts University, Amherst, MA

Maur Maurenberg

MAVR Massachusetts Vital Record

Max Maximillion

May Maria, Marie, Mary

MAY Mayo

Mayflower General Society of Mayflower Descendants, 4 Winslow St., P.O. Box 3297, Plymouth, MA 02361

mb minute book

MB (1) Manitoba, Canada (2) marriages and burials (3) *Medicinae Bachelor* (Bachelor of Medicine) (4) megabyte(s) (5) municipal borough

MBA Master in/of Business Administration

MBC Missionary Baptist Church

MBCR Massachusetts Bay General Court

MBCR *Records of the Goverment and Council of the Massachusetts Bay in New England*

MBE (1) Member, Order of the British Empire (2) Most Excellent Order of the British Empire

Mbk Minute book

mbn marriage banns

mbr member

MBR Member of the Order of the British Empire

mbrp/mbrshp membership

MBS Multilingual Biblioservice

MBUG-PC Monterey Bay Users Group—Personal Computer (California)

MC (1) Adams and Weis, Magna Charta Sureties 1215 (2) map coordinates (3) Marion County, Ohio (4) Marriage certificate (5) Master of Ceremonies (6) Medical Corps (7) Member of Congress (8) Methodist Church (9) Military Cross (10) Minor's Certificate

MCA Microfilm Corporation of America

MCC (1) Massachusetts Cultural Council (2) Microfilm Corporation of America

MCC Microfilm Card Catalog

mcd married contrary to discipline

MCD (1) minor civil division (2) Municipal Civil District

MCE Master of Civil Engineering

MCGS Mendocino Coast Genealogical Society, P.O. Box 762, Fort Bragg, CA 95437

MCGS Milwaukee County Genealogical Society, P.O. Box 2737, Milwaukee, WI 53227

MCh *Magister Cheir* (Master of Surgery)

mcht merchant

MCL (1) Marietta College Library, Marietta, Ohio (2) Master of Civil Law

MCMV Mine Countermeasures Vessel

mcpl municipal

MCPL Mid-Continent Public Library, 317 West 24 Highway, Independence, MO 64050

mct merchant

md (1) maid (2) married

Md Maryland

MD (1) *Medicinae Doctor* (Doctor of Medicine) (2) Middle Dutch (3) Military District

MD *The Mayflower Descendant* (journal of the Massachusetts Society of Mayflower Descendants, 100 Boylston Street, Suite 750, Boston, MA 02116-4610)

MD Maryland

MDAR Massachusetts Daughters of the American Revolution

Md Arch Maryland Archives (Hall of Records), 350 Rowe Blvd. Annapolis, MD 21401

Mddx/Mx Middlesex, England

MDG *Maryland and Delaware Genealogist*

MdHi/MdHs Maryland Historical Society, 201 West Monument Street, Baltimore, MD 21201

M Div Master of Divinity

mdl middle

MDL Mayflower Descendant Legacy

Mdn maiden

MDR (1) Madeira (2) Manorial Documents Register (British)

MDS Master of Dental Surgery

MdSCPA Maryland State College, Princess Ann

mdse merchandise

Mdsg Merchandising

MDSX Middlesex County, NJ

mdws meadows

MDX Middlesex, England

Me (1) Maine (2) Maître

ME (1) Methodist Episcopal Church (2) Middle English

ME/Me (1) Maine (2) Mechanical Engineer

ME/Meth Methodist

MEA Meath

Mec/Meck Mecklenburg, Germany

MEC Methodist Episcopal Church

mech mechanics

Mech Mechanical

Meck, Sc./MSCH Mecklenburg-Schwerin

MeckS/Meck, St./MSTR Mecklenburg, Strelitz

M Econ Master of Economics

MECS Methodist Episcopal Church South

MecSc Mecklenberg-Schwerin

med (1) median (2) medical (3) medicine (4) medieval (5) medium

Med Medical, Medicine

MEd Master of Education

MedA medical assistant

MEDFO Medford, OR

Media Media Specialist

Medit Mediterranean

MedO medical officer

MedS medical superintendent

MeHS Maine Historical Society, 485 Congress Street, Portland, ME 04101

Mei Meins

MEK Mecklenberg

Mel Melheim on Rhine

MEL Michigan Electronic Library

Melb Melbourne, Australia

Melch Melchior, Melcher

MELVYL Union catalog for the University of California library system

mem (1) membership (2) membrane (3) memoir (4) memorandum (5) memorial(s)

mem/memb member

Mem Member

MemH member of household

memo memorandum

MEMPH/MemT Memphis, TN

men mention made of the person named

Mendz Mendez

Meng Middlesex, England

Menn Mennonite

ment (1) mention (2) mentioned

mer (1) mayor (2) meritorious

Mer/MER Merionethshire, Wales

merc/merch merchant

merchntclk merchant clerk

MERI/Merion Merioneth, Wales

Mesg messenger

mess messuage

Messa Messach

Messrs Messieurs (plural of mister)

Messrs/Mess"/Mssrs Messieurs

Met Metropolitan

Meta Margaret

Metall Metallurgical, Metallurgy

Metaphys Metaphysics

Met.B metropolitan borough

METEM International Society of Toronto for Hungarian Church History (Toronto, ON)

Meteor Meteorology

meter rdr meter reader

Meth Methodist

meth prchr Methodist preacher

M.'et'L. Maine' et' Loire

M.'et'M. Meurthe' et' Moselle

Metrop Metropolitan

MeVS Maine Office of Vital Statistics, Maine Department of Human Services, State House Station II, Augusta, ME 04333-0011

MEX Mexican War veteran

MEX/MEXI Mexico

Mex Mexican

Mex.$ Mexican peso

Mex. S.O. Mexican Survivors' Originals

Mex W.C. Mexican Widows' Certificate

MeyS Meyerstadt, Germany

mf (1) manufacture (2) mulatto female

MF *Mayflower Families* (General Society of Mayflower Descendants, 4 Winslow Street, P.O. Box 3297, Plymouth, MA 02361)

MF (1) microfiche (2) microfilm (3) Minor's File

MFA Master of Fine Arts

MFF Missing Folk Finder

mfg manufacturing

MFIP *Mayflower Families in Progress*, General Society of Mayflower Descendants, 4 Winslow St., P.O. Box 3297, Plymouth, MA 02361

m'form microfilm, microfiche, microform

mfr manufacturer

Mfrank Mittel-Franken, Bavaria, Germany

mfrs manufactures

MG (1) Manchester Guardian (2) megabyte

MG/M.G./mg Minister of the Gospel

MGC Michigan Genealogical Council, P.O. Box 80953, Lansing, MI 48908-0953

MGen Major General

MGI *Michiana Genealogical Index*

Mgm Montgomeryshire, Wales

Mgmt Management

mgr (1) manager (2) monsignor

Mgr Manager

MGRP Molecular Genealogy Research Project, Sorenson Molecular Genealogy Foundation

MGS Minnesota Genealogical Society, P.O. Box 16069, Saint Paul, MN 55116-0069

MGS Mobile Genealogical Society, P.O. Box 6224, Mobile, AL 36660-6224

MGS Montgomery Genealogical Society, 3110 Highfield Drive, Montgomery, AL 36111

Mgt (1) Management (2) Margaret, Margret, Margretha

Mgy Margery

MGY Montgomeryshire, Wales

MH (1) meetinghouse (church) (2) *Michigan History* (3) *Minnesota History*

MHA Marine Historical Association, Mystic, Connecticut

MHA Master's Degree in Healthcare Administration

MHA Mormon History Association

MHB *Minnesota History Bulletin*

MHG Middle High German

MHGR *Maine Historical and Genealogical Recorder*

MHGS Midwest Historical and Genealogical Society, 1203 North Main, P.O. Box 1121, Wichita, KS 67201

MHI Military History Institute. *See also* United States Army Military History Institute, 22 Ashburn Drive, Carlisle Barracks, Carlisle, PA 17013-5008

MHM *Michigan History Magazine*

Mhn Monaghan, Republic of Ireland

MHR *Missouri Historical Review*

MHRAB Massachusetts Historical Records Advisory Board

MHS Maine Historical Society

MHS Massachusetts Historical Society, 1154 Boylston Street, Boston, MA 02215

MHS Minnesota Historical Society, 345 West Kellogg Blvd., St. Paul, MN 55102-1906

MHS Colls *Massachusetts Historical Society Collections*

MHSSL Missouri Historical Society, St. Louis, MO

mHZ Mega Hertz

mi (1) mile(s) (2) migrated from one place to another (3) monumental inscription (tombstone)

Mi Mistress

MI (1) Military Intelligence (2) Monumental Inscriptions

MI/Mich Michigan

MIA missing in action

MIBiol Member of the Institute of Biology

Mic Micah

Mich Michaelmas, the Feast of St. Michael (Christmas)

Mich/Mi Michigan

Mich/Michl Michael, Michel

micro (1) microfilm (2) microfiche

Micro Microform

Microbiol Microbiology

Mid (1) Middle (2) Midshipman

MID/Midd/Middx/MidE Middlesex, England

Midl Midland(s)

MidW midwife

Mig¹ Miguel

MiH *Michigan History*

MiHC *Michigan Historical Collections*

MiHM *Michigan History Magazine*

MII *Mormon Immigration Index* (compact disc)

Mike Michael

mil (1) militia (2) military (3) mother-in-law

mil/milit military

m-i-l/m.i.l./M-in-l mother-in-law

MIL Military

Mil (1) Milan (2) Military

Mil Dis Rec Military Discharge Records

Milit Military

mill (1) miller (2) milliner

Mil Ord of Crusades Military Order of the Crusades, 014 Bladdyn Road, Ardmore, PA 19003

Mil Ord, Loyal Legion Military Order of the Loyal Legion of the United States, 1805 Pine Street, Philadelphia, PA 19103

MilPL Milwaukee Public Library, 814 West Wisconsin Avenue, Milwaukee, WI 53233

milt military

Milw/MilW Milwaukee, Wisconsin

Mima Jemima

MIME (1) Member of Institution of Mining Engineers (2) Multipurpose Internet Mail Extensions

Mimeo Mimeographed

min (1) mineral (2) mineralogy (3) minister (4) ministry (5) minor (6) minority (7) minute(s)

m-in-l mother-in-law

minm minimum

Minn/MN Minnesota

minr (1) milliner (2) minor

min. ret. minister's return

MInstCE Member, Institute of Civil Engineers

MInstT Member, Institute of Transport

m.int marriage intentions

MIP Maine Index Project

mIRC chat software (*IRC* software for Windows)

MIRV Multiple Independently-targetable Re-entry Vehicle

mis missioner

misc miscellaneous

Misc Miscellaneous

MisD mistress's daughter

MiSL Michigan State Library, East Lansing, MI 48824

miss mission

Miss/MS/MSA Mississippi

MisS mistress's son

MIT Massachusetts Institute of Technology, 77 Massachusetts Avenue, Cambridge, MA 02139-4307

MiU Michigan State Library, East Lansing, MI 48824

MJBA *Maryland Journal and Baltimore Advertiser*

MJur *Magister Juris* (Master of Law)

Mk Mark

MkCl Muskingum College Library, New Concord, OH

mkr maker

mkt market

mktg marketing

Mktg Marketing

ml(s) mill(s)

M¹ Michael, Michel

ML (1) marriage license (2) Marriage Licence Records (3) Master of Laws (4) military land (5) modern language (6) Mother-in-law

MLA Maine Library Association, Community Drive, Augusta, ME 04330

MLA Member, Legislative Assembly

MLA Modern Language Association

MLC Member, Legislative Council

mldr molder

mle mile

MLE Military Land Entry

MLG Middle Low German

MLIS Master of Library and Information Science

MLitt Master of Letters

MlkC milk carrier

MlkM milk man, milk boy

mlle Mademoiselle

Mll/Wgt Millwright

MLN Midlothian, Scotland (*see* Edinburgh)

Mlnr milliner

MLo Midlothian, Scotland

M. Loth/MLOT Midlothian, Scotland

MLS Master of Library and Information Science

MLT Malta

MLW Military Land Warrant

mm (1) matri-monium (2) millimeter(s) (3) mulatto male (4) *mutatis mutandis* (necessary changes being made)

MM (1) Messieurs (2) Minuteman (3) Monthly Meeting (Society of Friends, Quaker)

MM Mariners Museum, Newport News, VA

M & M Mr. and Mrs.

MMan (1) militiaman (2) minuteman

Mme Madam

MMFF Missouri Mormon Frontier Foundation, P.O. Box 3186, Independence, MO 64055

MMGS Mid-Michigan Genealogical Society, P.O. Box 16033, Lansing, MI 48901-6033

MMM Member, Order of Military Merit (Canada)

mn (1) *more novo* (in the new manner) (2) man (3) minister

Mn Modern (MnI: Modern Irish, etc.)

MN (1) Merchant Navy (2) middle name

MN/Minn Minnesota

Mnc Manchester, England

mnd mound

MND(C) Multi-National Division (Central)

MND(SW) Multi-National Division (South West)

MnE Modern English

mng managing

mngr manager, manageress

MNHP Morristown National Historical Park, Morristown, NJ

MnHS Minnesota Historical Society, 345 Kellogg Blvd. West, St. Paul, MN 55102-1906

Mnl Manila, Phillipines

MNM Monmouthshire, Wales

MNO Monaco

mnr manor

mns mines

MNS Massachusetts News Service

MnSAr Minnesota State Archives, St. Paul, MN

mnst minister

MNT Montgomeryshire, Wales

mntd maintained

MNTG/Montg Montgomery, Wales

mo (1) microfilm of original (2) month (3) mother (4) mustered out (of military service)

m/o mother of

Mo/MO Missouri

MO Minor's Original

MO (1) Major Ordinance (2) (gravestone) (3) Medical Officer (4) Military Merit (Canada) (5) Money Order, *see also* MNO (6) Mother

MOA (1) Making of America (digital library) (2) Memorandum of Agreement

MOB Master of Organizational Behavior

Mobil Mobile, Alabama

mobles movables

MOCA Maine Old Cemetery Association, P.O. Box 641, Augusta, ME 04332-0641

MoCAT *Monthly Catalog* (of the U.S. government)

mod moderator

MoD Month of Death

Mod E Modern English

Modem Modulator/Demodulator (transmit data to and from a computer)

MOFW Military Order of Foreign Wars of the United States

MOG Monaghan

Moh Mohegan dialect

MOH (1) Medal of Honor (2) Medical Officer of Health

MoHS Missouri Historical Society, Research Library and Archives, Jefferson Memorial Building, Forest Park, St. Louis, MO 63112-1099

MOHS *A Guide to Manuscripts at the Ohio Historical Society*, Andrea D. Lentz, ed.

moiety one-half

Molec Molecular

MOLLUS Military Order of the Loyal Legion of the United States, 1805 Pine Street, Philadelphia, PA 19103 (Headquarters, 600 S. Central Ave. Glendale, CA 91204)

MOLO Mid-Eastern Ohio Library Association

MoLS mother-in-law's son

mon monument, tombstone

Mon (1) Monday (2) Monmouthshire, England (3) Monroe

MON Montenegro

Monagn Monaghan, Ireland

MONM/Monms Monmouth, England

mono monotype

Mons Monsignor

Mont (1) Montgomery (2) Montreal

Mont/MT Montana

MONT (1) Montenegro (2) Montgomeryshire, Wales

mo/o mother of

MOPSUMs Monthly Operations Summaries

mor mother

Mor/MOR Moray (*see* Elgin), Scotland

Mor Moroccan, Morocco

Mor/Morav/MORA Moravia

MORA Moray, Great Britain

Mor Arch Moravian Archives, 4 East Bank Street, Winston-Salem, NC 27101

morg (1) morganatic (2) morgen

morn morning

MORO Morocco

mors death, corpse

mort (1) mortgage/mortgaged (2) mortality (3) mortally

Mort Mortimer, Morton

mos (1) married out of Society of Friends (2) months

Mos (1) Moscow (2) Moselle

MOS Military Occupation

MoSA Missouri State Archives, P.O. Box 778, Jefferson City, MO 65102

Mosbch Mosbach, Baden

MoSGA Missouri State Genealogical Association, P.O. Box 833, Columbia, MO 65205-0833

MoSHS Missouri State Historical Society, 1020 Lowry Street, Columbia, MO 65201-7298

MoSL Missouri State Library, P.O. Box 387, Jefferson City, MO 65102-0387

Most Rev. Most Reverend

MOT Montelena/Monteleug

mot/moti/moto motion

MotA Mother's Aunt

MotC Mother's Cousin

MotD Mother's Daughter

MotF Mother's Father

moth mother

Moth Mother

MotH Mother's Help

MotL Mother-in-law

MotP Mother of Patient

MotS Mother's Son

MotU Mother's Uncle

MOU Married Out of Unity (Quaker married a non-Quaker)

mov move, moved

MOWW Military Order of the World Wars, 435 North Lee Street, Alexandria, VA 22314

MOZ Mozambique

mp map

MP/M.P. (1) Member of Parliament (British) (2) Military Police

MPA Master of Public Administration

MPCR Maine Province and Court Records

MPd Master of Pedagogy

MPE Master of Physical Education

MPEG Moving Picture Experts Group

mph miles per hour

MPH Master of Public Health

MPHC Michigan Pioneer and Historical Collections

MPLA Mountain Plains Library Association

Mplr Montpelier Public Library, Montpelier, VT

MPR Military Personnel Records (*see also* NPRC)

MQ *The Mayflower Quarterly*

mr (1) missionary rector (2) mother

Mr./Mr Mister or Master

MR (1) Marriage Record (2) Miscellaneous Registers (3) Mississippi River (4) Municipal Records

MRA Royal Arcanum

Mrbo Maribo, Denmark

mr cooper master cooper

Mrcr Dwyer-Mercer County Library, Celina, OH

mrd married

MRE Master of Religious Education

mr gun master gunner

MRIN Marriage Record Identification Number (used in *Personal Ancestral File,* genealogy software program)

mr-in-l mother-in-law

mris mistress

Mrk Mark

mrkd/mrked marked, branded (as in cattle)

MRL Master Repository List (*The Master Genealogist,* genealogy software program)

M-Rmdl More & Romsdal, Norway

mrnr mariner, seaman

MRR *National Archives Microfilm Resources for Research*

Mⁿ/Mrs. Mistress; identifying that the woman is married or an unmarried woman of high social standing

mr sgt Master sergeant

MrSID proprietary image format (LizardTech)

ms mews

ms/mss (1) male servant (2) *manuscriptum (-a)* (3) manuscript(s)

Ms (1) Manuscript (2) miss

MS (1) maiden surname (2) Manuscript (pl. MSS), *manuscriptum(-a)* (3) Master of Science (4) Merchant Service (merchant navy) (5) Michigan Survey

MS/M.S. male servant

MS/Miss. Mississippi

MS/MSc Master of Science degree

MSA Maine State Archives, 84 State House Station, Augusta, ME 04333-0084

MSA Massachusetts State Archives, Columbia Point, 220 Morrissey Blvd., Boston, MA 02125

MSA metropolitan statistical area

MSCH Mecklenburg (Schwerin)

MSDa mother's stepdaughter

MsDAR Mississippi Daughters of the American Revolution

MS-DOS Microsoft Disk Operating System

MSGA Missouri State Genealogical Association

Msgr. Monsignor

M/Sgt. Master Sergeant

MshU James E. Morrow Library, Marshall University, Huntington, WV 25755

MSI medium-scale integration

MSIA Master of Science in Industrial Administration

Msis mother's sister

MSL Maine State Library, State House Station 64, Augusta, ME 04333

MSM Microsoft *Messenger*

MSMD Massachusetts Society of Mayflower Descendents, 100 Boylston Street, Suite 750, Boston, MA 02116-4610

msn mission

MSN Microsoft Network

msngr messenger

MSOG Massachusetts Society of Genealogists, P.O. Box 215, Ashland, MA 01721-0215

MSPA Master of Science in Public Administration

MSPH Master of Science in Public Health

mss hand- or typewritten manuscript(s)

MS&S Massachusetts Soldiers and Sailors of the Revolutionary War

MsSAr Mississippi Department of Archives and History, 100 South State Street, Jackson, MS

MST Mountain Standard Time

Mstr (1) master (2) master of a ship (3) Meister

MSTR Mecklenburg-Strelitz, Germany

Mstu medical student

MsU (1) Michigan State University (2) Mississippi University

MSVSA Model State Vital Statistics Act and Regulations

MSW Master of Social Work/Welfare

mt (1) married to (2) mountain

Mt Mount

MT early November, the Michaelmas term of court

MT (1) machine translation (2) Military Tract (Illinois) (3) Montana

MT Military Task

mtce maintenance

mtd mounted

mtDNA mitochondrial DNA (deoxyribonucleic acid)

Mte Mate on a ship

mtg (1) meeting (2) mortgage

Mts Montgomery County, Ohio

mtge mortgage

mtg hs meeting house

MTGS Middle Tennessee Genealogical Society, P.O. Box 190625, Nashville, TN 37219-0625

Mth Meath, Republic of Ireland

MTh Master of Theology

M'tha Martha

MtHS Montana Historical Society, Memorial Building, 225 North Roberts Street, Helena, MT 59620

Mtitck Mattituck

MTLA Micropublishers' Trade List Annual

MtlM mantle maker

mtn mountain

Mtn Mountain

M Tn Memphis, Tennessee

MTP Master Title Plat(s) (General Land Office)

mtr motorman, motor

mtrn matron

Mtrs mistress

mu musician

Mu/MU Mulatto

MU Walter Havighurst Special Collections, Miami University, Oxford, OH 45056

MUL Marshall University Library, Huntington, WV 25775

mun/munic municipal

Mun (1) Munica (Munich) (2) Municipal

Mun Munster (Münster), Germany

mus (1) museum (2) music (3) musical (4) musician

Mus (1) Museum (2) Music

MUS Muscat

MusB Bachelor of Music

MusD Doctor of Music

Musicol Musicology

MusT/Mus Tch music teacher

mut mutual

mv *more vetere* (in the old way)

MV Moravia (Mähren)

mvd moved

MVD Soviet Ministry of Internal Affairs

MVGI Miami Valley Genealogy Index (Ohio)

MVHR *Mississippi Valley Historical Review*

MVO Member of the Royal Victorian Order

MVR Motor Vehicle Record

MW (1) Maine Wills (2) mother's will

MWA Modern Woodsmen of America

Mx Middlesex, England

My (1) Mary (2) May (3) major (4) Montana Territory

MyB Myersbad

MYBP million years before the present

my/d my daughter

Myo Mayo, Republic of Ireland

myth mythology

N

n (1) name (2) *natus* (born) (3) near (4) nephew (5) *nomen* (name) (6) north (7) northern (8) note, footnote (pl.nn.) (9) noun

N (1) census (source in *IGI*) (2) National News Service (3) Navy (4) Negro, Negroes (5) nephew (6) niece (7) Norse (8) North (9) number

N/NN (1) *nomen/nomina* (name(s), indicates the actual name is not known) (2) note(s)

N Car North Carolina

N Dak North Dakota

N1, NFC Negroes of the first age class

N2, NMC Negroes of the second age class

N3, NLC Negroes of the third age class

na not attending meeting

na/nat (1) national (2) natural (3) naturalize(d)/naturalization

NA National Archives and Records Administration, 700 Pennsylvania Ave. NW, Washington, DC 20408

NA National Archives of Ireland

NA (1) *non allocatur* (not allowed) (2) North Africa (3) North America (4) Native American (5) naturalized citizen (e.g., an immigrant who is a naturalized citizen); this abbreviation may be listed in a U.S. census schedule

NA National Archives of Ireland

NAACP National Association for the Advancement of Colored People, Washington Bureau, 1025 Vermont Ave NW, Suite 1120, Washington, DC 20005

NAC National Archives of Canada, Ottawa, Ontario

NACC North Atlantic Co-operation Council

NACo National Association of Counties

N.Afr North Africa

NAFTA North American Free Trade Agreement

Nag Nagasaki

NAGPRA Native American Graves Protection Act

NAHA Norwegian-American Historical Association, St. Olaf College, Northfield, MN 55057

NAI/NAIR Nairn, Scotland

NAIL National Archives and Records Administration Archival Information Locator

NAILDD North American Interlibrary Loan and Document Delivery

NAIP North American Immigrants Project

NAIPI National Association of Independent Private Investigators

NAL Native American Lineages (Board for Certification of Genealogists)

NAM (1) National Association of Manufacturers (2) North America

NAMA/NA North American Manx Association

Namr Name religious

N-An Netherlands Antilles

Nan Nancy

nany nanny

Nap Naples

NAP National Archives-Mid-Atlantic Region, 900 Market St., Philadelphia, PA 19107-4292

NAPHSIS National Association for Public Health Statistics and Information Systems, 1220 19th St. NW Ste 802, Washington, D.C. 20036

NAR/NARA National Archives and Records Administration, 700 Pennsylvania Ave. NW, Washington, DC 20408

NARB National Archives Regional Branches

narr narrative

Narra. Narragansett dialect

NARS National Archives and Records Service, Washington, DC (*see* NARA)

Nas/NAS/Nassa Nassau/Nausau

NAS National Academy of Science

NAS no author or compiler shown in the source listing

NAS National Archives of Scotland (Scottish Records Office, formerly known as Old Register House)

NASA National Aeronautics & Space Administration

NASSAR National Society for Armenian Studies and Research, Inc., 6 Divinity Avenue, Cambridge, MA 02138

NasT Nastata

nat natural, i.e., illegitimate; a natural son or daughter is an illegitimate son or daughter

nat (1) naturalization (2) *natus, nata* (born)

Nat (1) National (2) Natural

NAT naturalization

nat/natl national

Nat Arch National Archives and Records Administration, 700 and Pennsylvania Ave. NW, Washington, DC 20408

NAtd night attendant

NATF National Archives form number (form used to request records from the National Archives)

Nat Gallery National Gallery

Nath/Nathl/Nath¹/Nathan¹ Nathaniel

Nathan Nathan, Nathaniel

Nat Hist Natural History

Nathⁿ Nathan

Nat Huguenot National Huguenot Society, 9033 Lyndale Avenue South, Suite 108, Bloomington, MN 55420-3535

Nati Nationality

Natl National

Natl Gen Soc Qt *National Genealogical Society Quarterly*, National Genealogical Society, 4527 17th Street North, Arlington, VA 22207-2399

NATO North Atlantic Treaty Organization

NATS National Air Traffic Services Limited

natu naturalization

Natu Naturalization

Nau Nausau/Nassau

naut nautical

NAVA National Archives Volunteer Association

Nb Northumberland, England

NB (1) New Brunswick (uncommon usage: North Britain, i.e. Scotland), Canada (2) North Britain (3) *nota bene* (take careful note; mark well and pay particular attention to that which follows)

NB/Neb Nebraska

Nbaye North Bayern

NBL Northumberland

NBrun/NB New Brunswick, Canada

Nbtn Norrbotten, Sweden

nc name change (likely a court record)

NC (1) Civil Reference Aid (National Archives) (2) non-conformist (3) North Carolina (4) North Central

NCA National Cemetery Administration

NCAC National Capital Area Chapter, Association of Professional Genealogists, P.O. Box 11601, Washington, DC 20007

NCC National Conference Chair, e.g., Federation of Genealogical Societies National Conference Chair

NCDAH North Carolina Division of Archives and History, 109 East Jones Street, Raleigh, NC 27601-2807 (mailing address, 4610 Mail Service Center, Raleigh, NC 27699-4610)

nce niece

NCES National Center for Education Statistics, 555 New Jersey Ave NW, Washington DC 20208-5574

NCFR National Council on Family Relations

NCGS North Carolina Genealogical Society, P.O. Box 22, Greenville, NC 27835-0022

NCHS National Center for Health Statistics, 6525 Belorest Road, Hyattsville, MD 20782-2003

NCIC National Cartographic Information Center

nck neck

ncm *non compos mentis* (mental unsoundness)

NCO non-commissioned officer

NCOD No Code

NCPC National Personnel Records Center, Civil Personnel Records. *See* NPRC.

NCPO National Congress of Patriotic Organizations

NCRR National Center for Research Resources, NCRR, National Institutes of Health, Bethesda, MD 20892-5662

NCSA National Center for Supercomputing Applications, NCSA, University of Illinois at Urbana - Champaign, 152 Computing Applications Bldg, 605 East Springfield Ave., Champlaign, IL 61820-5518

NCSA National Computer Security Association

NCU North Carolina University, Chapel Hill, NC

NCURA National Council of University Research Administrators, One Dupont Cir. NW Ste. 220, Washington DC 20036

NCV North Carolina Volunteer(s)

NCy North Country (England)

nd/ndt no date, no date of publication indicated (the date of the original is not known)

ND/NDak North Dakota

NDau natural daughter

NDHS North Dakota Historical Society, 612 East Boulevard Avenue, Bismarck, ND 58505-0830

NDHSGR North Dakota Historical Society of Germans from Russia, 1008 E. Central Ave., Bismarck, ND 58501

Ndlw needlewoman

né original, former, or legal name of a man

née as born; precedes the maiden name of a married woman

ne(e) born (as); used to introduce the maiden name of a wife

NE/N. E. (1) nephew (2) New England (3) North East

NE/Nebr/Neb/Nb Nebraska

NEA (1) National Education Association 1201 16th St. NW, Washington DC, 20036 (2) *New England Ancestors* (New England Historic Genealogical Society, Boston, MA) (3) New England Archivists (4) Newspaper Enterprises Association

Neb/Nebr Nebraska

nebr neighbor

NEBS New England Business Service

NECG *The New England Computer Genealogist*, New England Historic Genealogical Society, *The Computer Genealogist*, 101 Newbury St., Boston, MA 02116-3007

NED *A New English Dictionary (The Oxford English Dictionary)*

neg (1) negative (2) neglecting attendance

NEG *New England Genealogy*

NEH National Endowment for the Humanities

NEHGR/NEH&GR *The New England Historical and Genealogical Register*, New England Historic Genealogical Society, 101 Newbury St., Boston, MA 02116-3007

NEHGS New England Historic Genealogical Society, 101 Newbury St., Boston, MA 02116-3007

NEHGS New England Historic Genealogical Society (Sales), One Watson Place, Framingham, MA 01701

NEI *non est inventus* (recently deceased) notation by an officer or court that a person sought was not found

nel/neph-l-l/nepl nephew-in-law

NEL (1) Nephew-in-law (2) Netherlands

NENGS Northeastern Nebraska Genealogical Society, P.O. Box 169, Lyons, NE 68038

NEO-CAG North East Ohio-Computer Aided Genealogy Group

nepC nephew's child

nepD nephew's daughter

neph (1) nephew (2) sometimes grandchild

nepS nephew's son

nepW nephew's wife

NEQ *The New England Quarterly*, Meserve Hall, Northeastern University, Boston, MA 02115

NERGC New England Regional Genealogical Conference

Nerv Aff Nervous Affection

NeSHS Nebraska State Historical Society, Division of Library/Archives, P.O. Box 82554, Lincoln, NE 68501-2554

Net/Neth Netherlands

NET (1) New Electronic Titles (2) No Electronic Theft Act

NetBEUI NetBIOS Extended User Interface

NETH Netherlands

Neth Arch Netherlands Archives, The Hague

Netherlands Soc of Phil Netherlands Society of Philadelphia

Neur Brain Neuralgia of Brain

Neurophys Neurophysiology

Neurosci Neuroscience

Neust Neustadt

neut neuter

Nev/NV Nevada

new newspaper

NewB/New Bruns New Brunswick

Newbu Newburg, OH

New Eng New England

New Eng National Society of New England Women, P.O. Box 367, Women Union City, TN 38261-0367

New Era *The New Era* (LDS publication)

Newf/NF Newfoundland, Canada

NEWGS Northeast Washington Genealogical Society, 195 South Oak, Colville, WA 99114

NewH New Hampton

New Hamp New Hampshire

New Jers New Jersey

New^m Newman

New M/New Mex New Mexico

NewOr New Orleans

news newspaper

Newsp Newspaper

NewZ/NEZ New Zealand

NEXUS former bimonthly newsmagazine of the New England Historic Genealogical Society, 101 Newbury Street, Boston, MA 02116-3007 (now *New England Ancestors*)

NEYM New England Yearly Meeting (Society of Friends/Quakers)

Nf Norfolk, England

NF (1) National Forest (2) Neue Folge (New Series)

NF/NFD/NFL Newfoundland, Canada

NFACE National Forum on Archival Continuing Education

NFDA National Funeral Directors Association

nfi no further information

nfk nothing further known

NFK/NORF/Norf Norfolk, Great Britain

Nfld Newfoundland, including Labrador (Canada)

nfr/nfrf no further reference or record found

NG (1) National Guard (2) New England (3) no good (4) Norse-Gaelic (5) not given

NGDC National Geophysical Data Center

nger engineer

NGO non-governmental organization

NGR New Grenada

NGRA New Granada

NGS National Park Service

NGS National Genealogical Society, 4527 17th Street North, Arlington, VA 22207-2399

NGS-BBS National Genealogical Society— Bulletin Board System (now defunct)

NGS/CIG National Genealogical Society Computer Interest Group, 4527 17th Street North, Arlington, VA 22207-2399

NGS/CIS National Genealogical Society Conference in the States

NGSQ *National Genealogical Society Quarterly*, 4527 17th Street North, Arlington, VA 22207-2399

NGV Dutch Genealogical Society

NH New Hampshire

NHA Nantucket Historical Association, P.O. Box 1016 Nantucket, MA 02554

NHACS Negro Historical Association of Colorado Springs, P.O. Box 16123, Colorado Springs, CO 80935

NHAM/Norf/Northants/Northton Northamptonshire, England

Nhant Northampton, England

N.H. Arch New Hampshire Archives, 71 South Fruit Street, Concord, NH 03301-2410

NHCHS New Haven Colony Historical Society, 114 Whitney Avenue, New Haven, CT 06510

NHD National History Day

NHGOS New Hampshire Society of Genealogists, P.O. Box 2316, Concord, NH 03302-2316

NHGR *New Hampshire Genealogical Record*

NHHS New Hampshire Historical Society, 30 Park Street, Concord, NH 03301

NHOGA New Hampshire Old Graveyard Association, New Hampshire Society of Genealogists, P.O. Box 2316, Concord, NH 03302-2316

NHPD New Hampshire Provincial Deeds

NHPP Provincial Papers, Documents and Records Relating to the Province of New Hampshire from 1866 to 1722

NHPRC National Historical Publications and Records Commission, Washington DC 20408-0001

NHS National Huguenot Society, 9033 Lyndale Avenue South, Suite 108, Bloomington, MN 55420-3535

NHS Newfoundland Historical Society (St. John's, Newfoundland)

NHS Newport Historical Society, 82 Touro Street, Newport, RI 02840

NHSG New Hampshire Society of Genealogists, P.O. Box 2316, Concord, NH 03302-2316

NHSL New Hampshire State Library, 20 Park Street, Concord, NH 03301

NHSOG New Hampshire Society of Genealogists, P.O. Box 2316, Concord, NH 03302-2316

NHSP New Hampshire Province and State Papers

Nhumb/NHUM/Northumb Northumberland, England

NHVR New Hampshire Vital Records

ni (1) Intent of Naturalization (2) no issue

ni/Ni/NI niece

NI Native Infantry

Niag Niagara

NIAU Northern Iowa University, 1227 West 27th Street, Cedar Falls, IA 50614

NIBSCO National Interreligious Service Board for Conscientious Objectors

NIC/Nica/NICA/Nicer Nicaragua

Nich/Nich'/Nic' Nicholas

Nicl Niklaus, Niclaus

NIDS *National Inventory of Documentary Sources* (reference source available on microfiche). Finding aids and indexes for the United States, United Kingdom, Ireland, and other countries. Published by Chadwyck-Healey. Index on CD-ROM.

NIE Newspapers in Education

niec/ni niece

NieC niece's child

NieD niece's daughter

Niedbn Niederbayern, Bavaria

NieH niece's husband

NieL/Nil niece-in-law

NieS niece's son

NIFGS National Institute for Genealogical Studies (University of Toronto)

NIGR National Institute on Genealogical Research, P.O. Box 14274, Washington, DC 20044-4274

NIGRAA National Institute on Genealogical Research Alumni Association, P.O. Box 14272, Washington, DC 20044-4274

Nil niece-in-law

nil nothing found, no information located

NINCH Networked Cultural Heritage

Nip Nipmuck dialect

NIPR *National Index of Parish Registers* (British)

N. Ire Northern Ireland

NIS Network and Information Services

NISL Nevis Island

NISO National Information Standards Organization

NiSv niece's servant

Nita Anita, Juanita

NIWM National Inventory of War Memorials

NJ New Jersey

NJArRM New Jersey Archives and Records Management

NJBAr New Jersey State Library, P.O. Box 520, Trenton, NJ 08625-0520

NJHS New Jersey Historical Society, 230 Broadway, Newark, NJ 07104

NK/N.K. not known (may be found in census schedule)

NK *Notable Kin*, by Gary Boyd Roberts

nl/Nl nephew-in-law

NL Netherlands

NL Newberry Library, 60 West Walton Sheet, Chicago, IL 60610

NLC National Library of Canada, 395 Wellington Street, Ottawa, Canada K1A 0N4

NLCHS New London County Historical Society, 11 Blinman Street, New London, CT 06320

NLRB National Labor Relations Board

NLW National Library of Wales, Aberystwyth, Ceredigion, Wales SY23 3BU

nm nonmember (i.e., nonmember of a church)

nm(s) name(s)

n/m not married

NM (1) no marker (gravestone) (2) Military Reference Aid (National Archives)

NM/NMex New Mexico

nmed named

NMGS New Mexico Genealogical Society, P.O. Box 8283, Albuquerque, NM 87198-8283

nmi no middle initial

NMM National Maritime Museum, Greenwich, London, England SE10 9NF

nmn no middle name

NMU New Mexico University, Albuquerque, NM

N.'Mul Nordur' Mulasysla

nn (1) no name (2) notes

Nn Nun

NN *Nomen nescio* (name not known)

NNA National Newspaper Association

NNE North Northeast

NNRR Textual Reference Branch, National Archives and Records Administration, Washington National Records Center, Washington, DC 20409

NNS Newhouse News Service

NNW North Northwest

no (1) none, no relation (2) north (3) number

No None (no relation)

No. (1) north (2) northern (3) number

NO (1) New Orleans, LA (2) North

NOA North America

No. Brab North Brabant

N.'Oestr Niederoesterreich

No. Holl. North Holland

noia *nomina* (names)

noie *nomine* (by name)

nois *nominis* (of the name)

NOK New Order of Knights (*see* KKK)

Noll/Nolly Oliver

nol. pros. *nolle prosequi* (which see)

nom nominative

Noncom Non-Commissioned Officer

non copos mentis not sound of mind

non obs *non obstante* (notwithstanding)

non seq *non sequitur* (it does not follow)

NOR/Nor/NORW Norway, Norwegian

Nora/Norah Eleanor, Elinor, Honor, Honora, Leonora

Nordld Nordland

NorE/Norf Norfolk, England

Norm Norma, Norman

NortA North America

Norw Norwich

Norw/NRY Norway

NOS not on [library] shelf

not noted

notK not known

not md not married

notp not of this parish

not pub/notry pblc notary public

NOTT/Nottm/Notts (1) Nottingham, England (2) Nottinghamshire

nov/n.o.v notwithstanding the verdict of a jury judgment

Nov/Novmbr/Novm/Novmb/N November

no. vo. *nolens volens* (with or without consent)

NovS/NovSc Nova Scotia, Canada (*see also* N.S.)

np (1) newspaper publisher or worker (2) no page (3) no papers in packet (4) no place of publication indicated

np/n.pub (1) no publication place (2) no publisher shown

NP (1) Negro Polls (2) New Providence (3) no protest (4) Notary Public (5) *The Ohio NISI PRIUS Reports*

N. pag no pagination

NPC National Program Chair

npl no place

npn/NPN no page number

np or d no place or date

npp no place of publication

NPR National Public Radio

NPRC National Personnel Records Center (1) Civilian Records Facility, 111 Winnebago Street, St. Louis, MO 63118-4199 (2) Military Records Facility, 9700 Page Avenue, St. Louis, MO 63132-5100

NPS National Park Service

NPT Non-Proliferation Treaty

N. pub no publisher

N & Q Notes and Queries (England)

NQF National Queries Forum, P.O. Box 593, Santa Cruz, CA 95061-0593

nr non-resident of area shown

nr/NR (1) near (2) not related (3) none recorded or not recorded (4) (naturalization) not reported (often found in recent U.S. census schedules, e.g., citizenship not reported, or vital records)

NR North Riding

NRA (1) National Recovery Administration (2) National Register of Archives (British)

NRA(S) National Register of Archives (Scotland), HM General Register House, 2 Princes Street, Edinburgh, Scotland EH1 3YY

NRF no record found (i.e., used on a research log)

NRH New Register House, Edinburgh, Scotland

NRHS National Railway Historical Society

Nrld Nordland, Norway

Nrn Nairnshire, Scotland

NrsC nursed child

nrsd nursed

NrsG nursegirl

nrsl nursling

NrsM nursemaid

Nrsy nursery

NRY (1) North Riding of Yorkshire, England (2) Norway

ns/NS (1) new series (2) new style (3) north side

NS (1) Cape Breton Island, Canada (2) Naval Service (3) New Style, referring to the Gregorian calendar (4) Nova Scotia, Canada

NSA National Speakers Association, 150 South Priest Drive, Tempe, AZ 85281

NSA National Student Association

NS Amer of Royal Desc National Society of Americans of Royal Descent

NS Arch Public Archives of Nova Scotia, Halifax, Nova Scotia

NSC Navy Survivor's Certificates

NSCD National Society, Colonial Dames of America, Dumbarton House, 2715 Q Street NW, Washington, DC 20007

NSCD-17 National Society, Colonial Dames of the Seventeenth Century, 1300 New Hampshire Avenue NW, Washington, DC 20036-1595

NSCDA/NSCol Dames National Society of the Colonial Dames of America, Dumbarton House, 2715 Q Street NW, Washington, DC 20007

NScot Northern Scotland

NSDAR National Society, Daughters of the American Revolution, 1776 D Street NW, Washington, DC 20006-5392

NSDCGS North San Diego County Genealogical Society, Inc., P.O. Box 581, Carlsbad, CA 92008-0581

NSDCH National Society, Dames of the Court of Honor

NSE *New Standard Encyclopedia*

NSF National Science Foundation

NSGC National Society of Genetic Counselors

NSO Navy Survivor's Originals

NSon natural son

NSP Newbury Street Press, 101 Newbury Street, Boston, MA 02116-3007

NSSAR National Society of the Sons of the American Revolution, 1000 South Fourth Street, Louisville, KY 40203

NSSD Pilgrims National Society, Sons and Daughters of the Pilgrims, 3917 Heritage Hills Drive #104, Minneapolis, MN 55437-2633

NSTC Nineteenth-century Short Title Catalogue (bibliography)

NSTL National Software Testing Laboratory

NStud Northern Studies

NS Vrs Nova Scotia Vital Records

NSW New South Wales, Australia

Nt Nottinghamshire, England

NT (1) Nebraska Territory (2) New Testament (Bible) (3) Northwest Territories, Canada (4) Note

Nth/NTH (1) Netherlands (2) Northamptonshire, England

Nthbld Northumberland, England

Nthest Northeast

Nthestn Northeastern

N.'Thing Nordur Thingeviarsysla

Nthn Northern

Nthwst Northwest

Nthwstn Northwestern

N-Tlg Nord-Trondelag, Norway

NTM Northumberland

N.' Tronglg Nord Trondelag

NTT Nottinghamshire

nu/Nu nurse

NUC (1) *National Union Catalog: Pre-1956 Imprints* (London, 1968-81) (2) *National Union Catalog*, Library of Congress

NUCMC *National Union Catalog of Manuscript Collections* (Library of Congress) national bibliographic database

num (1) numeral (2) numerically

numb numbered

Numb Number

nunc *nuncupative* (unwritten, an oral will)

nupt were married

Nur Nurenberg, Germany

NurB nurse's baby

NurC nurse's child

NurD nurse's daughter

NurH nurse's husband

nurs nurse

Nurs Nurse, Nursing

NurS nurse's son

Nutr Nutrition

NV Nevada

Nva/Sco Nova Scotia, Canada

NVG Dutch Genealogical Society

NvSHS Nevada State Historical Society, 1650 North Virginia Street, Reno, NV 89503

NVQ National Vocational Qualification

NvU Nevada University, Reno, NV

nw (1) new (2) northwest

NW (1) Northwest (2) Northwest Territories, Canada (3) Norway, Norwegian

NWA North Wales

NWale North Wales

NWU National Writers Union

NwB New Brunswick, Canada

Nwest Terr Northwest Territories, Canada

NWFP North West Frontier Province (India)

NWMP Northwest Mounted Police (Canada)

NWO Navy Widow's Originals

NWOQ *North West Ohio Quarterly*

NWP North-Western Province

NWT/NW Terr (1) Northwest Territories, Canada (2) Northwest Territory

NXN/nxn no Christian name

NY New York

NY Arch New York Archives, New York Department of Education, Cultural Education Center, Albany, NY 12230

NYC New York City, NY

NYCRO North Yorkshire County Record Office

NYGB New York Genealogical and Biographical Society, 122 East 58th Street, New York, NY 10022-1939

NYGBR *The New York Genealogical and Biographical Record*, 122 East 58th Street, New York, NY 10022-1939

NYG&BS/NYGBS New York Genealogical and Biographical Society, 122 East 58th Street, New York, NY 10022-1939

NYHS New York Historical Society, 170 Central Park West, New York, NY 10024

NYPL New York Public Library, U.S. History, Local History and Genealogy Division, Fifth Avenue and 42nd Street, New York, NY 10018-2788

NYSA New York State Archives, New York State Education Department, Cultural Education Center, Albany, NY 12230

NYScC New York Public Library, Schomburg Collection, Fifth Avenue and 42nd Street, New York, NY 10018-2788

NYSL New York State Library, Cultural Education Center, Albany, NY 12230

NYT *New York Times*

NYYM New York Yearly Meeting Young Friends (Quakers)

NZ/NZD/NZEA New Zealand

O

Oo (1) oath (2) officer (3) only

o/oe/oi/oy/oye/oey grandson or nephew (Scottish)

O (1) October (2) Officer (3) Ohio (4) Old (OC: Old Celtic, etc.) (5) Oriental (6) Orthodox (7) Oxfordshire, England

O' (1) A prefix to ancient Irish family names followed by the genitive case of the name of the ancestor, as O'Neil (nom. Niall). Before surnames of females, O' is replaced in Irish by ni, daughter. It prefixes H before a vowel, as Oh Airt, O'Hart. The apostrophe is due to the mistaken idea that O stands for of. (2) whatever follows

OA Oberamt

OA Ontario Provincial Archives, Toronto

OAH Ohio Academy of History, Elliott Hall, Ohio Wesleyan University, Delaware, OH 43015-2398

OAHQ *Ohio Archaeological and Historical Quarterly*

OAP Old Age Pension

OARA Oregon Adoptive Rights Association

OAS Organization of American States

OASIS Online Archival Search Information System

OAU Organization of African Unity

ob/OB (1) obit (died) (2) order book(s)

ob/obit obituary

OBA Office of Business Analysis

OBE Order of the British Empire

Oberbn Oberbayern, Bavaria

Oberfr Oberfranken, Bavaria

Oberhn Oberhessen, Hess-Darmstadt

ob inf *obit infantia* (died in infancy)

ob inf set died whilst still a minor

obit obituary, notice of a person's death

obj (1) object (2) objective

ob juv *obit juventus* (died in childhood)

Obk order book

obs (1) observer (2) obsolete (3) obsolete name

Observ Obervatory

ob. s.p. died without issue

ob. s.p.m. died without male issue

Obstet Obstetrics

obt (1) *obit* (2) obedient (e.g., "Your Obt. Servant")

ob unm *obit* (died unmarried)

oc (1) Old country (2) ope consilio (an accessory, usually criminal) (3) opere citato (only child)

OC (1) Officer, Order of Canada (2) Orphan's Court (3) outside cover (of a book)

OCA Archives, Oberlin College, Oberlin, OH

occ (1) occasionally (2) occupation (3) occupied (4) occurs/-ing

OCCGS Orange County California Genealogical Society, Huntington Beach Public Library, 7111 Talbert Avenue, Huntington Beach, CA 92648

Occu Occupation

Occup Occupational, Occupations

OCD (1) Office of the Civilian Defense (2) Discalced Carmeline Nun(s)

Oceanog Oceanographic, Oceanography

OCFA Ontario Cemetery Finding Aid, Ontario, Canada

OCI Ohio County Index (West Virginia)

OCLC Online Computer Library Center, 6565 Frantz Road, Dublin, OH 43017-3395

OCP Ohio Company Purchase

OCR Optical Character Recognition

OCRP Oxford Colonial Records Project (University of Oxford, Oxford, England)

OCS Officer Candidate School

Oct/O October

OCTA Oregon-California Trails Association, 524 South Osage Street, Independence, MO 64050

OCU Operational Conversion Unit

ocup occupant, occupier

OCWGJ *Ohio Civil War Genealogy Journal*, Ohio Genealogical Society, 713 South Main Street, Mansfield, OH 44907-1644

OD (1) Officer of the Day (2) olive drab (uniforms) (3) outside diameter

ODDC Old Darlington District Genealogical Chapter of the South Carolina Genealogical Society, P.O. Box 175, Hartsville, SC 29551-0175

ODCI *Ohio Death Certificate Index* (Ohio Historical Society, 1982 Velma Avenue, Columbus, Ohio 43211)

ODH Ohio Department of Health, Division of Vital Statistics, Ohio Departments Building, Room 6-20, 65 South Front Street, Columbus, OH 43266-0333

ODLQC Open and Distance Learning Quality Council (British)

OE (1) Old England (2) Old English, Anglo-Saxon

OED *Oxford English Dictionary*

OEMP Ottoman Empire

OEN Overland Emigrant Names

OEO Office of Economic Opportunity

OES (1) Oesterreich (Austria) (2) Order of the Eastern Star

Of Officer (rank unknown)

ofc office

off/offi (1) office (2) official

Off (1) Offaly, Republic of Ireland (2) Office, Official

offc (1) office (2) officer

offD officer's daughter

offg officiating

offl official

Offnbg Offenburg, Baden

offr officer

Offr Officer

OFFRI&PP Order of First Families of Rhode Island & Providence Plantations

OffS officer's son

OffW officer's wife

Ofkp office keeper

OFPA Order of the Founders and Patriots of America, 15 Pine Street, New York, NY 10005

OFr Old French

OFS Orange Free State (South Africa)

OfsS officer's sister

oft often

OFT *Online Family Tree* (software on Ancestry.com)

OGF One Great Family (Internet database)

OGQ *Ohio Genealogical Quarterly*

OGRE Online Genealogical Research Engine

OGRES Online Genealogical Research Service

OGS Ohio Genealogical Society, 713 South Main Street, Mansfield, OH 44907-1644

OGS Oklahoma Genealogical Society, P.O. Box 12986, Oklahoma City, OK 73157-2986

OGS Ontario Genealogical Society, 40 Orchard View Blvd., Suite 102, Toronto, Ontario, Canada M4R 1B9

OGS Oregon Genealogical Society, P.O. Box 10306, Eugene, OR 97440-2306

OGS Ozarks Genealogical Society, P.O. Box 3945, Springfield, MO 65808-3945

OGS-CIG Computer Interest Group of the Ohio Genealogical Society, 713 South Main Street, Mansfield, OH 44907-1644

OGS REP *Ohio Genealogical Society: Report*, quarterly

OGSRP *The Report*, Ohio Genealogical Society, 713 South Main Street, Mansfield, OH 44907-1644

Ogtld Ostergotland, Sweden

OH (1) Ohio (2) *Ohio History*

OHF Ontario Heritage Foundation (Toronto, ON)

OHG Old High German

OHMS On His (or Her) Majesty's Service

OHN Ohio History Network

OHP Ohio Historic Preservation Office, 567 East Hudson Street, Columbus, OH 43211-1030

OHPA Ohio Historic Preservation Office, 567 East Hudson Street, Columbus, OH 43211-1030

OHQ (1) *Ohio Historical Quarterly* (2) *Ohio State Archaeological and Historical Quarterly*

OHS Ohio Historical Society, 1982 Velma Avenue, Columbus, OH 43211

OHS Oregon Historical Society, 1200 SW Park Avenue, Portland, OR 97203

OhSHS Ohio State Historical Society, 1982 Velma Avenue, Columbus, OH 43211

OhSL State Library of Ohio, Genealogy Division, 274 East First Avenue, Columbus, OH 43201

OhR Ohio River

OHRPF Ohio Records and Pioneer Families, Ohio Genealogical Society, 713 South Main Street, Mansfield, OH 44907-1644

OHS Oklahoma Historical Society, 2100 North Lincoln Blvd., Oklahoma City, OK 73105

OHS Ohio Historical Society, Columbus, OH

OHS Ontario Historical Society

OHS Oregon Historical Society, Oregon History Center, 1200 SW Park Avenue, Portland, OR

OHS State Archives, Ohio Historical Society, Columbus, OH

OhU Ohio State University, Columbus, OH

OIEAHC Omohundro Institute of Early American History and Culture, P.O. Box 8781, Williamsburg, VA 23187-8781

OI Ohio Infantry

OI Ordinance Index™ (duplicate of information in the *International Genealogical Index*, but with LDS temple ordinance dates)

O.Ijsel Overijssel (Overyssel), Netherlands

OISL Orkney Island

OJ *Overland Journal, Oregon - California Trails Association*

OK okay

OK/Okla Oklahoma

OkHS Oklahoma Historical Society, 2100 North Lincoln Boulevard, Oklahoma City, OK 73105-4997

OKI Open Knowledge Initiative

OKI Orkney Islands, Scotland

Okia/Okla Oklahoma

Ol Oliver, Olive

OL (1) *Laws of Ohio* (2) Oriental-American Indian (3) online

OLAP Online Analytical Processing

Old/OLD/OLDE/Olden/Oldnbg Oldenburg, Germany

Old Plymouth Col Desc National Society of Old Plymouth Colony Descendants, Rt. 2, 24 Samoset Road, East Sandwich, MA 02537

OLIB Online Library Catalog

OLIS Oxford Library System Online Catalog (Oxford, England)

Ollie/Olly Oliver

OLM Old-Lore Miscellany of Orkney, Shetland, Scotland

OLS Online Search

OM (1) Order of Merit (2) organized militia

OMM Officer, Order of Military Merit (Canada)

omnibusdrv omnibus driver

ON Old Norse

ON (1) Canada West, Canada (2) Ontario, Canada

ONAHRC Ohio Network of American History Research Centers

ONC Office of National Statistics (England)

Oncol Oncology

OneC one of a community

ONGQ *Old Northwest Genealogical Quarterly*

Onon Onondaga

ONR Office of Naval Research, 800 North Quincy Street, Arlington, VA 22217-5660

ONS Office for National Statistics, General Register Office, Overseas Registration Section, Trafalgar Road, Southport England PR8 2HH

ONS Ottawa News Service

Ont Ontario, Canada

OO Order of Ontario

OOP out of print

op (1) operating (2) operator (3) opus; work (4) out of print (5) Overseer of the Poor

OPAC Online Public Access Catalog, a computerized library catalog

OPC (1) Orthodox Presbyterian Church (2) Online Library Catalog

op. cit. *opere citato* (in the work cited, previously cited)

OPCS Office for Population Censuses & Surveys, now ONS (British)

OPEI Office of Public Education and Interpretation

oper/opr/oprtr operator

Opfalz Oberpfalz, Bavaria

OPHAF Ohio Public Health Association Forum

OPLIN Ohio Public Library Information Network

OPM Office of Personnel Management

OPM Office for Public Management

opp opposite

opr operator

OPR Old Parish Registers

OPR Old Parochial Register(s) (Church of Scotland) parish registers. Housed at New Register House, Edinburgh, Scotland (microfilmed).

Ophth Ophthalmology

OPLANs Operational Plans

optn optician

optom optometrist

OQ Officer, National Order of Québec

or Ohio State Representative

Or/or (1) gold (heraldry) (2) Orphan

OR (1) Ohio Roster Soldiers of 1812 (2) Orderly

OR/Oreg/Ore Oregon

Or orator

orch orchard

ord (1) ordained (2) orderly (3) ordinance (4) ordinary

ord/ordr/ordrd order(ed)

Ord Ct Ordinary Court

ordl orderly

Ordl Ordination (LDS)

OrdlSgt Orderly Sergeant

Ordn Ordination

Ord of Acorn Colonial Order of the Acorn

Ord of Amer Ancestry Order of Americans of Armorial Ancestry, 2700 East of Armorial Minnehaha Parkway, Minneapolis, MN 55406

Ord of Crown in Amer Order of the Crown in America

Ord of Crown in Charlemagne Order of the Crown of Charlemagne in the United States of America, 7177 Williams Creek Drive, Indianapolis, IN 46240

Ord of Lafayette Order of Lafayette

Ord of Stars & Bars Order of the Stars and Bars

ORes Ohio Researcher, Allstates Researchers, Murray Utah, periodical (defunct)

org/orgn (1) organization (2) organizing

organ organized politically

Orgn Organization

orgr organizer

OrHS Oregon Historical Society, 1200 SW Park Avenue, Portland, OR 97205

orig (1) origin (2) original (3) originally

Ork/ORK/ORKN Orkney, Scotland

Orl Orleans

ORLLs Operations Reports/Lessons Learned

orp orphan

ORPF *Ohio Records and Pioneer Families*, publication of the Ohio Genealogical Society, 713 South Main Street, Mansfield, OH 44907-1644

orph/orpht/orpns orphan(s), orphanage

Orph Ct Orphans Court

orp/o orphan of

OrSAr Oregon State Archives, 800 Summer Street NE, Salem, OR 97310

ORSSAR Oregon Society of the Sons of the American Revolution

ORULS Oregon Union List of Serials

ORVF Ohio River Valley Families

os (1) Ohio State Senator (2) old series (3) old style (4) only son (5) original secession (6) organizational source

OS (1) Old Saxon (2) Old Style calendar (prior to 1752) date, referring to the Julian calendar (3) operating system (4) Ordinate Survey (5) Ordinance Survey (6) Osthofen

OSCE Organisation for Security and Co-operation in Europe

OSI Open Systems Interconnection

OSL Oregon State Library, State Library Building Winter and Court Streets NE, Salem, OR 97310-0641

oslr ostler

Osn Osnaberg, Germany

osp/ob.s.p. *obiit sine prole* (died without issue)

Osrfd/Ostf Ostfold, Norway

OSS Office of Strategic Service

Ost Ostfriesland, Germany

osteo osteopath

Osteo Osteopathic

OSTI Office of Scientific and Technical Information

ostler grd ostler & gardner

Ostpr Ostpreuseen, Prussia (East Prussia)

OT (1) Old Tenor (2) Old Testament (Bible)

OTB On the Bookshelf

OTD On This Day (event database genealogy software utility)

oth/othr other(s)

Othm Othmar

OTHSA Orphan Train Heritage Society of America, 4912 Trout Farm Road, Springdale, AR 72762

Otolaryngol Otolaryngology

otp (1) of this parish (2) of this/that place

OTS (1) Officers' Training School (2) On The Sea

ou out of unity

OU (1) Archives and Special Collections, Alden Library, Ohio University, Athens, OH 45701-2978 (2) Oxford University (England)

OUAM Order of United American Mechanics

OUP Oxford University Press

OUZn Ohio University Library, Zanesville, OH

OV Ohio River

OVA Ohio Volunteer Artillery

OVAL Ohio Valley Area Libraries, 252 West Thirteenth Street, Wellston, OH 45692

OVC Ohio Volunteer Cavalry

over overman

Overs overseer(s)

OVI Ohio Volunteer Infantry (Civil War), e.g., 20th OVI

OVIL Ohio Vital Information for Libraries Center

o.v.m. *obiit vita matris* (died in lifetime of mother)

OVM Ohio Voluneer Militia (Military)

ovp *obiit vita patris* (died in lifetime of father)

owb old will book

OWI Office of War Information

ownr owner

Ox Oxford

OXF/OXFO/Oxon Oxfordshire, England

Oxon (1) of Oxford, England (2) Oxfordshire (3) *Oxoniensis*, of Oxford

OXSIL Oxfordshire Surname Interest List, England

Oy grandchild

oz. ounce

Oz Australia

P

p (1) British pound (2) LDS Controlled Extraction indicates christenings (or births) extracted in R-Tab program (Family History Department, Salt Lake City, UT) (3) pagination/page(s) (4) parent(s), parentage (5) parish (6) past (7) pater (8) patient (9) pence (10) penny (11) pensioner (usually Army or Navy) (12) per (13) perch (14) poll(s) (15) Polynesian (16) populus (17) post, after (18) posted as a parent (19) pro (20) probably (21) profession of the person mentioned (22) 1840 Revolutionary War veteran census

p/pp(s) page(s)

P2P peer-to-peer

P90, P120 Pentium 90, Pentium 120, etc.

P (1) Pacific News Service (2) Patient (3) Precinct

Pa Partner

PA (1) papers filed for naturalization. The individual prepared first papers for naturalization (in this case, "PA" is not an abbreviation for Pennsylvania) (2) partner (3) per annum. (4) petition (abbreviation often found in recent U.S. census schedules) declaration of intent filed (e.g., an immigrant who has petitioned a court for citizenship) (5) Power of Attorney (6) public address (7) purchasing agent

PA/Pa Pennsylvania

Pa Arch Pennsylvania Archives, P.O. Box 1026, Harrisburg, PA 17108-1026

PAAMS Principal Anti-Air Missile System

PAAS Proceedings of the American Antiquarian Society

Pac/Pacif Pacific

PAC Public Access Catalog (library catalog)

p. adj. participial adjective

PAF *Personal Ancestral File*, genealogy software program developed by the Family and Church History Department, Salt Lake City, Utah.

PAK Pakistan

PAL/PALE Palestine

PALA Palatinate

Pal-Am/PALAM Palatines to America, Capital University, Box 101, Columbus, OH 53209-2394

PALE Palestine

Paleon Paleontology

Palp/Heart Palpitation of Heart

pam/pamph pamphlet

Pam Pamela

PAM Pamphlet Accompanying Microfilm (National Archives)

PAN Panama

PANS Public Archives of Nova Scotia, 6016 University Avenue, Halifax, NS Canada B3H 1W4

par (1) parade (2) paragraph (3) parallel (4) parent(s), parentage (5) parish (6) parson

par/pce/ps piece

para paramour

Para/PARA Paraguay

Para/Epilg Paralysis Epiglottis

Par Clk Parish Clerk

paren parentheses

Parl Parliament, Parliamentary

PARP Planning and Review Process

par reg parish register(s)

pars (1) parents (2) parsonage

part (1) parliamentary (2) participant (3) participle

Partic Participant, Participates

pas pastor

pass (1) passage (2) passenger (3) passim, throughout (4) passive

pat (1) patent(ed) (2) paternal (3) patriot (Revolutionary War Service)

Pat Patrick

path (1) pathological (2) pathologist (3) pathology

Pathol Pathology

Patk/Patrk Patrick

PauC pauper's child

PauD pauper's daughter

Paug Paugassett dialect

paup pauper

PauS pauper's son

PauW pauper's wife

p/b place of birth

PB *Patriarchal Blessing Index*

PB (1) pamphlet box (2) publisher

PBA pamphlet box, small

PBC Primitive Baptist Church

PBCGS Palm Beach County Genealogical Society, Inc., West Palm Beach Public Library, 100 Clematis Street, P.O. Box 1746, West Palm Beach, FL 33402

pbk paperback

Pbl Peeblesshire, Scotland

PBO Presiding Bishopric's Office

PBoy postboy, postman

pc (1) personal computer (2) piece (3) precinct

p.c. (1) per cent (2) post card

PC (1) Panama Canal (2) parent & child on archive records (3) Pickaway County (4) Police Constable (5) Privy Council (British) (6) Probate Court

PCA Presbyterian Church in America

PCC (1) Parochial Church Council (2) Prerogative Court of Canterbury (Church of England)

PCC Prerogative Court of Canterbury (England). The probate court of the Province of Canterbury. The senior ecclesiastical court in England.

pccPAU Paraguay

PCD Kodak Photo CD

pce piece

p:cells parcels, usually of land (with or without a crossed p)

pchd purchased

PCHS Platte County Historical Society, P.O. Box 103, Platte City, MO 64079

PCLP Presbyterian-Canada and Lower Provinces

P-Cn Panama Canal Zone

PCR *Records of the Colony of New Plymouth, in New England*

PCX Personal computer file format

PCY Prerogative Court of York (England). Probate court of the Province of York.

pd/pd (1) paid (2) the day after

p/d place of death

PD (1) physical description (2) Police Department

PDA personal digital assistant (i.e., handheld assistant)

PdB Bachelor of Pedagogy

PdD Doctor of Pedagogy

PDF portable document format (extension for files in Adobe's *Acrobat* format). Often known as a PDF file.

P-DG président-directeur général

PDL professional development leave

PdM Master of Pedagogy

PDM Pamphlet Describing Microfilm (National Archives)

pdob place, date of birth

pdod place, date of death

pds/# pounds of weight

pe petition

Pe/Pec Peculiar Court

PE (1) portable executable (2) Presiding Elder

PE Procurement Executive

PE/PEI Prince Edward Island, Canada

PEE/Peeb/PEEB Peebles, Scotland

PEF Perpetual Emigration Fund

PeHS Historical Society of Pennsylvania, 1300 Locust Street, Philadelphia, PA 19107-5699

PEI Prince Edward Island, Canada

PEM/Pemb Pembrokeshire, Wales

PEMB/Pembs Pembroke, Wales

Pene/Penny Penelope

Penn/Penna Pennsylvania

Penna Pennacook dialect

pens (1) pension (2) pensioned (3) pensioner

Pensr Pensioner

penult penultimate, last but one

peo people

per (1) by means of (2) perhaps (3) periodical

Per (1) Percival (2) Periodical

PER (1) Perth, Scotland or Perthshire (2) Peru

perf (1) perfect (2) perforated (3) performed

Perf Performance, Performing

perh perhaps

period periodical

perm (1) permanent (2) permission

pers (1) peers (Norman) (2) personal, personally (3) personnel

Pers Personnel

PERS (1) Persia (2) Persian

per se by itself, in itself

PERSI *PERiodical Source Index*, Allen County Public Library, 900 Webster Street, Fort Wayne, IN 46802. An index to many current and retrospective genealogical and historical periodicals.

pers knowl personal knowledge

person¹/p'son¹ personal

pert pertaining

PERT Perth, Great Britain

Perths Perthshire, Scotland

PERU Peru

Peruv Peruvian

PeSL Pennsylvania State Library, P.O. Box 1601, Harrisburg PA 17105

Pet Peter

pet/petitn/petn petition

petd petitioned

petr petitioner

Petrol Petroleum

PEU Peru

pf printed forms

PFAL Pfalz

Pfc Private first class (Army)

PFC Presbyterian Free Church

pfect perfect

PFI Private Finance Initiative

PfP Partnership for Peace

Pfr. Pfarrer (minister)

PFR Pocket Family Researcher

pg (1) page number (2) preacher of the gospel

Pg Portugal

PG President General

PG Professional Genealogist

PGCS (1) Publisher's Genealogical Coding Service (2) Publisher's Genelogical Coding System

PGM *The Pennsylvania Genealogical Magazine*

PGP pretty good privacy (computer encryption program)

PGRS Proceedings of the First (Second, etc.) Priesthood Genealogy Research Seminar (held on the campus of Brigham Young University, Provo, Utah)

PGS Pinellas Genealogical Society, P.O. Box 1614, Largo, FL 34649-1614

PGS Paradise Genealogical Society, Paradise, CA

PGSA Polish Genealogical Society of America, 984 North Milwaukee Avenue, Chicago, IL 60622

PGS CA Polish Genealogical Society of California, P.O. Box 713, Midway City, CA 92655-0713

PGSM Polish Genealogical Society of Michigan, Detroit Public Library, Burton Historical Collection, 5201 Woodward Avenue, Detroit, MI 48202

PGST Polish Genealogical Society of Texas, 218 Beaver Bend, Houston, TX 77037

ph/Ph (1) physician (2) telephone

Ph Phillip

ph/pish/parsh parish

PH Purple Heart

PharB Bachelor of Pharmacy

PharD/PharmD Doctor of Pharmacy

pharm pharmacist

Pharm Pharmacology, Parmacy

PharmM Master of Pharmacy

PhB *Philosophiae Bacalaureus* (Bachelor of Philosophy)

PhD *Philosophiae Doctor* (Doctor of Philosophy)

Phe Phelipe

PhG Graduate in Pharmacy

PHI Philippine Islands

Phil (1) Philemon (2) Philip (3) Philippians (4) Philippine (5) philosophy

Phila/Phi/Phil Philadelphia

Phill Phillip

Philos Philosophy

PhiP Philadelphia, Pennsylvania

PHL/PHIL Philippines

PhM Master of Philosophy

PHMC Pennsylvania Historical and Museum Commission

Phon Phone number

photo photograph

photog (1) photographer (2) photography

Photog Photographic, Photography

PHR *Pacific Historical Review*

PHS Historical Society of Pennsylvania, 1300 Locust Street, Philadelphia, PA 19107-5699

PHS *The Publications of the Harleian Society*

Phthisis/Pul Phthisis Pulmonales

PHW Personal History Writer

phy/phys/physcn physician

Phys Physical

Physiol Physiological, Physiology

PI (1) Preliminary Inventory (e.g., National Archives preliminary inventory) (2) The Republic of the Philippines, Phillipine Islands (3) Place interred

Pi *par interim*

PIC Picton Press, P.O. Box 250, Rockport, ME 04856

PICS Platform for Internet Content Selection

PID Parentage in doubt

PIED Piedmont

PIHL Publications of the Illinois State Historical [Library] Society

PIL Portuguese Islands

PILI *Passenger and Immigration Lists Index*, edited by P. William Filby, et al. (Detroit: Gale Group)

p IL insco President-IL Insurance Co.

Pilot River Pilot

PIN Personal Identification Number

Pip Philip, Philipa, Phillipa

PIRA Provisional Irish Republican Army

pish parish

Pit/PitP Pittsburgh, Pennsylvania

PiU Pittsburgh University, Pennsylvania

PJHQ Permanent Joint Headquarters

PJK Probate Judge of the Peace

pjp probate justice peace

PJP Probate Judge of the Peace

pk (1) packet (estate file) (2) park (3) peck

Pk (1) park (2) peak

PKC public key cryptography

pkg package

PKI public key infrastructure

PKP Phi Kappa Phi

pkr packer

Pkwy/pky Parkway

PKZIP file compression utility (program)

pl (1) place (2) plate (3) plural

Pl Place

PL (1) Place (2) Poland, *see* POL (3) Public Laws

PLA Port of London Authority

Plac Place

Plan Planning

Plant/plant Plantation

PLB Poor Law Board

PLC Public Library of Cincinnati

PLCH Public Library of Cincinnati and Hamilton County, History and Genealogy Department, 800 Vine Street, Cincinnati, OH 45202-2071

Plcmt Placement

PLD Poland

Pldg Paulding Public Library, Paulding, GA

Pleas Pleasance

plen plenipotentiary

plkroadagt plank road agent

PLM Personalized Mailing List

plmb plumber, plumbing

plms palms

pln(s) plain(s)

PLOW Palatinate, Lower, Germany

plr pillar

plshr polisher

plstr/plster plasterer

plt/pltf plaintiff

Plt Plantation

plu/plu/plur pluries, a 3rd or subsequent writ, warrant, or court order

PLU Poor Law Union(s) (British)

plum plumber

PlwB ploughboy

PlwM ploughman

Ply Plymouth

Ply Col Rec Records of the Colony of New Plymouth

Plz Plaza

p.m. postmaster

PM (1) Patriarchs Militant (Independent Order of Odd Fellows) (2) Paymaster (3) Peabody Museum, Salem, MA (4) *piae memoriae* (of pious memory) (5) Police Magistrate (6) Postmaster (7) *post meridiem* (afternoon) (8) *Post Mortem* after death (8) Preparative Meeting

P.M. Principal Meridian (federal township and range survey system)

Pmb Pembrokeshire, Wales

PMC (1) Presidential Memorial Certificate (2) Professional Management Conference (e.g., APG Professional Management Conference) (3) Protestant Methodist Church

PMG Postmaster General

PMHSM Papers of the Military Historical Society of Massachusetts

PML (1) Personalized Mailing List (2) Presidential Memorial Certificate

PML Pierpont Morgan Library, 29 E. 36th Street, NY

PM's Clk Pay Master's Clerk

Pmst paymaster

p Mu insco President-Mutual Insurance Company

pn pension

PN Place-Name

pnes pines

PNG (1) Papua New Guinea (2) portable network graphics

pni pagination not indicated

PNQ *Pacific Northwest Quarterly*

PNRISSHS Personal Narratives Rhode Island Soldiers and Sailors Historical Society

PNSR Soldier Pensioned

pntr painter

pnts pointsman

po property owned at the place listed

p.o. Post Office

p/o parents of

P/O Pilot Officer

PO/P.O. (1) Pacific Ocean (2) Petty Officer (3) Poland, Polish (4) Poll Book (5) Post Office (6) President's Office (LDS Church)

poa/POA power of attorney

POA Pennsylvania Oaths of Allegiance, William Henry Egle

POB Post Office Box

POC Pacific Ocean

POD Professional and Organizational Development Network in Higher Education

PodD Doctor of Podiatry

POE (1) preponderance of the evidence (2) port of entry

P of A Power of Attorney

POINT (1) Pursuing Our Italian Names Together (2) Polish Genealogical Society of America

POL/Polan/PLD/Plnd/POLA (1) Poland (2) Polish

pol political

polc police, police constable

Poli Political

Polit Sci Political Science

PolW police officer's wife

Polytech Polytechnic

POME Pomerania (Pommern), Prussia

Pomm (1) Pommerania (2) Pommern, Prussia

poorhsekpr Poor House Keeper & farmer

pop population

Pop Population

POP (1) Point of Presence (2) Post Office Protocol (3) Preserve Our Past (4) Preserving Our Past

popn population

por/Por porter

Por/POR Portugal

Po.R Puerto Rico

PorD porter's daughter

PorS porter's son

port porter, portree

Port/PORT (1) Portugal (2) Portuguese

Portr portrait

Ports Portsmouth, Ohio

Portu/PORT Portugal

PorW porter's wife

pos/poss possible/possibly

POSA Patriotic Order of the Sons of America

POSE Posen

poss (1) possessive, possession (2) possible/possibly

poss/of possession of

post after

Post Postal code

Poth pathologist

PotM potman

POW (1) prisoner of war (2) Prince of Wales

powr any power to act for another, as in power of attorney

pow res power reserved

pp (1) pages (2) parcel post (3) parish priest (4) past participle (5) past president (6) pauper (7) post paid (8) privately printed

Pp Pauper

P&P past and present

ppa per power of attorney

PPFA Palatinate, Pfalz

PPGS Pikes Peak Genealogical Society, P.O. Box 1262, Colorado Springs, CO 80901

PPI/ppi pixels per inch

PPLS pixels per line segment

p:pole/p:poll per person

ppose propose

PPP Point-to-Point Protocol (computer term)

P.P.propria-persona in propria persona (litigant who represents himself)

PPR Principal Probate Registry (England)

PPS post postscriptum (a later postscript)

PQ/Que Québec, Canada

P&QS Pleas & Quarter Sessions

pr proved

pr/prob/prob' probate or probated

pr/prs two or a pair, a number of pairs

Pr (1) Press (2) Prisoner (3) Prussia

PR (1) Commonwealth of Puerto Rico (2) Parish Register (3) Physicians' Records/Returns (4) Prussia

PR/pr (1) parish register(s) (2) prairie (3) preacher (4) prisoner (5) printed book (6) probate record(s), probated (7) proved (8) public relations (9) the day before

PR Puerto Rico

p^r/p^2 pair, per

Pragu Prague (Praga)

Pr Appt Prior Appointment

Praus Prausen (Preußen, Prussia)

prbn probationer

prc (1) Probate Record, case number (2) proclamation (marriage) (3) produced a certificate

prcf produced a certificate from

PrCo Providence College, Rhode Island

PRCT (1) percent (2) percentage

PRDH *Répertoire des Actes de Baptême, Mariage, Sépulture, et des Recensements du Québec Ancien* (published by Programme de recherche en démographie historique—Université de Montréal)

pre before

Preb Prebendary (England), office and title of a priest

prec/precd preceding

Prec Precinct

prede precede

Pr Edw Isl Prince Edward Island

pref (1) preface (2) prefix

p.regist^r probate register

prem premature

prep (1) preparatory (2) preposition

Prep Preparation, Preparatory

prepd prepared

pres (1) presence (2) present (3) presented (4) president (5) presumed

Pres/Presb/Presby Presbyterian

Pres President

presv preservation

Presv Preservation

pret preterit

prev previous

PRF Pedigree Resource File (lineage-linked pedigrees on compact discs). Family and Church History Department, Salt Lake City, UT.

prfrdr proofreader

PRHE Palatinate, Rhenish

PrHes Prussia, Hesse

pri/Pri (1) principal (2) price

PRIC Puerto Rico

Pries Prieson

prim (1) primitive (2) Primitive Baptist

prin/princ principal

pris prisoner

Pris/Prissy Priscilla

priv (1) private (2) privilege

Priv Private

priv pr privately printed

priv pub privately published

pr md previously married

PrMd parlormaid

prnt parent

prntr printer

pro (1) probate record (2) proprietor (3) proved (4) province (5) provost

pro/prob (1) probate (2) probation (3) probationary

PRO Public Record Office, Ruskin Avenue, Kew, Richmond, Surrey, England TW9 4DU

prob (1) probable (2) probably

PROB Prerogative Court of Canterbury, England

Prob Probate

probal probable

prob. Ct./ProbCt probate court

proc (1) proceedings (2) procurator

Proc Process, Processing

ProCD ProPhone (national telephone directory on CD-ROM)

procl/procla/prol proclamation

Proc. Mass. Soc *Proceedings of the Massachusetts Historical Society*

Procs. Proceedings

prod produce, production

ProD proprietor's daughter

prof/Prof. (1) professional (2) professor

Prof Professional, Professions

profl professional(s)

prog program

Prog Program

PROG NAME program name

proj project

Pro Judge Probate Judge

prom (1) professionnel(le) (2) promontory (3) promoted

pron pronoun

PRONI Public Record Office of Northern Ireland, Belfast

prop property

prop/propr proprietor

proprhouse proprietor of the house

ProS proprietor's son

pros. Atty. prosecuting attorney

prot protector

Prot Protestant

Prot. E. Protestant Episcopal

pro tem *pro tempore* (for the time being)

prov (1) proved (2) provided (3) province/provincial (4) provost

Prov Province

prov/provis provision

Prov. Laws Acts and Resolves of the Province of the Massachusetts Bay

prox *proximo* (next month)

PRP Professional Registered Parliamentarian

PRRN Public Record Retriever Network

PRRS Public Record Research System

Prs/PRs Parish Registers

PRS (1) Pedigree Referral System (2) Prussia

PRSA Public Relations Society of America, 33 Irving Place, New York, NY 10003-2376

prsfdr press feeder

PRSH Parish

prsmn pressman

prsr presser

prst priest

Prst Praesto, Denmark

PRT/prt (1) Portugal (2) priest

prt brwr partner in brewery

prtg protègée, protégè

PRU Prussia

Prue Prudence

Pruss/PRUS/PRUSS Prussia/Prusia

Prv/prvt private

prvd proved

ps (1) previously submitted (LDS), indicates that the name of a person has been submitted for temple ordinance work (2) pieces (3) purchased goods at a sale

PS Pilgrim Society, Plymouth, MA

PS&OL Patron Sheets and Ordinance Lists (microfiche, Family History Library)

PS/ps (1) Patriotic Service (2) *postscriptum* (3) postscript (4) primary sources (5) Public Services (6) Public School

PSA Persia

PSA public service announcement

PSAX Saxony (Province of Saxony)

psd p = pound, s = shilling, d = pence, denominations of English money

psentmt a presentment, or charge, made by a grand jury

psh parish

pshr parishioner

psnr pensioner

PSon principal son

psych psychology

Psychi Psychiatry

Psychiat Psychiatrist, Psychiatry

Psychol Psychology, Psychological

PST Pacific Standard Time

pt (1) part (2) part of roll of film (3) partition case (4) patient (5) petition (6) point (7) port (8) *pro tempore* (for the time) (9) pint

pt/pts part(s)

Pt (1) Patient (2) Patten

PT (1) Part Time (2) Petitioner's List (3) Portugal

p&t plain and true

PTA Parent-Teacher Association

pte private

ptf/plt Plaintiff

PTFS Progressive Technology Federal Systems

Pth Perthsire, Scotland

PTLDC Provincial and Territorial Library Directors Council (Canada)

PtnD partner's daughter

ptnr partner

PtnS partner's son

ptnt patient

PtnW partner's wife

pto please turn over (the page)

p.t.p. *post tribus proclamationibus* (after calling the banns three times)

PTS Postal Transportation Service

PtWi patient's wife

P2P peer-to-peer

pty proprietary

pu/Pu/pupl pupil

PU Prussia, Prussian

PUASAL Proceedings of the Utah Academy of Sciences, Arts & Letters

pub/publ (1) public (2) published, publication, publisher, published by (3) published inventory, guide, directory

Pub Public

Publ (1) Public (2) Publisher, Publishing

pubn publication(s)

pubr publisher

Pub Rel Public Relations Head

Puer Fev Puerperal Fever

PUL Princeton University Library, Princeton, NJ 08540

Pul Affec Pulmonary Affection

Pul Con Pulmonary Consumption

PUPP Palatinate, Upper

pur purveyor

PUR Puerto Rico

purch purchase, purchasing

Purch Purchasing

Put So Th Putrid Sore Throat

pvd proved

PVR Premature Voluntary Release

PVRL Parish and Vital Records List (Family History Library, Salt Lake City, UT)

pvt private

Pvt Private (military)

Pvtr Privateer

pw per week

PW The Presbyterian Witness and Evangelical Advocate (Halifax, Nova Scotia)

PWA Public Works Administration

PWCGS Prince William County Genealogical Society, P.O. Box 2019, Manassas, VA 20108-0812

PWCIIC POW/Civilian Internee Information Center, United States

PWGSC Public Works and Government Services Canada

PWI Prince of Wales Island

PX Post Exchange

py per year/annum

pymt payment

Q

q (1) a query (2) qu. or qts. (3) quarterly (4) queen

Q Quarto, oversized book

Q. Quarterly

Q/QC/Qe/Que/QUEQB Québec, Canada

Q & A question(s) and answer(s)

qaly qualifying

Qbc Québec, Canada

q c quit claim

QC (1) Quad Cities (2) Québec, Canada (3) Queen's Council (British)

QED *quod erat demonstrandum* (which was to be demonstrated, which was to be proved)

qen wherefore execution (q.v.) should not issue

Qkr Quaker

Qld Queensland

Q-Link Quantum Computers, Vienna, VA (BBS online service)

Qly Quarterly

QM (1) Quarter Master (2) Quarterly Meeting (Quakers)

QMC Quartermaster Corps

QMD Quartermaster's department

QMG Quartermaster General

QMGen Quartermaster General

QMORC Quartermaster Officers Reserve Corps

Qm.Sgt/QMSgt Quartermaster Sergeant

QMst quartermaster

qrtr/qtr/qr quarter

qt quart

Qt/Qtly/qtrly quarterly

Qtm Quartermaster

qs quod sacrs

QS Quarter Sessions

qt quart

Qtr Quarter

Qtr Mstr Quarter Master

qu qualities

QU (1) Lower Canada, Canada (2) Québec, Canada

quad (1) quadrant (2) quadrennial (3) topographical map

Qual Quality

quar a stone quarry

quart (1) quarter (2) quarterly

QUE/Que Québec, Canada

Qust Queenstown, Ireland

qv/QV *quod vide* (refer to, which see)

qy query

R

R/r (1) on a Revolutionary War pension jacket, R means "rejected" (2) Rabbi (3) Range: on a Rectangular Survey map (legal land description (4) record (5) rector (6) reigns, reigned (7) recto (8) Regiment (9) *regina*; queen (10) regular censuses (11) rejected (12) removed (13) Republican (14) resident, resides (15) residing (16) *rex*; king (17) right (in stage directions) (18) river (19) road (20) room(s) (21) roomer (22) Royal (23) rural (24) Rutland, England

R2aa-14 letter preceding 2aa on a female's card; represents the letter of the alphabet in which the sheet was filed (Family History Library)

ra/Ra raising

RA (1) Rear Admiral (2) Recreation Area (3) Royal Academician (4) Royal Artillery (British) (5) Russia

RA Royal Artillery

RAuxAF Royal Auxiliary Air Force

RAC Royal Automobile Club (British)

Rad/RAD (1) Radnor (2) Radnorshire, Wales

RAD (1) rapid application development (2) Records Adjustment Department

Radiat Radiation

Radiol Radiologic, Radiological

RADN Radnor, Great Britain

RAF Royal Air Force

RAFVR Royal Air Force Volunteer Reserve

RAL Reuss Altere Linie

RALL Reuss Altere Linie

RAM (1) Random Access Memory (computer term) (2) Royal Arch Masons

RAMC Royal Army Medical Corps

Ran Randolph

Rang Rangarvallasysla

RAOGK Random Acts of Genealogical Kindness

rat rated

Rau Rause

Ray Rachel, Raymond

rb Record Book

Rb Robert

RB Rigle Brigade

RBaue Rein Bauer

RBH Rutherford B. Hayes Presidential Center, Spiegel Grove, Fremont, OH 43420

RC (1) Red Cross (2) Reserve Corps (3) Roman Catholic (4) Roman Catholic Church

R&C Ross & Cromarty, Scotland

RCAF Royal Canadian Air Force

rcd/rec (1) record (2) recorded

rcdr/rcor recorder

Rcdr Deeds Recorder of Deeds

Rcdrs/Rcds records, recorders

RCE Register of Corrected Entries (Scotland)

RCGS Riley County Genealogical Society, 2005 Claflin Road, Manhattan, KS 66502-3415

Rch Research

RCHM Royal Commission on Historical Monuments (British)

Rcm Roscommon, Republic of Ireland

R-Cn Republic of the Congo

rcp Roman Catholic priest

rcpt receipt

rcut recruit

rd (1) relinquished right as administrator of estate (2) road

Rd (1) release of dower rights (2) Road

Rd Richard

R & D Research & Development

RD (1) Registration District (2) Revolutionary Daughter (3) Rural Deaneries (British) (4) Rural Delivery

RDF Research Data Filer (a program in *Personal Ancestral File* 2.31, and older versions). This program is not available in *PAF* 3.0 or 4.0 or later.

rdg ridge

rdnt resident

rdr reader

re:/re regarding

RE Royal Engineers (British)

Read Readable

re-af reaffirmed

REAH *Reading Early American Handwriting*, by Kip Sperry (Baltimore: Genealogical Publishing Co., 1998)

real est real estate

realestagt real estate agent

ReaP Reading, Pennsylvania

Rear Adm. Rear Admiral

reb rebellion

Reb/Rebª Rebecca

rec (1) receive, received, receiving (2) record(s) (3) recording

rec/recᵈ (1) record(s) (2) recorded

Rec Record, Recording

recd/rec'd/recᵈ**/recv**ᵈ received

rec'd by corr received by correspondence

rec of mem record of members

recoll recollections

Record *The New York Genealogical and Biographical Record*

recpt (1) receipt (2) receptionist

Recr Recreation

recrq received by request

Recrt (1) Recruit (2) Recruiting

rect/rec rector, rectory

recᵗ receipt

REED Reverse Emulsion Electrophoretic Display

ref (1) refer (2) reference (3) reformed

Ref Reference

refers reference

reffrd referred

refgr refrigeration, refrigerator

REFIS Related Entity Financial Information System (Family History Centers)

refl reflexive

Refn Reference number

Ref.Pres.Ch. Reformed Presbyterian Church

reg (1) regiment (2) region (3) register(s) (4) registration (5) regular

reg/regᵗ**/regist**ᵗ**/regt** (1) regiment (2) register

Reg Regula

Reg/Reggie/Reggy/Rex Reginald

REG (1) *The New England Historical and Genealogical Register* (2) Regiment

regd registered

Reg Gen Registrar General

Reg in Chan Register in Chancery

Regis Registration

Register *The New England Historical and Genealogical Register*

reg'l regional

regn region

regnal year the date most often used in medieval documents referring to the number of the year of the reign of the monarch at the time the document was dated

regnl regional

Reg of Wills Register of Wills

Regr Registrar

regt regiment

regtl regimental

rehab rehabilitation

Rehab Rehabilitation

ReiB Reichenberger

Reinb Reinbiern

reinstd reinstated

rej rejected

rel (1) related, relative(s) (2) relations (3) relationship (4) released (5) relict (6) religion (7) religious

Rel Related, Relations

rela relative

RelC religious condition

reld relieved

relecta widow

relectus widower

relfc released from care for

Reli Religion

Relig Religion, Religious

rel-i-l relative-in-law

rel/o relict of

RelO religious order

relrq released by request

rem (1) remain (2) remainder (3) remained (4) reminiscences (5) remove (6) removed

Rema Remarks

REME Royal Electrical and Mechanical Engineers

remove removed

Remit/Fev Remittent Fever

ren (1) *renatus, renata* (baptized) (2) renounced, renunciation

REN renewal

ren cov renewed covenant

RENF/Renf Renfrew, Scotland

renun renunciation

rep (1) repair (2) report (3) representative (4) reprint(ed)

Rep (1) Representative (2) Republican

repl replacement, replaced

repr (1) repair, repairman (2) reprint, reprinted

Repr Reproduction, Reproductive

Reprod Reproduction

republ republished

repud repudiated

req/reqt (1) request (2) requested

Req Requirement

res (1) research (2) reservation (3) reserve (4) reservoir (5) residence (length of, in county, lived at) (6) resident (7) resides, resided (8) residue (9) resign (10) resolution

Res (1) Research (2) Reservoir (3) Resources

RES Reservation, Reserve

res. aids research aids

resd (1) reserved (2) resigned

Resi Residence

res leg residuary legatee

resrt resort

Restaur Restaurant

restr restaurant

ret (1) retail (2) returned

ret/retd retired

Ret/Far retired farmer

Reti Retirement

ret mbrp retained membership

Ret/Wvr retired weaver

ReuO Reuss-Olden

REUS Reuss

rev (1) revenue (2) reverend (3) reversed (4) review (5) revised (6) revision (7) revived use

Rev (1) Revelation (2) Reverend (3) Revolution/Revolutionary (4) Revolutionary War

REV Reservation

rev. ed. revised edition

Revol Revolutionary War, American Revolution

Rev vet Revolutionary War veteran

RevW/Rev War Revolutionary War, American Revolution

RF research folder

RFA Royal Fleet Auxiliary

RFC (1) Request for Comment (2) Royal Flying Corps

RFD Rural Free Delivery

RFG Refuge

RFV *Resource File Viewer* (computer software, Family and Church History Department, Salt Lake City, UT)

RFW Renfrew or Renfrewshire, Scotland

RG (1) General Register Office, Public Record Office, Kew, Surrey, England (2) Record Group (e.g., National Archives and Records Administration record group number) (3) Registered Genealogist (4) Registrar General

Rgl Rogaland, Norway

RGRE Reuss Griez

RGS Rochester Genealogical Society, P.O. Box 10501, Rochester, NY 14610-0501

Rgstr Registrar

RHA Royal Horse Artillery (British)

Rheinh Rheinhessen, Hess-Darmstadt

Rheinl/Rhinel Rheinland, Prussia

Rhi Rhine

RhiB Rhine Bion

RHIN Rhineland (Rheinland, Rheinprovinz)

RhiR Rhine Bier/Beir

RHistS Royal Historical Society (British)

RHL Rhodes House Library (Bodleian Library, University of Oxford), South Parks Road, Oxford, England OX1 3RG

RHO Rhodesia

Rhode Isl Rhode Island

RHP Register House Press, Scottish Record Office, HM General Register House, Princes Street, Edinburgh, Scotland EH1 3YY

RHQ Regional Headquarters

ri rise

RI Rhode Island

RiaB (1) Rian Baron (2) *Rogers Index* (The Filson Club)

R.I. Arch. Rhode Island Archives, Providence, RI

Ric/Rich/Richd/Rich^d/R^d Richard

RIC Reference Information Circular (National Archives)

RIC Research Information Center (Family History Library, Salt Lake City, UT)

RIC Royal Irish Constabulary

Rich/Richd Richard

Richf Richfield, Ohio

RICON Rhode Island Consortium of Genealogical and Historical Societies

RicV Richmond, Virginia

RIGR *Rhode Island Genealogical Register*, Rhode Island Families Association, P.O. Box 1414, Ashburn, VA 20146-1414

RIGS Rhode Island Genealogical Society, P.O. Box 433, Greenville, RI 02828

RIHS Rhode Island Historical Society, 110 Benevolent Street, Providence, RI 02906

RIN Record Identification Number (used in *Personal Ancestral File®* genealogy software program)

rinq relinquished

RIP Reference Information Paper (National Archives)

R.I.P. *requiescat in pace* (rest in peace); sometimes found on gravestones

RISL Rhode Island State Library, Providence, RI

RITA Regional Income Tax Agency

RIU Research and Intelligence Unit

riv river

Riv River

RIVR,NS *Rhode Island Vital Records, New Series*

RJUL Reuss Jungere Linie

rk rock

RK Roman Knights

Rkbg Ringkobing, Denmark

RL regional libraries

RLAC Research Libraries Advisory Committee

RLC Royal Logistic Corps

RLDS Reorganized Church of Jesus Christ of Latter Day Saints, 1001 West Walnut, Independence, MO 64050-3562 (now Community of Christ)

RLDSLA Library-Archives and Museum, Reorganized Church of Jesus Christ of Latter Day Saints (Community of Christ), Independence, MO 64050-3562

RLG Research Libraries Group. *See* RLIN

RLIN Research Libraries Information Network; Research Libraries Group. Computerized bibliographic database of over 85 million titles, including the acquisitions of the Library of Congress since 1968.

RLL Roots Location List

rlnq relinquished

rly railway

rm (1) ream (of paper) (2) reported married

Rm (1) room (2) roomer

RM Royal Marines (British)

RM Royal Marines

RMC Royal Military College

RMOKHSJ Religious and Military Order of Knights of the Holy Sepulchre of Jerusalem

RMR Royal Marines Reserve

RMS Royal Military Surveyor (British)

rmt reported married to

RN (1) Record Number (Family History Library Catalog computer number) (2) Registered Nurse (3) Reuters News Agency (4) report number (5) Royal Navy (British)

RNA ribonucleic acid

RNAS Royal Naval Air Station

rnch(s) ranch(s)

Rnds Randers, Denmark

RNE Register of Neglected Entries (Scotland)

Rnf Renfrewshire, Scotland

Rngr Ranger

RNR Royal Naval Reserve

RNSHS Royal Nova Scotia Historicl Society

RNVR Royal Naval Volunteer Reserve

RO (1) Record Office (2) Recruiting Officer (3) Romania

road ngner engineer on road

RO-AUM Rosocrucian Order (Masonic)

Rob/Robt/Rob'/Ro' Robert

Robt° Roberto

roc received on certificate

ROC (1) Ross & Company (2) Ross & Cromarty

rocf received on certificate form

ROCR Ross & Cromarty, Great Britain

Roddy Roderick, Rodney

Rodrig² Rodriguez

ROG Rogassen

rol received on letter

rolf received on letter from

Rom (1) Roman(s) (2) Romance

ROM (1) Read Only Memory (computer term) (2) Romania

ROMA Romania

Rom.Cath. Roman Catholics

Ron/Ronnie/Ronny Ronald

R-Or Rio Del Oro, NM

Ros Ross and Cromarty, Scotland

Ros Rosamund, Rosemary

ROS Roscommon

Rosetta Rose

Rosie Rosamund, Rose, Rosemary

ROST Rostock

Rot. Roll, Rolls (*rotalus*); a term used for many types of early records

ROTC Reserve Officers' Training Corps

Rox/ROX/ROXB/Roxb Roxburgh or Roxburghshire, Scotland

Roxy Roxana

ROY Royal Navy

RP/rp Revolutionary War pensioner

RP (1) Reformed Presbyterian (2) Reformed Presbyterian Church

RP&A Records Preservation and Access Committee

rpd/rpt reported

rpds rapids

Rph Ralph, Randolph

RPI Research Publications, Inc., Woodbridge, CT

rpm revolutions per minute

rpt (1) reprint(ed) (2) report, reported

Rpt Reports

Rpt respited (no accompanying inventory). Term found in Prerogative Court of York (England)

rq request(s), requested

rqc requested certificate

rqct requested certificate to

rqcuc requested to come under care (of meeting)

rr railroad employee or incorporator

r.r./RR railroad

RR (1) railroad (2) Rent Role (3) Right Reverend (4) Rural Route

RRB Railroad Retirement Board

rr bggmstr railroad baggage master

rr cndctr railroad conductor

RR GR Railroad Grade

rr ngner railroad engineer

rrq request, requests, requested

r.s. railroad street

RS (1) Residence List (2) Residents List (3) Revolutionary Soldier

RSA Republic of South Africa

RSCG Reuss Schleiz Gera

RSCH Reuss Schleiz

rsch/rsh research

rshr researcher

RSL RootsWeb Surname List, Roots Surname List

RSL Royal Staff Corps (British)

RSM *Records Submission Manual* (former LDS handbook)

RSNMA Royal Scottish Naval and Military Academy

RSOF Religious Society of Friends (Quakers)

Rsrch Research

rst (1) reinstated in membership (2) rest

RSTV (1) Rite of St. Vita (2) Rite of St. Vaclara

RSV Revised Standard Version (of the Bible)

RSVP please reply

rt (1) right, as in a right of dower (2) route

Rt/Rt. Honab Right Honorable, a title

R-Tab Records Tabulation

RTC (1) Real Time Clock (personal computer) (2) relationship to claimant

Rte Route, U.S. or state numbered road

RTF Rich Text Format (computer format)

R Tkt Reader's Ticket

R Tr Radio Tower

RtSU Rutgers State University, New Brunswick, NJ

RU Rumania

RUC Royal Ulster Constabulary

RU/RUS/RUSS Russia, Russian

Rud Rudolf, Rudolph

rudimnts/rudmnts rudiments

Rufe Rufus

Rum Rumania(n)

Rupt Rupture

RUS/RUSS Russia(n)

RUSA Reference and Users Services Association

RUT/Rutl/Rutlds Rutland, England

Ruther Rutherford

RUTL Rutlandshire, Great Britain

RVA Richmond, Virginia

RVN Republic of Vietnam

RVNAF Republic of Vietnam Armed Forces

Rvr River

Rvrhd Riverhead

RW (1) Red War (2) Revolutionary War

R. W. Revolutionary War

RWGR *Revolutionary War Graves Register* (National Society of the Sons of the American Revolution)

RWGuide RootsWeb Guide

RWR *RootsWeb Review*

Ry Railway

ry sta railway station

S

s (1) section (2) sepulture (burial) (3) sepultus (4) shilling (5) siecle (century) (6) single (7) soldier (8) son(s) (9) son of (Quaker) (10) south (11) speculation (12) spinster (13) substantive (14) succeeded (15) successor (16) surveyed (17) survivor

S (1) sale (2) Saturday (3) section (4) Selig, (of persons) (late, deceased) (5) Sister (6) Son (7) South (8) State or colonial census (9) Sunday (10) Supplement (usually found at the end of the printed register) (11) survivor (in a Revolutionary War pension jacket)

S. south

s/ or s/o son of

S/Sergt/Sgt Sergeant

S1 First Sergeant

S2 Second Sergeant

S3 Third Sergeant

S4 Fourth Sergeant

S5 Fifth Sergeant

S6 Sixth Sergeant

S7 Seventh Sergeant

S8 Eighth Sergeant

S Car South Carolina

S Dak South Dakota

sa (1) sailor (2) *secundum artem* (3) see also (4) *sine anno* (without year) (5) *sub anno* (under the year)

s-a twice annually

Sa (1) Saxony (2) Shropshire, England

Sa/Sat Saturday

SA (1) corporation (2) Selective Availability (3) Société Anonyme (4) South Africa (5) South America (6) Spanish America (7) Survivor's Application

Sᵃ, Sⁿ Señora (title)

SAA Society of American Archivists, 527 S. Wells, 5th Floor, Chicago, IL 60607

Sac Sachs/Sachs Weimer/Sachsen

SacC Sachs Coburg/Saxe Coburg

SACEUR Supreme Allied Commander Europe

Sachs Sachson

SACLANT Supreme Allied Commander Atlantic

Sacogo Sachsen-Coburg-Gotha, Thuringia

sae/SAE self-addressed envelope

SAF South Africa

SAFHS Scottish Association of Family History Societies, 15 Victoria Terrace, Edinburgh, Scotland EH1 2JL

SAG *Swedish American Genealogist*, Swenson Swedish Immigration Research Center, Augustana College, Rock Island, IL 61201-2273

SAHS Swiss American Historical Society, 6440 North Bosworth Avenue, Chicago, IL 60626

sail sailor

sal/Sal saleslady

Sal (1) Salary (2) Salmon

SAL San Salvador

Sal/Sallie/Sally Sarah

SAL/Salop Shropshire, England

SALT Saxony Altenburg, Germany

SALT Subject, Author, Locality, Title (catalog search)

Saltbg Sachsen-Altenburg, Thuringia, Germany

Salv El Salvador

Salzbg Salzburg

Sam Samson, Samuel

Sam Sameria, Samaritan, Samoa

SAM/SAME South America

Samein Sachsen-Meiningen, Thuringia, Germany

SAmer South America

Saml/Sam¹ Samuel

samt. together with

san sanitary

s and coh son and coheir

s and h son and heir

SAN (1) Sandwich Islands (2) Standard Address Number

San Jacinto Desc San Jancinto Descendants

SAR National Society of the Sons of the American Revolution, 1000 South Fourth Street, Louisville, KY 40203

SAR Search and Rescue

SAR Sons of the American Revolution

SAR Sardinia

SAR Sark, Channel Islands

SARA New York State Archives and Records Administration

SARD Sardinia

Sarum Salisbury, England or Maryland, US

SAS Saskatchewan, Canada

SAS Special Air Service

SASE self-addressed, stamped envelope

Sask Saskatchewan, Canada

SASS Society for the Advancement of Scandinavian Study

Sat (1) Saturday (2) Saturn

sauv savage (Indian)

sauvagesse savage (feminine) (Indian)

Sav (1) savings (2) Savior

SAV Savoy

Savage James Savage, *Genealogical Dictionary of the First Settlers of New England*, 4 vols. (1860–62, reprint. Baltimore: Genealogical Publishing Co., 1981)

Saweim Sachsenl–Weimar-Eisenach, Thuringia, Germany

SAX/Sax/SAXO Saxe, Saxony, Saxon

SaxC Saxe Coburg/Sachs Coburg

Saxe Sachsen, Prussia

Saxe Sachsen or Saxe

SAXO Saxony, Kingdom of

SaxW/SaxeW Saxe Weimer

say used with a date indicating a great degree of uncertainty

sb (1) settlement because (2) step brother (3) stillborn

s/b should be

sb. spouse born

SB (1) Bachelor of Science (2) source book of documents (3) Stepbrother (4) subfile

SBA Small Business Administration

SBA Sovereign Base Area

SBAGS South Bend Area Genealogical Society, 209 Lincoln Way E, Mishawaka, IN 46544

SBC Southern Baptist Convention

SBCGS Santa Barbara County Genealogical Society, P.O. Box 1303, Santa Barbara, CA 93116-1303

SBCGS South Bay Cities Genealogical Society, P.O. Box 11069, Torrance, CA 90510-1069

SBCL Saint Bonifazius Catholic Union

SBDa stepbrother's daughter

SBHLA Southern Baptist Historical Library and Archives, Nashville, TN 37203-3620

Sbl/SBL stepbrother-in-law

SBL Society B. Lafayette

SBro stepbrother

SBS Special Boat Service

SBSn stepbrother's son

SBWi stepbrother's wife

sc (1) scene (2) science (3) *scilicet* (namely) (4) *sculpsit* (carved by) (5) state census (6) Supreme Court (held in each county)

Sc (1) Scotland (2) Settlement Certificate

SC (1) Schomburg Center for Research in Black Culture (2) Scotland (3) Sergeant Commissary (4) Society of the Cincinnati (5) South Carolina (6) South Central (7) Southern News Service (8) Staff Corps (9) Summit County, Ohio (10) Survivor's Certificate(s)

SCA Leonardo Andrea Collection of South Carolina genealogies

SCAN Scottish Archive Network

Scand/SCAND/SCAN Scandinavia(n)

Scarl Fev Scarlet Fever

scatt scattering or scattered

scc sworn chain carrier

SCC Samuel Eliot Morison, *Records of the Suffolk County Court*

SCC Southern California Chapter, Association of Professional Genealogists (APG), P.O. Box 9486, Brea, CA 92822-9486

SCCAPG Southern California Chapter, Association of Professional Genealogists (APG), P.O. Box 9486, Brea, CA 92822-9486)

SCCHGS Santa Clara County Historical and Genealogical Society, Santa Clara Central Library, 2635 Homestead Road, Santa Clara, CA 95051-5387

SCCOGS Southern California Chapter, Ohio Genealogical Society, P.O. Box 5057, Los Alamitos, CA 90721-5057

ScD Doctor of Science

SCDAH South Carolina Department of Archives and History, 8301 Parklane Road, Columbia, SC 29223

SCGS Shelby County Genealogical Society, 17755 State Route 47, Sidney, OH 45365-9242

SCGS South Carolina Genealogical Society, P.O. Box 16355, Greenville, SC 29606

SCGS Southern California Genealogical Society, 417 Irving Drive, Burbank, CA 91504-2408

sch school

Sch School

Sch/SCH Schleswig Schlessien Schleweig Schumbold

SchB Schalbag

Schd stepchild

sched schedule

schl scholar, student

SchL Schaumberg-Lippe

Schles Schlesien, Prussia

Schles' Holst Schleswig-Holstein

Schlho Schleswig-Holstein, Prussia

Sch.' Lippe Schaumburg-Lippe

SchM school mistress, schoolmaster

scho school

schs schedules (e.g., Veterans Schedules)

SCHS Shelby County Historical Society, P.O. Box 376, Sidney, OH 45365-0376

SCHS South Carolina Historical Society, Fireproof Building, 100 Meeting Street, Charleston, SC 29401

Sch/Tchr School Teacher

SCHW Schwarzburg, Germany

Schwa Schwabia

Schwab Schwaben, Bavaria, Germany

Schwe Schwere

Schwru Schwarzburg-Rudolstadt, Thuringia, Germany

Schwso Schwarzburg-Sondershausen, Thuringia, Germany

Schwz Schwarzenborn, Germany

Schwzw Schwarzwald, Wüerttemberg, Germany

Schy Schuyler

sci science

Sci Science, Scientific

Sci scientific

sci. fa. *scire facias* (and it is ordered that)

Sci Fict Science Fiction

SCIP Society of Competetive Intelligence Professionals

Scis Sciences

scj *Supreme Court Journal*

Scl stepchild

SCL Sclavonia

scm *Supreme Court Minutes*

ScM Master of Science

SCMAR *The South Carolina Magazine of Ancestral Research*, P.O. Box 21766, Columbia, SC 29221

ScMd scullery maid

Sco/Scot Scotland, Scottish

SCOB Supreme Court Order Book

SCOG Saxony Coburg Gotha

SCOT Scotland

Scou stepcousin

SCP Suffolk County, Massachusetts, probate records

scr scrivener

SCR Scottish Church Records (FamilySearch™)

SCR Security Council Resolution

SCRE Scottish Council for Research in Education

script scriptor

SCRO Staffordshire County Record Office, Stafford, England

SCRO St. Croix

Scro Dysp Scrofula Dysipales

scru scruple

SCRU Santa Cruz

SCSAr South Carolina State Archives, Columbia, SC

SCSI small computer system interface (a parallel interface standard)

scst grind scissor grinder

sct secretariat(s)

SCT Scotland

scts scouts

SCU South Carolina University, Columbia, SC

Sculp Sculpture

SCV Sons of Confederate Veterans

SCW (1) Society of Colonial Wars (2) South Central Wisconsin

SCWFO Society of Civil War Families of Ohio (Ohio Genealogical Society, 713 South Main Street, Mansfield, Ohio 44907-1644)

sd/s^d (1) said (2) *sine die* (without setting a day for reconvening)

s'd said, in legal documents

sd (1) school director, board member, etc. (2) spouse died

s.d. will dated

Sd Sohn des, Sohn der (son of)

Sd/SD/SDau stepdaughter

SD soldier died

SD (1) Doctor of Science (2) Secure Digital (3) Senated Document (4) Spirit of Democracy, Woodsfield, Monroe Co., OH (5) supervisor's district (e.g., U.S. census)

SD/SDak South Dakota

SDA Seventh Day Adventist

SDaL/Sdl stepdaughter-in-law

SDC State Data Center

SDDa stepdaughter's daughter

SDFH Society of the Descendants of the Founders of Hartford

sdg siding

SDGS San Diego Genealogical Society, 1050 Pioneer Way, Suite E, El Cajon, CA 92020-1943

SDI Signer of the Declaration of Independence

Sdl/SDL stepdaughter-in-law

Sd/o stepdaughter of

SDOM Santo Domingo

SDOP Sons and Daughters of Oregon Pioneers, P.O. Box 6685, Portland, OR 97228

SDRAM Synchronous Dynamic Memory (computer term)

SDS Students for a Democratic Society

SDSHS South Dakota State Historical Society, South Dakota Archives, Cultural Heritage Center, 900 Governors Drive, Pierre, SD 57501-2217

SDSn stepdaughter's son

se (1) southeast (2) surname exchange

se/Se servant

SE (1) Sea (2) Settlement (3) Settlement Examination (4) Southeast, Southeastern

SEA at Sea

SEA Southeast Asia

SeaCap Sea Captain

SEAGS Southeast Alabama Genealogical Society, P.O. Box 143, Dothan, AL 36302

seal sealing (LDS)

SeaW seaman's wife

Sebast Sebastian

sec (1) second (2) secretary (3) section (4) sector (5) *secundum* (according to) (6) security

Sec (1) Secklendorf (2) Secondary

SeCl servant's child

Secr/Secy/sec'y secretary

Secr Secretarial

secs securities

sec state secretary of state

sect section

sectn boss section boss

secty/secy secretary

Secur Security

SED Senate Executive Document

SEER System for Evaluating the Effectiveness of RVNAF, Vietnam War Era

sel (1) selected (2) *selig* (of persons) (late, deceased)

Sel Sellmont

SEL Selkirk, Scotland

Seli Silesia

SELK/Selk Selkirk, Scotland

sell seller

Sem (1) Semester (2) Seminary

sen/senr/sr/sen^r/s^r senior

Sen (1) senate (2) Senator (3) Seneca

SEN Senegal

sent (1) sentence (2) sentry

SENTRI Secure Electronic Network for Travelers Rapid Inspection

sep (1) Latin form used as separate Christian name from date shown (2) separate(d)

Sep/Sept/S September

seqq sequentia

ser (1) series (2) servant

ser. (1) series (2) Congressional publication serial number

Ser Serials, Serials Librarian

SerB servant's baby

SERB Serbia

SerC servant's child

SerD servant's daughter

serg/sergt sergeant

SerH servant's husband

SerM servant's mother

SerN servant's nephew or niece

ser no serial number

SerS servant's son

sert/serv/servt servant

serv serve -ice,-ant

Serv Service, Services

serW servant's wife

ses/sess session

Sess. Clk. Session Clerk (Presbyterian)

set settled

set/sett settlement, settlement record

settl (1) settled (2) settler

sev/sevl several

sevt servant

Sew Disp Sewage Disposal

SEY Seychelles

Sf/SF (1) step father (2) Suffolk, England

SF (1) San Francisco (2) State Forest (3) stepfather (4) Survivor's File

SF Special Forces

SFal servant's father-in-law

SFat stepfather

SFBA JGS San Francisco Bay Area Jewish Genealogical Society, 4430 School Way, Castro Valley, CA 94546-1331

S-Fj Sogn & Fjordane, Norway

Sfl/SFL stepfather-in-law

SFPL San Francisco Public Library, 100 Larkin St. San Francisco, CA 94102-4733

sg (1) singular (2) sealing (LDS)

SG Society of Genealogists, 14 Charterhouse Buildings, Goswell Road, London, England EC1M 7BA

SG/Surg Surgeon (or Assistant)

SGC/SGCh step-grandchild

sgd signed

Sgd/SGD step-granddaughter

SGDL step-granddaughter-in-law

SGI St. George Island

SGML Standard Generalized Markup Language

SGMo step-grandmother

S&GP Serial and Covernment Publications Division, Library of Congress

Sgs/SGS/SGSn step-grandson

SGS Sasketchewan Genealogical Society, P.O. Box 1894, Regina, Saskatchewan S4P 3E1

SGS *Scottish Gaelic Studies*

SGS Scottish Genealogy Society, 15 Victoria Terrace, Edinburgh, Scotland EH1 2JL

SGS Seattle Genealogical Society, 8511 15th Avenue, NE, P.O. Box 1708, Seattle, WA 98111

Sgt Sergeant (military)

Sgt. Maj. Sergeant Major

sh (1) share (2) ship (3) shortly

SH Schkcswig

s & h/s. & h. son and heir

Sha Shanbry

SHAEF Supreme Headquarters, Allied Expeditionary Forces

Shak Shakespeare

SHAN Shanghai, China

Sh/Bt/Mk shoe and boot maker

shd shode

SHE Shetland Islands

shef sheriff

Shef/Sheff Sheffield

shep shepherd

SHET/Shet Shetland Islands, (Zetland) Scotland

SHFS Saskatchewan History and Folklore Society

shgs shillings

SHHAR Society of Hispanic Historical and Ancestral Research, P.O. Box 490, Midway City, CA 92655-0490

SHI Shetland Isles, Scotland

ship shipping

shl(s) shoal(s)

Shn Shanburgh, Canada

SHNA Scripps-Howard Newspaper Alliance

Shoe/Mkr Shoemaker

ShoL shoplad

SHOL Schleswig Holstein (Rudolstadt)

SHols South Holstein

ShoM shoemaker master

shop (1) shopman (2) shopping (3) shopwoman

ShpA shop assistant

Shp/Cptr ship carpenter

ShpG shop girl

ShpK shopkeeper

SHPO State Historic Preservation Office

ShpW shop walker

shr(s) (1) sheriff (2) shore(s)

SHR *Scottish Historical Review*

shrff dept sheriff deputy

SHRO/SHR Shropshire, Great Britain

Shrops Salop (Shropshire, England)

sh. sh. Sharpshooters

SHSI State Historical Society of Iowa, Des Moines and Iowa City, IA

SHSM State Historical Society of Missouri, 1020 Lowry Street, Columbia, MO 65201-7298

SHSW State Historical Society of Wisconsin, 816 State Street, Madison, WI 53706

sht mtl sheet metal

Shurtleff Nathaniel B. Shurtleff, *Records of the Governor and Company of the Massachusetts Bay in New England*

si/sis (1) sister (2) sister (of)

Si sister

SI (1) Sand Island (2) Sandwich Islands (3) Sister (4) Smithsonian Institution, Washington, DC (5) Staten Island (New York)

SIAM Siam

sib sibling(s)

Sib Sibyl, Sybil

Sib. Siberia(n)

Sibl Sibling

sic written thus, as copied, as shown in original: (often inserted after an obvious error)

SIC Sicily

SIC standard industrial classification

SICI/SIC Sicily

Sid Sidney, Sydney

SIE Sierra Leone

sig (1) signal (2) signature (3) signed (4) Signor

SIG Special Interest Group(s)

SiGD sister's granddaughter

SIGG Society of Indexers Genealogical Group, The RidgeWay, Kenton, Newcastle-upon-Tyne, England NE3 4LP

Signmaker Lincomatic Banner Maker

SiGs sister's grandson

sil/Sil/SIL (1) sister-in-law (2) sometimes means stepson (3) son-in-law

Sil Silvester

SiLD sister-in-law's daughter

SILE Silesia (Schlesien)

Silic Silicia

SilM sailmaker

Sim/Simmy/Sim^n Simeon, Simon

sin sine

SIN Singapore

sine without

sine die without delay, indefinitely

sing singular

Sing Singapore

SInm special inmate

SIP Surname Index Project

SIRS online database of articles from newspapers, periodicals, etc.

sis/sist sister

SIS (1) Special Information Services (2) Supplementary Information Services

SisC sister's child

SisD sister's daughter

SisH sister's husband

SisL/Sis-i-l/Sis-il sister-in-law

sis/o sister of

SisN sister's niece

SisR sister in religion

SisS sister's son

SITREPs Situation Reports

SIW Self-Inflicted Wound

SJ Society of Jesus

SJC Supreme Judicial Court

SJD Doctor of Juridical Science

SJI San Juan Islands

SK/Sask Saskatchewan, Canada

Skarab Skaraborg, Sweden

Skbg Skanderborg, Denmark

SKIT St. Kitts, West Indies

Skm Stockholm, Sweden

sl/SL (1) *sine loco* (without place) (2) slain (3) son-in-law

Sl South America

SL Savitz Library, Glassboro State College, Glassboro, NJ

SL Scotland

SL (1) Select List (e.g., National Archives select list) (2) Special List (National Archives)

Sla/Slav/SLAV (1) Slavic (2) Slavonia (3) Slavonian

s.l.a.n. *sine loco, anno, vel nomine* (without place, year, or name of publication)

SLBM Submarine-launched Ballistic Missile

SLC Family History Library, 35 North West Temple Street, Salt Lake City, UT 84150

SLC Salt Lake City, Utah

SLCL St. Louis County Library, 1640 South Lindbergh Blvd., St. Louis, MO 63131-3598

sld sealed (LDS)

SldC soldier's child

SldD soldier's daughter

SldN soldier's niece

Sldr soldier

S/Ldr Squadron Leader

SldS soldier's son

SldW soldier's wife

Sle Sleswick

SLEIF Statue of Liberty Ellis Island Foundation

slg (1) sealing (2) *sine legit* (without legitimate issue)

Slgc Sealing child

Slgp Sealing parent

Sli Sligo, Republic of Ireland

SLI/SLIG Salt Lake Institute of Genealogy, Utah Genealogical Association, P.O. Box 1144, Salt Lake City, UT 84110

SliI Sligo County, Ireland

SLIP Serial Line Internet Protocol (Computer term)

Slippe Schaumburg-Lippe, Germany

Slk Selkirkshire, Scotland

SLK Slovakia

SLMn slaughter man

Sln/Kpr saloon keeper

sl/o slave of

SLO Slovakia

SLO State Library of Ohio, 274 East First Avenue, Columbus, OH 43201

s.l.p. *sine legitima prole* (died without issue)

slphr sulphur

SLPL Saint Louis Public Library, 1301 Olive St., St. Louis, MO 63103

slr sailor

sls sales

SlSn sister-in-law's son

SLT *Salt Lake Tribune*, Salt Lake City, UT

Sly Sylvester

sm saw mill

s-m twice monthly

sm/sma small

Sm/SMot stepmother

SM (1) Master of Science (2) schoolmaster (3) Sergeant Major (4) service mark of the Board for Certification of Genealogists (5) South America (6) step-mother

SMan salesman

S.'Manld Sodermanland

SMAR St. Martins

S.'Marit Seine' Maritime

SMCGS San Mateo County Genealogical Society, 25 Tower Road, P.O. Box 5083, San Mateo, CA 94402

SMD General Society of Mayflower Descendants, 4 Winslow Street, Plymouth, MA 02360

SMD Senate Miscellaneous Document

SMEI Saxony Meiningen

SMGd granddaughter's stepmother

SMjr sgt. major

Sml/SML/SMoL stepmother-in-law

Smmr Comp Summer Complaint

Smn Seaman

smnry seminary

SMO/Smoa Samoa Islands

SMOTJ Sovereign and Military Order of the Temple of Jerusalem

SMTP Simple Mail Transfer Protocol (computer term)

SMSA Standard Metropolitan Statistical Area

smstrs seamstress

Smstrss Seamstress

smt summit

Smth smith

SMtr sub-matron

SMU Southern Methodist University, Dallas, TX 75275

S.'Mul Suder' Mulasysla

sn (1) san (2) santa (3) santo (4) sine (5) stranger

s.n. *sine nomen* (infant who died without being given a name)

Sn stranger

SN (1) Santo Domingo (2) Sweden

SNA Scottish National Archives, Edinburgh, Scotland

SNA-AUM Shrine of North America (Masonic)

Snaef Snaefellsnessysla, Iceland

SNCA Society of North Carolina Archivists, P.O. Box 20448, Raleigh, NC 27619

SNep step-nephew

sngl single

SNI Step-niece

SNie step-niece

SnLD son-in-law's daughter

SnLS son-in-law's son

SnLW son-in-law's wife

SnML son's mother-in-law

SNP State Nature Preserve

snr senior

SnSi son's sister

SNur sick nurse

SnWS son's wife's sister

s/o son of

So (1) soldier (2) Somerset, England (3) South (4) Southern (5) Source

SO (1) Sergeant Ordnance (2) Son (3) South (Dixie) (4) Survivors' Originals

SOA Society of Ohio Archivists, 10825 East Boulevard, Cleveland, OH 44106

SOA (1) South Africa (2) South America

soc/Soc/socs society, societies

Soc Social, Societies, Society

Soc, Cincinnati The Society of Cincinnati

Soc Gen Society of Genealogists, 14 Charterhouse Buildings, Goswell Road, London, England EC1M 7BA

sociol sociology

Sociol Sociology

socl social

Soc of Col Wars General Society of Colonial Wars, 840 Woodbine Avenue, Glendale, OH 45246

Soc of Whiskey Rebellion Society of the Whiskey Rebellion of 1794, 3311 Columbia Pike, Lancaster, PA 17603

Soc Sec Social Security

SOcu sole occupant

Soc, War of General Society of the War of 1812, P.O. Box 106, Mendenhall, PA 19337

Sodmld Sodermanland, Sweden

SOF/S.Af South Africa

SOG/SoG Society of Genealogists, 14 Charterhouse Buildings, Goswell Road, London, England EC1M 7BA

SoHCUNC Southern Historical Collection, University of North Carolina, Chapel Hill, NCSOI South Island

Sok jurisdiction (Scotland)

sol/sold/soldr soldier

Sol Solomon

SOLEIF Statue of Liberty – Ellis Island Foundation

SOLINET Southeastern Library Network

solr solicitor

Som/Soms Somerset, England

SOM/SOME/Somst Somersetshire, England

SoMsU Southern Mississippi University, Hattiesburg, MS

son son

SON Sonora

SonC son's child

SonD son's daughter

SonF son's father

SonL/son-i-l son-in-law

SonS son's son

Sons & Dau National Society Sons and Daughters of the Pilgrims of Pilgrims

Sons of Rep Sons of the Republic of Texas

Sons Union Veterans Sons of the Union Veterans of the Civil War, 411 Bartlett Street, Lansing, MI 48915

SonW Son's wife

Source Guide Family History SourceGuide™

SOS (1) Secretary of State (2) international distress signal

SOT Spirit of the Times, Batavia, Clermont County

Sour Source

Southern Dames of Amer National Society Southern Dames of America, 414 North Walnut Street, P.O. Box 43, Florence, AL 35631

Southton Hampshire

Sov Col Soc Amer of Royal Desc Sovereign Colonial Society, Americans of Royal Descent, P.O. Box 27112, Philadelphia, PA19118

sp (1) *sine prole, sans progeny* (without issue, childless) (2) spinster (3) spouse(s) (4) spring

Sp Spain, Spanish

SP (1) James Balfour Paul, *Scots Peerage*, 9 vols. (1904–1914) (2) sealing to parents (LDS) (3) Shore Patrol (4) signed photograph (5) South Pacific (6) Spanish (7) spring (8) State Papers (9) State Park (10) Symmes Purchase

SP/SPA/Spa/SPN/SPAI Spain, Spanish

sp? spelling is questionable

SPA Secure Passsword Authentication

SPAGS Stevens Point Area Genealogical Society

SPAI Spain

SPAM unsolicited junk e-mail

SPAR Women's Coast Guard Reserves

SPC Sales Product Catalog

SPCK Society for the Propagating (Promoting) of Christian Knowledge (British), Holy Trinity Church, Marylebone Road, London, England NW1 4DU

SP Dom State Papers, Domestic

spec (1) special (2) specialist

Spec Special

spell (1) spelling (2) spelled

spg(s) spring(s)

SPG Society for the Propagation of the Gospel (British), Partnership House, 157 Waterloo Road, London, England SE1 8XA

SPHQ *Swedish Pioneer Historical Quarterly*

spin spinster

spkr speaker

spl (1) *sine prole legitima* (without legitimate issue) (2) special

SPL Seattle Public Library, 1000 Fourth Avenue, Seattle, WA 98104

spm *sine prole mascula* (without male issue)

SPN Spain

SPNEA Society for the Preservation of New England Antiquities, 141 Cambridge Street, Boston, MA 02114

Spnl Dis Spinal Disease

spnr spinner

SpPL Spokane Public Library, West 906 Main Avenue, P.O. Box 1826, Spokane, WA 99210-1826

spr (1) spinster (2) sponsor

sprs/Spr(s) springs

sps *sine prole supersite* (without surviving issue)

spur *spurius, spuria* (illegitimate)

spy spy

sq/sqr square

Sq (1) Squadron (2) Square (3) St. Helena

SQ Sergeant Quartermaster

sqd squad

sqdn squadron

SQL Stuctured Query Language

sq. mi. square mile(s)

sr senior

Sr/Sʳ/Sᵒʳ (1) Senior (2) Señor (3) servant (4) Sir (5) sister (6) soror (7) Surrey, England

SR General Society Sons of the Revolution, 600 South Central Avenue, Glendale, CA 91204

SR (1) Scholarly Resources (2) Senate Report (3) Senior (4) Seven Ranges (5) son of the Revolution (6) Supplementary (or Special) Reserve

SR Scottish Rite (Masonic Order)

Sra Señora

SRAM Static Random-Access Memory

SRB Serbia

src source

SRD Superintendent Registrar's District (British)

SRG Scottish Research Group, Edmonton, Alberta, Canada

SrgnMte Surgeon's Mate

SrgO surgical officer

SrgS sergeant's son

Srgt sergeant

sr-in-l sister-in-law

SRK Isle of Sark, Channel Islands

srnms surnames

sr/o sister of

SRO Scottish Record Office, HM General Register House, Princes Street, Edinburgh, Scotland EH1 3YY

SRO standing room only

srs seniors

SRT Sons of the Republic of Texas, SRT Office, 1717 Eighth Street, Bay City, TX 77414

srtr sorter

SRUD Schwarzburg Rudolstadt, Germany

srv (1) served (2) service

SRY Surrey

ss/SS (1) *scilicet* (2) south side (3) steamship (4) *supra scriptum* (as written above, or a form of greeting used to open charters, etc.)

s/s same stone (two or more names on same gravestone)

Ss Sandwich Island

SS (1) Saints (2) Scottish Studies (3) sealing to spouse (LDS) (4) stepson

SSA Social Security Administration, Baltimore, MD 21201

SSAN Social Security Account Number (Social Security Administration, Baltimore, MD 21201)

SSBN Ship Submersible Nuclear (Nuclear-powered ballistic missile submarine)

SSC Solicitor in the Supreme Court (British)

SSDB Social Security Death Benefits (Social Security Administration, Baltimore, MD 21201)

SSDI *U.S. Social Security Death Index* (available through www.ancestry.com and on compact disc)

SSDMF Social Security Death Master File

SSE South Southeast

SSGHS South Suburban Genealogical and Historical Society, South Holland, IL

Ssgt staff sergeant

SSHRCC Social Sciences and Humanities Research Council of Canada, University of Ottawa, Ontario, Canada KIN 6N5

Ssi/SSi/SSI stepsister

Ssi stepsister-in-law

SSI South Sea Islands

SSI *Social Security Index* (available through FamilySearch™, the Internet, and on compact discs)

Ssil/SSiL stepsister-in-law

SSis stepsister

SSL Secure Socket Layers (computer term)

SSL stepson-in-law

SSN/Ssn Social Security Number (Social Security Administration, Baltimore, MD)

SSnC stepson's child

SSnD stepson's daughter

SSnL stepson-in-law

SSnS stepson's son

SSnW stepson's wife

Ss/o stepson of

SSon stepson

SSON Schwarzburg-Sondershausen, Germany

SSR Soviet Socialist Republic

SSRB Senior Salaries Review Body

SSRC Social Science Research Council, 810 Seventh Avenue, New York, NY 10019

SST supersonic transport

SSW South Southwest

SSX Sussex

st (1) school teacher (2) stanza (3) state (4) street (5) student

St (1) non-Biblical saints (2) Saint (when used as a prefix, e.g., St. Peter's Church) (3) sainte (4) street (5) student

St Stephen

St (1) Staffordshire, England (2) State

St/Bt/Plt steamboat pilot

ST (1) Scotland (2) stock in trade (3) State (4) State or colonial census

Sta/Sta (1) station (2) status

Stae State

sta eng stationary engineer

Staf staff

STAF/Staff Staffordshire, England

StaffOf staff officer

Staffordsh· Staffordshire, England

Staffs Stafford (England)

Stal Stake (LDS)

Stand. Dict. standard dictionary

STAR Strategic Technology and Resources (system)

Stat (1) statistical (2) statistician (3) statute

Stats Statistics

sta'y stationary

STB *Sacrae Theologiae Baccalaureus* (Bachelor of Sacred Theology)

StbB stableboy

StbH stable help

StBL stepbrother-in-law

StbM stableman

STC St. Croix

St Chm state chairman

std standard

STD *Sacrae Theologiae Doctore* (Doctor of Sacred Theology)

St David's Soc of N Saint David's Society of the State of New York, 17 West 23rd Street, New York, NY 10010

Ste (1) Saint (Sainte-feminine) (2) Suite

SteB Steinsberg/burg, Germany

sten stenographer

step step (a close legal relationship)

stepdau stepdaughter

Steph/Stephⁿ Stephen

stereo stereotyper

stew/stewd steward

STF Staffordshire, England

STG Scholarly Technology Group

stge storage

STH St. Helena Crown Colony

Sthest Southeast

Sthestn Southeastern

Sthld Southold

Sthmptn Southampton, England

Sthn Southern

STHO St. Thomas

Sthwst Southwest

Sthwstn Southwestern

STI stillborn

STI/STIR/Stirl Stirling, Scotland

StkH Stockhausen

Stkhm Stockholm, Sweden

stkp storekeeper

stkr stoker

Stl (1) Sentinel (2) Stirlingshire, Scotland

StL St. Louis, Missouri

S-Tlg Sor-Trondelag, Norway

StLGS St. Louis Genealogical Society

StLPL St. Louis Public Library, 1301 Olive Street, St. Louis, MO 63103

STM Master of Sacred Theology

stmboatman steam boatman

stmbtngner steamboat engineer

stmbtpilot steam boat pilot

stmftr steamfitter

STMP Simple Mail Tansfer Protocol

stn (1) station (2) *stilo novo* (new style of dating a document)

stn cutter stone cutter

St Nicholas Soc of NY The Saint Nicholas Society of the City of New York, Soc of NY 122 East 58th Street, New York, NY 10022

Stn/Msn Stone Mason

stnqurier stone querrier

stove tnmct stove & tin merchant

STP Professor of Sacred Theology

Stphⁿ Stephen

str setter

Strel Strelitz

strg stranger

Strkbg Starkenburg, Hess-Darmstadt, Germany

strm (1) storeroom (2) stream

strs seamstress

STS Staffordshire, England

st sprnkl street sprinkler

StSL stepsister-in-law

STT St. Thomas Island, U.S. Virgin Islands

Stu Steuben

stud study

Student mn student for ministry

studt student

Stu law student of law

stu med student of medicine

STUT Stuttgart

STV St. Vincent Island

stvdr stevedore

su surety

Su (1) superintendent (2) Susan, Susannah

Su/Sun Sunday

SU (1) Soviet Union (USSR) (2) Sutro Branch of the California State Library, San Francisco, CA 94132

sub/SUB (1) subdivision (2) as in sub-Sheriff, a deputy or chief assistant (3) submitted (4) subsistence (5) substitute (6) suburb

Sub Subscription

Subj Subject

subj subject, subjective

Sub-Lt Sub-Lieutenant

Subm Submitter

subp subpoena

subst substantive, substantial

Subst Substation

suc succeeded

succ (1) successively (2) succursale

sud sudden

SUD Sudan

Sue Sue, Susan, Susannah

suf suffix

SUF/SUFF/Suf/Suff Suffolk, Great Britain

suff/sufft/suftly sufficient, sufficiently

Suic by L Suicide by Loderium

suite suit, as at law

Sul Sultzburg

sum summer

summ summoned

Sun (1) step-uncle (2) Sunday

SUN Step-uncle

SUNY State University of New York, Buffalo, NY

suo juris in his (or her) right

sup (1) superintendent (2) superior (3) supply (4) *supra* (above)

Sup Supplies

superl superlative

supp/suppl supplement

Supr superintendent

supra above

Supss superioress

supt superintendent

suptcoalco Superintendent Madison County Coal Co.

supt gaswk Superintendent Gas works

Supv Supervising, Supervision

SupV supervisor

supvr supervisor

Supvr Supervisor

Supvry Supervisory

sur survived

SUR Surinam

SUR/SURR/Surr Surrey, Great Britain

SurA surgical assistant

surg surgeon

Surg Surgery, Surgical

SurGen The Surgeon General

SURI Surinam

sur mate surgeon's mate

surr (1) superior (2) surrender

Surr (1) Surrey, England (2) surrogate

surv survived

surv/svg survived, surviving

sus Suspended

Sus Susanna

SUS/SUSS/Suss Sussex, England

Sut Sutherland, Scotland

SUT/SUTH/Suth Sutherland, Scotland

SUV Sons of Union Veterans, 411 Bartlett Street, Lansing, MI 48915

SUVCW Sons of Union Veterans of the Civil War, 411 Bartlett Street, Lansing, MI 48915

sv *sub verbo, sub voce* (under the word)

Sv Sohn von (son of)

SV Sons of Veterans, 411 Bartlett Street, Lansing, MI 48915

Svbg Svendborg, Denmark

SVC Southern Virginia College, Buena Vista, VA

SVGA Super Video Graphics Adapter (Super VGA)

SVIN St. Vincent

SV-PAF-UG Silicon Valley PAF Users Group, P.O. Box 23670, San Jose, CA 95153-3670

svt servant

sw (1) semi-weekly (2) southwest (3) swear, swore

SW (1) Southwest, Southwestern (2) Southwest Territory (3) Switzerland

Sw Sweden

Sw.A Southwest Africa

SWA (1) South Wales (2) Swaziland

Swab/SWAB Swabia

Swal/SWale South Wales

swch switch

SWD/SWE/SWED/Swed/Swede Sweden

Swedish Col Soc The Swedish Colonial Society, 916 Swanson Street, Philadelphia, PA 19147

SWEE Saxony Weimar-Eisenach, Germany

Sweet William W. Sweet, *Religion on the American Frontier* (4 vols., 1926-46, repr. 1964)

Swei South Weimer

swep sweep

SWFLN Southwest Florida Library Network, Bonita Springs, FL

SWH Swarthmore/Haverford (Pennsylvania)

Swi/SWI/SWIT/SWT Switzerland

SwiD son's wife's daughter

SWiS son's wife's son

switchtndr switch tender

Switz/Swtz/Swit Switzerland

swmchnagt sawing machine agent

swmm saleswoman

SWOGS Southwest Oklahoma Genealogical Society, P.O. Box 148, Lawton, OK 73502-0148

SWT Switzerland

swtchmn switchman

swth sweetheart

SWZ/Switz Switzerland

Sx Sussex, England

SX Saxony, Germany

SXL Step-sister-in-law

Sxw Saxe Wissnar

SYFT *Shaking Your Family Tree* (Myra Vanderpool Gormley)

syn (1) his (2) synonym, synonymous

synop synopsis

SYR/SYRI Syria

sys system

SYSOP system operator(s)

Syst Systems

Sz Santa Cruz

T

t (1) testamentary (2) TOMUS (Boston University's online catalog system) (3) turns of microfilm handle (4) teaspoon (5) *tempore* (in the time of)

T (1) card already at LDS temple (2) National Archives microfilm series (3) tablespoon (4) Tag(e), day(s) (5) tax substitutes for censuses (6) Territorial census (7) Thursday (8) township (legal land description) (9) Treasury, Public Record Office, Kew, England (10) Tuesday

T/ temporary

T9 LDS temple originated family group

T99 Special handling, LDS temple code

T000001 110 year file (manual) used with Family History Library, Salt Lake City, UT

T000011 TIB Conversion number, Family History Library, Salt Lake City, UT

TA Territorial Army

T/A trading as, under the name of

Tafel Ahnentafel chart

TAFFS The Army Functional Filing System

tag label used in *PAF* notes (*Personal Ancestral File*)

TAG *The American Genealogist*, David L. Greene, P.O. Box 398, Demorest, GA 30535-0398

TAH Tahiti

TAI Taiwan

tak taken

TALL Technology Assisted Language Learning

talr tailor

Tanstaafl (1) There ain't no such thing as a free lunch (2) Bulletin board system name in Akron

TARI *Technical Assistance Reference Index*

TAS Tasmania

TAst trade assistant

TAT Tatnall tombstone Collection

tb tuberculosis

TBA The Bible Archives

TBLC Tampa Bay Library Consortium, Tampa, FL

tbsp tablespoon

TC Technology Center

TC The Constitutionalist, Newark, Licking Co.

TCHA Tippecanoe County Historical Association, Wetherill Historical Resource Center, Alameda McCollough Library, 909 South Street, Lafayette, IN 47901

t&c mct tin & copper merchant

tchr teacher

tchr bkkg teacher-book keeping

tchr lang teacher of languages

tchr rhet rhetoric teacher

TchS teacher's son

TClk telegraph clerk

TCP/IP Transmission Control Protocol/Internet Protocol (computer term)

TCWAAS Transactions of the Cumberland and Westmorland Antiquarian and Archaelogical Society, England

Td Tochter des, Tochter der (daughter of)

TD Territorial Decoration

TDD Telecommunication Device for the Deaf

TDGNHAS Transactions of the Dumfriesshire and Galloway Natural History and Antiquarian Society, Scotland

Teach Teaching

tech (1) technical (2) technician (3) technology

Tech Technical, Technologoy

techn technology

Technol Technological, Technology

Ted Theodore

TEG *The Essex Genealogist*

TEI Text Encoded Initiative

tel telephone

Tel Telephone

Telecom Telecommunications

teleg telegraph

telegr opr telegraph operator

telev television

TelG telegraphist

Telm Telemark, Norway

temp (1) temporary (2) *tempore* (living in time of) (3) temporarily

Temp Temple

temp lctr temperance lecturer

ten (1) tenant (2) tenure

Ten/Tenn/TN Tennessee

tent tenant

tent/tent tenement

ter/terr (1) terrace (2) territorial (3) territory

Ter Teroll

term terminal

Terr Territory

TERR territory

Terry Terence, Teresa, Theresa

TeSL Tennessee State Library and Archives, 403 Seventh Avenue North, Nashville, TN 37243-0312

Tess/Tessa Esther, Hester, Teresa, Theresea

test testified

test/testam'/testa testament

testr testator

Tex/TX Texas

TFE *The Family Edge* (genealogy software program)

TFEL Thin Film Electroluminescent

Tffn Tiffin-Seneca Public Library, Tiffin, OH 44883

TFGS The Fairbanks Genealogical Society, P.O. Box 60534, Fairbanks, AK 99706-0534

TFT Thin Film Translator

TG *The Genealogist*, American Society of Genealogists, Picton Press, P.O. Box 250, Rockport, ME 04856-0250

TGC *The Genealogical Companion* (freeware Windows print utility)

Tgph/Op Telegraph Operator

TGS Topeka Genealogical Society, P.O. Box 4048, Topeka, KS 66604-0048

TGS Tulsa Genealogical Society, P.O. Box 585, Tulsa, OK 74101-0585

TGSI Transactions of the Gaelic Society of Inverness, Scotland

Th/Thurs Thursday

TH Temple of Honor-Independent Order of Odd Fellows

TH (1) Territory of Hawaii (2) Town History

THA Thailand

THAGS Humble Texas Area Genealogical Society

THC Texas Historical Commission, P.O. Box 12276, Austin, TX 78711-2276

ThD Doctor of Theology

Theo Theodore, Theodosia, Theopolis

theol (1) theology (2) theological (3) theologian

Theol Theological, Theology

Theos Theopolis

Therap Therapeutic, Therapy

THI Thailand

Th'ine Thomasine

Thist Thisted, Denmark

tho though

Tho/Thos/Tho'/Th' Thomas

thot thought

thro/thru through

Thu/THUR (1) Thuringia (2) Thursday

Thur (1) Thueringen (not German) (2) Thursday

TI (1) Taiwan (2) title

TIALD Thermal Imaging Airborne Laser Designator

TIARA The Irish Ancestral Research Association, Dept. W, P.O. Box 619, Sudbury, MA 01776

TIB Temple Index Bureau (card index available at the Family History Library and Brigham Young University, on microfilm). Also known as the Temple Records Index Bureau. *See also* TRIB.

TIF Tagged Image File Format (graphic file format)

TIFF graphics file (graphical format)

til until

Tim/Timmie/Timmy/Timo Timothy

TIP Teacher Incentive Program

Tip/TIP Tipperary, Republic of Ireland

TIPCOA Tippecanoe County Area Genealogical Society, Wetherill Historical Resource Center, Alameda McCollough Library, 909 South Street, Lafayette, IN 47901

Tipp Tipperary, Ireland

Titl Title

TKep tent keeper

TKey turnkey

TKHS Transactions Kansas Historical Society

TLA Texas Library Association, 3355 BeeCave Road, Austin, TX 78746-6763

TLB Top Level Budget

TLC The Learning Company, One Athenaeum Street, Cambridge, MA 02142

tm temperance movement

TM (1) Teamster (military) (2) triple marker (gravestone)

TMA *The Midland Ancestor* (journal of Birmingham and Midland Society for Genealogy and Heraldry), England

TMG *The Master Genealogist* (genealogy software program produced by Wholly Genes, Inc., 5144 Flowertuft Court, Columbia, MD 21044)

TMGW *The Master Genealogist for Windows*

tmkpr timekeeper

Tm. Off Trademarks Office

tmpl temple

Tms Teamster

TMS (1) Tafel Matching System (e.g., tiny tafels) (2) Tiger Map Service (U.S. Bureau of the Census)

tn (1) tenant (2) ton (3) town (4) township

Tn Tenant

TN (1) Tennessee (2) Trade Name

tndr tender

Tng Tonga Islands

TNP Temple Names Preparation (LDS feature in *Ancestral Quest*)

tnry tannery

to/to-w to-wit, e.g., "He addressed the petition to the richest residents of the precinct, to., the Parks, the Harrisons, and others."

TO Township Officer

T.O. telegraph office

tob/tobo tobacco

TOB Tobago, West Indies

Tom/Tommie/Tommy Thomas

TON Tonga

top topographical

TOPA Transactions of the Oregon Pioneer Association

Topo. quad U.S. topographical quadrangle maps

TOR Temple Originated Records (LDS)

Toro Toronto, Canada

Torrey *Torrey's Marriage Index*

Tot/TOTL total

Tot/Parals Total Paralysis

TOW Tube-launched Optically-controlled Wire-guided bomb

Toxicol Toxicology

tp (1) this parish (2) title page

Tp Trooper

tp/twp/Twp township

t & p true and perfect

TPCGS Tacoma–Pierce County Genealogical Society, P.O. Box 1952, Tacoma, WA 98401

tpk/tpke turnpike

Tpk Turnpike

tpm title page mutilated

tpw title page wanting

tr (1) town record(s) (2) transferred (3) translated (4) translation (5) troop

Tr Trail

Tr. Trinitatis, Trinity (8th Sunday after Easter)

TR (1) Town Record(s) (2) traditional (3) transcribed will record

trad tradition

TRAM The Texas Research Administrators Group

trans (1) transactions (2) transcription (3) transfer/-red (4) transitive (5) translated (6) transport (7) transportor (6) transportation

trans/transl translator

transcr (1) transcribed (2) transcriber (3) transcript (-ion)

Transcript *The Boston Evening Transcript*

transfrd transferred

TRS *Name Index to Official Temple Records for Family File Entries* (microfiche, Family History Library)

trav traveler, traveling

trd trading

trea's treasurer

tres/treas treasurer/-y

Treas Treasurer

TRI Trinidad

trib tribune

TRIB Temple Records Index Bureau (on microfilm at Family History Library) *See also* TIB.

TRIGAT Third Generation Anti-Tank Guided Weapon

Trin Trinity

TRIN Trinidad

TRIP Tripoli

Tristⁿ Tristan

Trix/Trixie/Trixy Beatrice

TRK Turkey

trl trail

TRLN Triangle Research Libraries Network

trlr trailer

Trm Trumpeter

trmp tramp

trmr trimmer

trnmn trainman

trnr trainer

trop tropical

trp troop

trps troops

trpt trumpeter

trs trustee

Trudy Gertrude

ts (1) tombstone (2) typescript

T S tax sale

TS Typescript

T/S typescript

TS Treasury Solicitor, Public Record Office, Kew, Richmond, Surrey, England TW9 4DU

TSEL Texas State Electronic Library

TSGS Texas State Genealogical Society, 2507 Tannehill, Houston, TX 77008-3052

TSHA Texas State Historical Association, Sid Richardson Hall, University Station, Austin, TX 78712

TskM taskmaster

TSLA Tennessee State Library and Archives, 403 Seventh Avenue North, Nashville, TN 37243-0312

tsp teaspoon

tss typescript

tstr tester

TT True Type (font)

TT Tiny Tafel (family database standard)

TTY Teletypewriter

TTYL Talk To You Later

Tu Turkey

Tu/Tue/Tues Tuesday

TUN Tunisia

tunl tunnel

tunr tuner

Tuon tuition

Tur. Turnpike

TUR/Trky/TURK Turkey

Tusc Tuscarawas County Ohio OGS Chapter, P.O. Box 141, New Philadelphia, OH 44663-0141

TUSC Tuscany, Italy

tutr tutor

Tunx Tunxis dialect

TV Television

TVA Tennessee Valley Authority, 400 West Summit Hill Drive, Knoxville, TN 37902

tvrn tavern

tw tri-weekly

TWCU Tactical Weapons Conversion Unit

Twif traveler's wife

twin twin

twn town

Twn Clk Town Clerk

twp township

Twp/TWP Township

twr tower

tx tax record

TX (1) Tax List (2) Texas

TxSL Texas State Library, P.O. Box 12927, Austin, TX 78711-2927

TXSSAR Texas Society of the Sons of the American Revolution

Ty territory

typ typist

Typh Fev Typhoid Fever

typo typographical

Tyr (1) Tyrol (Austria) (2) Tyrone, Northern Ireland

U

u. und (and)

U (1) *ultimo* (last) (2) uncle (3) University (4) unstated

UAE United Arab Emirates

UALC Utah Academic Library Consortium

UAN Uniform Accounting Network

UAP (1) Universal Access to Publications (2) Universal Availability of Publications

UAS University Air Squadron

UB United Brethren

UBC Universal Bibliographic Control

uc (1) under care (Quaker meeting) (2) upper-case

UC Upper Canada (i.e., Haut-Canada or Ontario)

UCC United Church of Christ

UCGA Upper Cumberland Genealogical Association, P.O. Box 575, Cookeville, TN 38501-0575

UCLA University of California at Los Angeles

UCS Utah Computer Society

UCV United Confederate Veterans

u.d. (1) *ultimo die* (final day) (2) *und des, und der* (and of)

U.D. (1) University of Delaware Morris Library, South College Avenue, Newark, DE 19717-5267 (2) urban district

UDC United Daughters of the Confederacy, UDC Memorial Building, 328 North Boulevard, Richmond, VA 23220-4057

UDC (1) Universal Decimal Classification (2) Urban District Council

UDE *Universal Data Entry* (a computer program used by the Family and Church History Department, Salt Lake City, UT)

UDP User Datagram Protocol

UEL United Empire Loyalists

UELAC United Empire Loyalists Association of Canada, 50 Baldwin ST., Suite 202, Toronto, Ontario, Canada MST 1L4

UEN Utah Education Network

UF United Free Church (Scotland)

UFDL Ultimate Family Data Library

UFL P.K. Yonge Library, University of Florida, Gainesville, FL

Ufrank Unterfranken, Bavaria

UFT *Ultimate Family Tree* (genealogy software program, discontinued)

UGA Utah Genealogical Association, P.O. Box 1144, Salt Lake City, UT 84110

UGGS Utah Germanic Genealogy Society, P.O. Box 510898, Salt Lake City, UT 84151-0898

UGHM *Utah Genealogical and Historical Magazine* (1910-1940)

UGRR Underground Railroad

UGS Utah Genealogical Society. *See* GSU (Genealogical Society of Utah)

UHF Ulster Historical Foundation, 12 College Square East, Belfast, Northern Ireland BT1 6DD

Uhl Uhlenburg, Germany

UHQ *Utah Historical Quarterly*

UIC University of Illinois at Chicago, Chicago, IL

UID (1) unique identification (2) unique serial number (used in *Personal Ancestral File*)

UIS University of Illinois at Springfield, Springfield, IL

UJA United Jewish Appeal

UK (1) United Kingdom (2) Unknown

UKBC United Kingdom Based Civilians

UKOLN United Kingdom Office of Library Networking

UKOP United Kingdom Official Publications

UKR/UKRA Ukraine

Ul/uncL/uncle-i-l uncle-in-law

ULA Utah Library Association

Ulc Bowels Ulcerated Bowels

Uli Ulrich

ult *ultimo* (last, a date last month, used in letters-as "in your letter of the 13th ult.", ultimate, last month, last week, etc.)

UM 1) United Methodist (2) University of Michigan, Ann Arbor, MI

UMAC United Methodist Annual Conference

umar/unmar unmarried

UMC United Methodist Church

UMGBI *Upper Midwest German Biographical Index*, Don Heinrich Tolzmann (Bowie, Md.: Heritage Books, 1993)

UMI University Microfilms, Inc.

UMW United Mine Workers

un (1) union (2) unknown

UN (1) Unknown (2) United Nations

UN/unc/uncl uncle

UNAVEM United Nations Angola Verification Mission

UNBL University of New Brunswick Library, Fredericton, New Brunswick, Canada

UNC uncleared

UNCL University of North Carolina Library, Chapel Hill, NC

UNCLOS United Nations Convention on the Law of the Sea

UnCr under care

und/undr under

Undergrad Undergraduate

undwrtr underwriter

UNFICYP United Nations Force in Cyprus

UnGr undergraduate

UNHQ United Nations Headquarters

unident unidentified

UNIKOM United Nations Iraq Kuwait Observer Mission

unin union

Unincorp. Unincorporated

unit united, uniting

univ universal

univ/Univ University

Univ. Libr. University Library, West Road, Cambridge, England CB3 9DR

unk/unkn unknown

UNK (1) United Kingdom (2) unknown

UNKN unknown

unm/unmd unmarried

UnNr undernurse

UNO United Nations Organization

UNOMIG United Nations Observer Mission in Georgia

unorg unorganized

unp (1) unpaged (2) unpublished field notes, draft reports

UNPROFOR United Nations Observer Mission in Georgia

UNSCOM United Nations Special Commission

unpub unpublished

U of A/UA University of Akron, Akron, OH

U of C/UC University of Cincinnati, Cincinnati, OH 45221-0113

UOS United Original Secession

Up. Upper

UP (1) United Presbyterian Church (Scotland) (2) United Press (3) United Provinces (India)

UPA University Publications of America, 4520 East-West Highway, Bethesda, MD 20814-3389

UPC Universal Product Code

UPER UMI Periodical Abstracts

UPGS United Polish Genealogical Societies

uphol upholsterer

UPI United Press International

upl using profane language

UPL University of Pennsylvania Library, 3420 Walnut Street, Philadelphia, PA 19104

UPM United Presbyterian Minister

Upps Uppsala, Sweden

upr upper

U^a Ursula

URAG Uruguay

urb urban

URC United Reformed Church (Great Britain, mostly Congregational and Presbyterian)

URI Uniform Resource Indentifier

URL Uniform Resource Locator (an electronic address for web pages on the Internet)

URN Uniform Resource Names

Ur^a Ursula

URSN Unique Record Serial Number (*Personal Ancestral File*)

URU/UUG/URUG Uruguay

US United States

USA (1) Union of South Africa (2) United States Army (3) United States of America

USAAC United States Army Air Corps

USAAF United States Army Air Force

USAC United States Air Corps

USAF United States Air Force

USA Inf United States Army Infantry

USAMHI United States Army Military History Institute, Carlisle Barracks, PA 17013-5008

USAR United States Army Reserve

USARV U. S. Army, Vietnam

USB universal serial bus, e.g., USB port

USC (1) United States census (2) United States Citizen (3) U.S. Colony

USCA United States Code Annotated

US CAN United States and Canada

USC Art United States Colored Artillery

USCB United States Census Bureau

USCC United States Chamber of Commerce

USC Cav United States Colored Calvalry

USCG United States Coast Guard

USCGR United States Coast Guard Reserve

USC Inf United States Colored Infantry

USCL US Congress Lands

USCT United States Colored Troop(s)

USD United States dollars

USD 1812 National Society, U.S. Daughters of 1812, 1461 Rhode Island NW, Washington, DC 20005

us dp mrsh U.S. Deputy Marshall

USENET worldwide network

USES United States Employment Service

USF University of South Florida

USG United States Government

USGS United States Geological Survey

USGW US GenWeb Project (Internet)

Ushr usher

USHS Utah State Historical Society, 300 South Rio Grande, Salt Lake City, UT 84101-1143

Usi Usingen

USIA United States Information Agency

USIGS United States Internet Genealogical Society

USM United States Marines

USMA United States Military Academy

USMARC United States Machine Readable Cataloging

USMC United States Marine Corps

USMCR United States Marine Corps Reserve

USMD United States Military District

USN United States Navy

USNA United States Naval Academy

USNAC United States Naval Air Corps

USNAM United States Naval Academy Museum, 118 Maryland Avenue, Annapolis, MD 21402-5034

USNG United States National Guard

USNP United States Newspaper Program

USNPL United States Newspaper List

USNR United States Naval Reserve

USO United Service Organization, 901 M Street SE Building 198, Washington, DC 20374

USPG United Society for the Propagation of the Gospel (British), Partnership House, 157 Waterloo Road, London, England SE1 8XA

USPS United States Postal Service

USPTO United States Patent and Trademark Office

USS United States Ship or Steamer

USSR Union of Soviet Socialist Republic

USV United States Volunteers

usw *und so weiter* (and so forth)

USWPA United States Works Progress Administration

Ut Utah

UT (1) University of Toledo, Toledo, OH (2) Utah

Utah early Utah LDS sealing (Pre-Endowment House)

UTL University of Texas Library, Austin, TX, 78712

UTM Universal Transverse Mercator

Utr Hem. Uterine Hemorrhage

UTSCAR Utah Society, Children of the American Revolution

UTSDAR Utah Society, Daughters of the American Revolution

UTSSAR Utah Society, Sons of the American Revolution

ut sup *ut supra* (as above)

UVL University of Virginia Library, Charlottesville, VA 22903

UV-PAF-UG Utah Valley PAF Users Group (*Personal Ancestral File*)

UW University of Washington, Seattle, WA

ux/uxor/uz (1) Mrs. (2) *uxor* or *uxoris* (wife)

V

v (1) verse (2) *verso* (the back [of a page]) (3) vessel/ship (4) *vide* (see) (5) volume(s) (7) *von* (from)

v/vb verb

v/vs *versus* (against)

V (1) Vicar (2) Vice (3) Viscount (4) Volume

va vixit

VA (1) Department of Veterans Affairs (2) U.S. Veterans Administration (3) Vagrancy Arrival

VA/Va Virginia

V-Ag Vest-Agder, Norway

val value, valuation

Val (1) Valdeck/Waldeck (2) Valentine (3) Valerie

VALE Virtual Academic Library Environment

valt valet

var variant, variation, various, variously spelled

VARMC Veterans Affairs Records Management Center

Varmld Varmland, Sweden

VASSAR Virginia Society, Sons of the American Revolution

VAT Value Added Tax

V.'Bard Vestur' Bardastrandarsysla

VBCL Virginia Beach Central Library, 4100 Virginia Beach Blvd., Virginia Beach, VA 23452-1767

VBGS Virginia Beach Genealogical Society, P.O. Box 62901, Virginia Beach, VA 23466-2901

V.'bottn Vasterbotten

Vbth Vasterbotten, Sweden

vc victim of a crime

VC Victoria Cross

VC Viet Cong

VCH *Victoria History of the Counties of England*, Victoria County Histories

vCnc virtual Canadian Union Catalogue

VC/NVN Viet Cong/North Vietnamese

VCRP Virginia Colonial Records Project, The Library of Virginia, 11th Street at Capitol Square, Richmond, VA 23219

vctr victor

vCuc Virtual Canadian Union Catalogue

v.d. various dates

VDM *Verbi Dei Minister* (minister of the word of God), Voluns Dei Minister

VDT Visual Display Terminal

VDU Visual Display Unit

ve/vve widow

VE Vagrancy Examination

VE Victory in Europe

VEN/VENE/Venez Venezuela

ver (1) verify (2) version

verch daughter

verh. *verheiratet* (married)

verl. *verlobt* (engaged)

Verm Vermont

Vers Version

vet(s) veteran(s), veterinary

Vet Veteran

VET ADM Veterans Administratoin

Vet Corps of Artillery NY Veteran Corps of Artillery, State of New York Constituting the Military Society of the War of 1812, Seventh Regiment Armory, 643 Park Avenue, New York, NY 10021

vf (1) vertical file (2) *veuf* (widower)

VF Vertical Files

VFW Veterans of Foreign Wars, 406 West 34th Street, Kansas City, MO 64111

VG *The Virginia Genealogist*

VGA Video Graphics Adapter (array)

VgrD vagrant's daughter

VgrS vagrant's son

Vgrt vagrant

VgrW vagrant's wife

VGS Victoria Genealogical Society, P.O. Box 45031, Mayfair Postal Outlet, Victoria, BC Canada V8Z 7G9

VGS Virginia Genealogical Society, 5001 West Broad Street, Suite 115, Richmond, VA 23230-3023

VHS Virginia Historical Society, P.O. Box 7311, Richmond, VA 23211-0311

V./Hun Vestur/Hunavatnssysla

vi (1) verb intransitive (2) visitor

Vi (1) Vancouver Island, CA (2) Violet (3) visitor

VI Virgin Islands

via viaduct

vic vicinity

vic/vicr (1) vicar (2) vicarage

Vic/Vict Victoria

Vice Pres. Vice President

VicG vicegerent

VicP vice principal

vid. *viduus, vidua* (widower, widow)

vide see

VIE Vietnam

Vien Vienna

VIGR Virginia Institute of Genealogical Research

vil village

Villgn Villengen, Baden, Germany

vills villas

Vin/Vince/Vinny Vincent

Vinc'/Vinz'/Vinc^{nt} Vincent

VIP very important person

VIR St. Thomas, Virgin Islands

virdt/verd verdict, usually of a jury

Virg/Virg^a Virginia (woman's name)

Virga Virginia (the state)

Virgin Isl Virgin Islands

vis vista

Vis (1) Visiting (2) Visual

Vis., Visit. Visitations (of various English counties)

Vis/Visc/Visct viscount, viscountess

VisC visitor's child

VisD visitor's daughter

ViSL Virginia State Library, 11th Street at Capitol Square, Richmond, VA 23219-3491

VISL/VI Virgin Islands

visn visitation

VisN visitor's nephew or niece

VisS visitor's son

vist visitor

VisW visitor's wife

vit vital

Vit Stat vital statistics

ViU Virginia University, Charlottesville, VA

VIVA Virtual Library of Virginia

vix lived, also vixit

viz. videlicet (namely)

viz't namely, to wit, that is to say

VJ Victory over Japan

VL (1) ville (2) Vulgar Latin

vlg village

VLSMS Vehicle-Launched Scatterable Mine System

vlt vault

vly valley

v.m. *vita matris* (during mother's life)

Vmanld Vastmanland, Sweden

VMD (1) Doctor of Veterinary Medicine (2) Virginia Military District (located in Ohio)

VML Vector Markup Language

Vmst vice-master

VN veterans marker (gravestone)

VN Vietnam

Vna Vienna

V'Norld Vasternorrland, Sweden

VNZ Venezuela

VOAA Veterans of America Association

voc. vocative

VOC Vereenigde Ooost-Indische Compagnie (Dutch United East India Company)

VOCA Vermont Old Cemetery Association, P.O. Box 132, Townshend, VT 05353

Vocat Vocational

vol(s) (1) volume(s) (2) volunteer(s)

Vol Volumes, Volunteers

VOM Voluns Deus Minister (minister by the will of God)

voters/reg voter and voter registration records

vp *vita patris* (in the father's lifetime)

VP Vagrancy Pass

VP/Vpre vice president

VPG vice president general

Vpo Valparaiso

VPres Vice President

vr vital record(s)

VR (1) Vagrancy Removal (2) Village Register, West Union, Adams Co. (3) virtual reality (4) vital record(s), e.g., Dedham, Mass. VR (town vital records)

VRA Virginia Records Award (Virginia Genealogical Society)

VRI Virgin Islands

VRML Virtual Reality Modeling Language

vs./v. *versus* (against)

VS/V.S. Vital statistics

VSer visitor's servant

VSis visitor's sister

V.Skaft Vestur' Skaftafellssysla

VSnL visitor's son-in-law

Vstf Vestfold, Norway

v.t. verb transitive

Vt Vermont

VT Vermont

V-tapes Video Tapes

VtSL Vermont State Library, 135 Main Street, Montpelier, VT 05602

Vt Soc of Col Dames The Vermont Society of Colonial Dames

VtU Vermont University and State College, Burlington, VT

VTVR Vermont Vital Records

vulc vulcanizer

vv vice versa (as used between a first and a middle name which are reversed in some records)

Vw view

W

w (1) weekly (2) west (3) in Revolutionary War pension jacket, widow (4) widow, widowed, widower (5) wife (6) will (source in *IGI*) (7) with

w/ (1) wife of (2) with

w/1, w/2, w/3 wife no. 1, 2, 3

1.w. first wife

W (1) Ward (2) West (3) white (whites), Caucasian (4) wife (5) Last Will and Testament (6) Wiltshire, England

W/ wife of

W. west

W/Wed Wednesday

W3C World Wide Web Consortium

W12 War of 1812

wa (1) Ward (2) warden

w.a. with answers

Wa (1) Ward (2) Warden (3) Warwickshire, England

WA (1) Wales (2) Washington (3) Western Australia (4) Widow's Application

WA/Wash Washington

WAAC Women's Auxiliary Army Corps

WAAF Women's Auxiliary Air Force

wab will and administration record

WAC (1) washings, annointings, and confirmations (LDS temple ordinances) (2) Women's Army Corps

WAF Women in the Air Force

wag wagoner

WagB wagon boy

wagnmaster wagon master

WAGS Waseca Area Genealogy Society, Waseca County Historical Society Museum, Second Avenue and Fourth Street, NE, Waseca, MN 56093

WAGS Whittier Area Genealogical Society, P.O. Box 4367, Whittier, CA 90607-4367

wai/wait (1) waiter (2) waitress

WAI Web Accessibility Initiative

WAIS Wide Area Information Server (Service)

Wal/Wald/WalD/Walde/Waldck Waldeck, Hesse (Nassau), Germany

Wal Walter

WAL Wales

WALD Waldeck Hesse-Nassau, Germany

Waldsh Waldshut, Baden

WALE Wales

Wally Wallace, Walter

WalNY Wales, New York

Walt Walter

WAN wide area network

WAP wireless application protocol (computer term)

Wapp Wappinger dialect

WAR/WARW/Warw Warwickshire, Great Britain

ward ward, reared

warden pen warden penitentiary

WarH warehouseman

warrt warrant

War Ser war service

Warws/WARW (1) Warwick, England (2) Warwickshire

WasDC Washington, DC

Wash/Wa Washington

Wash. C.H. Washington Court House

Washington Fam Desc Washington Family Descendants

WaSHS Washington State Historical Society, 315 North Stadium Way, Tacoma, WA 98403

WaSL Washington State Library, P.O. Box 2475, Olympia, WA 98504-2475

WASP Women's Air Force Service Pilots

Wat Waterford, Republic of Ireland

Wat/Wattie/Watty/Walt Walter

Water Waterford, Ireland

Waters Henry F. Waters, *Genealogical Gleanings in England*, 2 vols. (1883-99. Reprint. Baltimore: Genealogical Publishing Co., 1981)

Watm watchman

Wau Wauldig

WAVES Women Appointed for Volunteer Emergency Service (US Navy)

WBHSM Wisconsin Black Historical Society Museum

WBI *World Biographical Index* (University Publications of America)

Wbk/WB will book (probate record)

WbrL wife's brother-in-law

wc with costs

w/c with consent of (Quaker)

WC (1) West Central (2) Widow's Certificate

W/Cdr Wing Commander

wch/wch which

WChd wife's child

WCLAR Washington Crossing Library of the American Revolution, Washington Crossing, PA

Wclev West Cleveland, Ohio

W/Cmdr Wing Commander

WCRA West Coast Railway Association (Vancouver, BC)

WCTU Women's Christian Temperance Union, Meade, KS 67864

wd/WD (1) the widow of (2) widow, widowed (3) will dated

Wd/WD ward

WD widow died

WD (1) War Department (2) Warranty Deed (3) West Indies

wdr widower

wds wounds

We (1) West Indies (2) Westmoreland, England

WE (1) Wales (2) West (3) West Indies

Web World Wide Web (Internet)

WEAG Western European Armaments Group

Wed Wednesday

WEE *World Education Encyclopedia*

Wei Weimer/Weighains

WEI Western Islands

weibl *weiblich* (feminine)

weil *weiland* (deceased)

WEIS Weissenberg, Germany

WEL/WLOT West Lothian (*see* Linlithgow), Great Britain

Welcome Soc of Pa The Welcome Society of Pennsylvania, 415 South Croskey Street, Philadelphia, PA 19146

Well Wellington

WELS Wisconsin Evangelican Lutheran Synod

Welsh Soc of Phila The Welsh Society of Philadelphia, 450 Broadway, Camden, NJ 08103

WEM Westmeath

Wer Wertenberg/Wurtemburg

Wes (1) Wessem (2) Westfall (3) Westphalia (Westfalen)

WES Westmoreland, England

WesD/WestD West Darmstadt

WesF Westfall

WesP/Wesp Westphalia

west western

WEST Westphalia (Westfalen)

Westf Westfalen, Prussia

Westm/Westmd/WMOR Westmorland, England

Westph Westfalen, Germany

Westpr Westpreussen, Prussia

WEU Western European Union

Wex Wexford, Republic of Ireland

Wexfd Wexford, Ireland

wf (1) the wife of (2) wharf (3) white female (4) wife

WF (1) West Florida (2) Widow's File

W.Fland West Vlaanderen

wf/o wife of

WFPI Welfare Fraud Prevention Initiative

WFT *World Family Tree* (Brøderbund, P.O. Box 760, Fremont, CA 94537-9824)

WGA Writers Guild of America

WGAt wife's grandaunt

WGC Wisconsin Genealogical Council

Wgm wagon master

WGmc West Germanic

Wgn wagoneer

Wgn/Mkr Wagon Maker

Wgnr waggoner

WGW WorldGenWeb (www.worldgenweb.org)

wh (1) where (2) which (3) white, Caucasiam (4) who (5) with

WHC Wisconsin State Historical Society Collections, 816 State Street, Madison, WI 53706

Whi Whitenburg/Wittenburgh/Whesterburg

Whit. Col. Whitaker Collection

WHLBA Wisconsin Local History & Biography Articles

whls boots wholesale dealer boots & shoe

whlsdrygds wholesale dry goods merchandise

whls gro wholesale grocer

whls mct wholesale merchant

WHM *Wisconsin Magazine of History*

whn when

whol wholesale

WHOM Women Historians of the Midwest, Minnesota Women's Bldg., 550 Rice Street, Suite 101, St. Paul, MN 55103

Whoop Cgh Whooping Cough

WHR Western Humanities Review

WHS Wisconsin Historical Society

whsemn warehouseman

wht white

wi witness

WI (1) West Indies (2) Wife

WIA Wounded in Action

WI/Wisc Wisconsin

Wic Wicklow, Republic of Ireland

Wiccia Worcestershire, England

Wick Wicklow, Ireland

Wickl Wicklow, Ireland

wid/widw/wido 1) widow (of) (2) widowed (3) widower

WID widow

wid necs widow's necessaries

wid/o widow of

widr widower

WifA wife's aunt

WifB wife's brother

WifC wife's cousin

WifD wife's daughter

wife wife

WifF wife's father

WifM wife's mother

WifN wife's nephew or niece

WifP wife's parent

WifS wife's sister

WifU wife's uncle

Wig Wigtownshire, Scotland

WIG Wigtown or Wigtownshire, Scotland

WiGD wife's granddaughter

WiGF wife's grandfather

WiGS wife's grandson

WIGT/Wigtwn Wigtown, Scotland

Wil Wilber, Wilbur, Wilfred

WIL/WILT/Wilts Wiltshire, Great Britain

WilD wife's illegitimate daughter

Wilf Wilfred

WilS wife's illegitimate son

w.i.h. went in hole

Wilf Wilfred

Wilf/Wilf^d Wilford

Wilh Wilhelm

Will/Willm/Wm William

Will Wilfred, Willard, William, Willis

Willa/Wilma Wilhelmina

Willie/Willy William

will pr will proved

Wilts Wiltshire (England)

WIN/WIn West Indies

Win Winifred

WinC Winthrop College, Rock Hill, SC

Winch Winchester

wind winder

WIND/WIN West Indies

Winfl^d Winfield

Winn Winnipeg

Winnie Winifred

WINS Windows Internet Name Service

WINSLO Worldwide Web Info Network, State Library of Ohio, Columbus, OH

Winthrop *Winthrop Papers*

Winton Winchester

WinZip Windows file compression program

WIP Washington International Report

WIPO World Intellectual Property Organization

Wir/Wirt/WIRT/WERT Wirtemburg/Wertenberg

Wis/Wisc Wisconsin

WiSB wife's stepbrother

Wisc Wisconsin

WiSD wife's stepdaughter

WISE Wales, Ireland, Scotland, England Family History Society

WiSHS Wisconsin State Historical Society, 816 State Street, Madison, WI 53706

WiSL wife's son-in-law

WiSM wife's stepmother

WiSn wife's son

WiSS wife's stepson

WISU Wichita State University Library, 1845 Fairmount, Wichita, KS 67260-0068

WiSv wife's servant

wit/wtn (1) witness (2) witnessed (3) witnesses

Wit Wittenberg, Germany

wits witness(es)

Wittl Wittlage

Wittn Wittenberg

WiU Wisconsin University, Madison, WI

WJ John Winthrop, *The History of New England from 1630 to 1649*, ed. James Savage, 2 vols. (Boston, 1853).

wk (1) walk (2) week (3) work

wk(s) (1) week(s) (2) works

WK Waldeck

wker worker

wkm/Wkm workman

wkr worker

wk's works

WL (1) Wales (2) Wilmington Institute Library

Wld Waldic

wldr welder

WHLBA Wisconsin Local History & Biography Articles

WLN (1) Washington Library Network (2) West Lothian, Scotland

Wlo/W.Loth/WLOT West Lothian, Scotland

wls wells

WLS Wales

wm white male

Wm/Wm William

WM Wesleyan Methodist

Wmak watchmaker

WMCP *William and Mary College Papers* (Earl Gregg Swem Library, College of William and Mary)

WMD Weapons of Mass Destruction

Wme/W.Meath Westmeath, Republic of Ireland

WMF Windows Metafile

WMG *Western Maryland Genealogy*

WmGS Williams County Genealogical Society, Bryan, OH 43506

WMH *Wisconsin Magazine of History*

WmHS Williams County Historical Society, 13660 Country Home Road, Bowling Green, OH 43401

WMOR Westmoreland

WMQ *William and Mary Quarterly*

Wmst workmistress

W.Mth West Meath, Ireland

WN (1) Caucasian-Negro (2) World News

Wndr wanderer

W. Nian West Niantic dialect

WNRC Washington National Records Center, National Archives and Records Administration, 4205 Suitland Road, Suitland, MD 20746-8001

WNS Women's News Service

wnt wants

WNT Winterthur Museum Library

WNW West Northwest

WNYGS Western New York Genealogical Society, P.O. Box 338, Hamburg, NY 14075

w/o (1) wife of (2) without

Wo Worcestershire, England

WO (1) presumed to mean white oak when found in old records (2) War Office (England) (3) Warrant Officer (4) widow's original

Women Desc Anc & Hon Artillery Co National Society, Women Descendants of the Ancient and Honorable Artillery Company

womn woman

Wood Wood County Public Library, 251 North Main Street, Bowling Green, OH 43402

WOR/WORC/Worc/Worcs Worcestershire, England

Worcs Worcester

WorldCat OCLC Online Union Catalog

Wort/Ger Wortenberg, Germany

WOW (1) Woodmen of the World (2) Worldwide Organization for Women

WP/wp (1) white poll(s), e.g., white poll tax (2) will probated (3) will proved or proven

wp will proved

w/pwr with power

WPA Works Progress Administration

WPB War Production Board

WPE *World Press Encyclopedia* (Gale)

WPG WordPerfect Graphic format

WPGS Western Pennsylvania Genealogical Society, 4400 Forbes Avenue, Pittsburgh, PA 15213-4080

WPGS Historical Society of Western Pennsylvania, 4338 Bigelow Boulevard, Pittsburgh, PA 15213-2695

WPH Westphalia

WPI Worcester Polytechnic Institute

WPL Westminster Public Libraries (Archives Dept.), Victoria Library, Buckingham Palace Road, London, England SW1

WPL (1) Public Library, Whitehaven, England (2) Worcester Public Library

wpm words per minute

WPNS Widow Pensioned

Wprus/WPRU West Prussia

WQUAR Winter Quarters

Wr mentioned or inherited in a will

WR (1) Western Reserve (northeastern Ohio) (2) West Riding (3) Württemberg, Germany

WRA War Relocation Authority (World War II, U.S. Department of War)

WRDA Wisconsin Register of Deeds Association

WrdM wardsman

wrdn warden

wrd/o ward of

wrdr warder

WrdW wardswoman

WRENS Women's Royal Naval Service

WRHS Western Reserve Historical Society, 10825 East Boulevard, Cleveland, OH 44106-1788

wrkd worked

Wrs Wrappers (paper binding)

W-Rs White Russia

WrSt Wright State University Archives, 3640 Colonel Glenn Highway, Dayton, OH 45431

WRsv Western Reserve Historical Society, 10825 East Boulevard, Cleveland, OH 44106-1788

WRY West Riding of Yorkshire, England

ws (1) west side (2) whiskey still

w(s)s warrant(s) signed

WS/W.S. (1) Writer to the Signet, a solicitor (2) West Saxon

WSC Worcester State College

WSDa wife's sister's daughter

WSGS Washington State Genealogical Society, P.O. Box 1422, Olympia, WA 98507-1422

WSGS Wisconsin State Genealogical Society, P.O. Box 5106, Madison, WI 53705-0106

wshr wmn washer woman

WSHS Wisconsin State Historical Society, Madison, WI

WSI (1) West Indies (2) West Sea Isles

WSis Wife's Stepsister

wsky drnkr whisky drinker

WSL William Salt Library, Stafford, England

WSSn wife's sister's son

Wsthmptn Westhampton, MA

Wstmld Westmorland, England

Wstn Western

WSU Wright State University, Special Collections and Archives, Paul Laurence Dunbar Library, Dayton, OH 45435-0001

WSW West Southwest

wt want(ed)

wt/Wt waiter

wt/wth/wth with

Wt Isle of Wight, England

WT (1) Water Tank (2) Western Territory

wtchmn watchman

wtn witness

Wtr (1) waiter (2) water

Wu/Wur/Wurt Württemberg, Germany

Wuertt/WUR/Wurt Württemberg, Germany

WURT Württemberg, Germany

Wut Wüttenberg, Germany

Wuv Wustenberg/Wistenburg

WV/WVa/W VA/W Va West Virginia

WVAr West Virginia Department of Archives and History, 1900 Kanawha Blvd East, Charleston, WV 23505-0300

WVGS Willamette Valley Genealogical Society, Oregon State Library, P.O. Box 2083, Salem, OR 97308

ww (1) widow (2) will written

WW World War

WW1/WW2 World War I, World War II

WWI-L World War I Military History List

Wwe Witwe (widow)

Wwer Witwer (widower)

ww/o widow of

wwr widower

WWrt wheelwright

WWW World Wide Web (a network of documents, files, and linked pages of information on the Internet)

WY/Wyo Wyoming

WyAR Wyoming State Archives and History Department, 2301 Central Avenue, Cheyenne, WY 82002

WYSIWYG What you see is what you get

X

X (1) a person who signed a document with an "X" (2) by, in dimensions (3) Christ (4) Christian (5) cross (6) equivalent to Xp (q.v.) (7) unknown (8) was not married

Xber December (10ber)

xch exchange

X-cut cross-cut

Xena Green County District Library, Xenia, OH

Xing crossing

XL Sister-in-law

Xmas Christmas

XML eXtensible Markup Language (computer term), a programming language

x/mo. times per month

XMS Extended Memory System

Xn Christian

Xnty Christianity

x. out crossout

Xp the Greek letters *chi* and *rho*, Chr(ist), often used as a part of someone's name as in Xpmann = Christmann or Xpian—Christian, sometimes found without the *rho* as in Xtopher = Christopher

XP eXtra Performance (Windows XP)

Xped christened

Xper/Xr Christopher

Xpofer Christopher

Xr (1) Christian (2) Receiver/Purchaser/Buyer/Grantee/Inherit/Endowee/etc.

XSL Extensible Stylesheet Language (computer term)

xt next, as in next friend

Xt (1) Christ (2) Transmitter/Seller/Grantor/Giver/Distribure/Endower/etc.

xt.court/xt.crt next term of court

Xtian/xtian Christian

Xty Christianity

x/wk times per week

x/yr times per year

Y

y (1) th, as in yᵉ (2) year(s) (3) yearly (4) young

Y Young Men's Christian Association

Y2K year 2000 computer issue, known as the "Millennium Bug"

YA Young Adult Librarian, Young Adult Services

YAS Yorkshire Archaeological Society, Claremont, 23 Clarendon Road, Leeds, England LS2 9NZ

YC Yacht Club

YCGSJ *York County Genealogical Society Journal*

yd (1) graveyard (2) yard

YD York Deeds

ydmn yardman

ydmstr yardmaster

yds yards

ye/ye (1) the (2) you (3) your

yearb yearbook

YEM People's Republic of Yemen

yeo/yeom yeoman/yeomanry

yᵉʳᵉ there

YG/YUG Yugoslavia

YGC Your Genealogy Conference, Provo, UT

YHCIL Youngstown Historical Center of Industry and Labor, P.O. Box 533, Youngstown, OH 44501-0533

yⁱˢ this

YIVO YIVO Institute for Jewish Research

YKS Yorkshire

ym them

YM Yearly Meeting (Quaker)

YMCA Young Men's Christian Association

-y-m-d years, months, days

YMHA Young Men's Hebrew Association

YN Yukon, Canada

yng young

yngr younger

yngs/yngst/yngste/young youngest

y.o.b. year of birth

y.o.d. year of death

Yo Pub Lib Youngstown Ohio Public Library, 305 Wick Avenue, Youngstown, OH 44503

yor/yr younger

YORK/Yorks/YRKS Yorkshire, England

yr. (1) year(s) (2) younger (3) your

Yr (1) Year (2) publication year

yrbk yearbook

YrdB yard boy

YrdM yardman

yre/yr(s) year(s)

yrly yearly

yrs yours

YS York State

yᵗ this

yst youngest

yt/yᵗ (1) that (2) yet

YT/YUK Yukon Territory, Canada

ytd year to date

YU/YUL Yale University Library, New Haven, CT 06520

YU/YUG/YUGO Yugoslavia

Yuc Yucatán

Yukon Terr Yukon Territory, Canada

YWCA Young Women's Christian Association

YWHA Young Women's Hebrew Association

Z

Zach Zachary

Zach/Zachʳ/Zacharᵃ/Zack Zachariah

Zam/Zamb Zambia

Zan/ZAN/Zanz Zanzibar

Zech Zechariah

Zeke Ezekid

Zeph Zephaniah

Zet/ZET Zetland/Shetland, Scotland

ZIP Zone Improvement Plan

ZLL Zion Lutheran Church

Znvl John McIntire Public Library, Zanesville

Zool Zoology

Zur/Zwick Zurich, Canton of Zwickau, Saxony

APPENDIX

SYMBOLS

[   ] original record illegible or missing

--- no information given, or unreadable

~ ca, circa, approximately

... information illegible

★ (1) date of birth/born (2) name omitted

(★) born illegitimate

= date of marriage

+ (1) date of death   (2) information in note field (3) or later

: commonly used to end an abbreviation

★ TIB (upper left) typed from an old-style LDS temple record

★★ TIB (upper left) typed from a family group record, but no copy was made at that time (archive record)

★★★ TIB (upper left) there is a question as to the correct parentage of the person described on the card

★★★ indicates that the LDS ordinance dates are listed in the computer parish print-out

'' ditto (the same), same as above

@ (1) at (2) individual and the principal name on the card appear as husband and wife on an archive record

? questionable interpretation, illegible, spelling in doubt, doesn't make sense

X killed

X baptized or christened

> after

< before

number, pound

p. penny

$/dol dollar

Mex.$ Mexican peso

Can.$ Canadian dollar

¢/c/ct cent

© copyright

£ pound sterling

I£ Isreali pound

% percent

c/o in care of

& and

&c/& ca/etc. and so forth (etcetera)

(feet) feet on microfilm spool

1st first

2nd second

3rd third

4th fourth

1:57 refers to research notebook or volume number 1, p. 57

47t refers to the # of turns equivalent to the 87 ft. or the "F"on the take up reel of the microfilm reading machine

(50673, pt 57) 50673 is the old Family History Library microfilm number, and pt 57 is the part number (use the new six or seven digit film numbers)

2aa-6 Family Group Record Sheets (no. following hyphen is no. of binder for that letter of the alphabet)

2ab-542 second thousand sheets of a large surname in 2aa

2B-414-17 same as form 2, but arranged by locality

2BA-103-17-295 bound LDS temple records; these records have been returned to the contributing families

2BC old lineage books - probably filed in 2aa

7/ 7 shillings

7BA-149-6 three generation pedigree charts

7R-44-6 No. 7 indicates pedigree charts. The letter represents the book; the number of the chart; & the last number, the number of the individual on the chart

51t refers to the number of turns equivalent to 51 ft. on the take-up spool of microfilm reading machine

97' refers to 97 feet of film on take-up spool of microfilm reading machine

725 *Controlled Extraction Eng-Gibson marriage Index*

710481251 batch processed in 1971 on the 48th day of the year, 12th batch that day, page 51

1812 A veteran of the War of 1812

1cou first cousin

1c 1r first cousin once removed

2c 1r second cousin once removed

2c 2r second cousin twice removed

2 gg dau second great-granddaughter

2 gg son second great-grandson

3 gg neph il third great-grandnephew-in-law

2-6-7 Form 2; family group records with four

1HuD first husband's daughter

1HuS first husband's son

1wif first wife

1WiS first wife's son

2Coh second coachman

2Cou second cousin

2Crp second corporal

2HuD second husband's daughter

1Lt 1st Lieutenant

2Lt 2nd Lieutenant

2Mst second master

2nep second nephew

2nie second niece

2sgt second sergeant

2son second son

2WiD second wife's daughter

2wif second wife

2WiM second wife's mother

2WiS second wife's son

3/m. three times a month

3/yr. three times a year

3cou third cousin

3son third son

4M 4 names on marker

/m married

/w widow/widower

/d divorced

/m★ married within the year

7br 7ber ' viibr ' viiber ' September

7bris viibris ' Septembris (of September)

8br 8ber ' viiibr ' viiiber ' October

8bris viiibris ' Octobris (of October)

9br 9ber ' ixbr ' ixber ' November

9bris ixbris ' Novembris (of November)

10br 10ber ' xbr ' xber ' December

10bris xbris ' Decembris (of December)

MEASUREMENTS

Length

in. or " inch

ft. or ' foot

yd. yard

rd. rod

mi. mile

Area

sq. in square inch

sq. ft square foot

sq. yd square yard

sq. rd square rod

sq. mi square mile

a. acre

Volume

cu. in cubic inch

cu. ft cubic foot

cu. yd cubic yard

Weight

gr. grain

s. or scruple

dr. or 3 dram

dwt. pennyweight

oz. ounce

lb. or # pound

cwt. hundredweight

tn. ton

Dry Measure

pt. pint

qt. quart

pk. peck

bu. bushel

gi. gill

bbl. barrel

Liquid Measure

min. minimum, minim

fl. dr. fluid dram

f.₃ fluid dram

fl. oz. fluid ounce

pt. pint

qt. quart

gal. gallon

gi. gill

qt. quart

gal. gallon

bbl. barrel

Base Units

m	meter
kg	kilogram
s	second
A	ampere
K	Kelvin
mol	mole
cd	candela

NUMBERS

Roman Numerals

I	one	XXVII	twenty-seven
II	two	XXVIII	twenty-eight
III	three	XXIX	twenty-nine
IV	four	XXX	thirty
V	five	XXXI	thirty-one
VI	six	XL	fourty
VII	seven	L	fifty
VIII	eight	LX	sisty
IX	nine	LXX	seventy
X	ten	LXXX	eighty
XI	eleven	XC	ninety
XII	twelve	C	one hunred
XIII	thirteen	CI	one-hundred-one
XIV	fourteen	CL	one-hundred-fifty
XV	fifteen	CCC	three hundred
XVI	sixteen	CD	four hundred
XVII	seventeen	D	five hundred
XVIII	eighteen	DC	six hundred
XIX	nineteen	DCC	seven hundred
XX	twenty	DCCC	eight hundred
XXI	twenty-one	CM	nine hundred
XXII	twenty-two	M	one thousand
XXIII	twenty-three	MDC	sixteen hundred
XXIV	twenty-four	MDCC	seventeen hundred
XXV	twenty-five	MDCCC	eighteen hundred
XXVI	twenty-six	MCM	nineteen hundred

Cardinal Numbers

1	unus
2	duo, duae
3	tres, tres, tria
4	quattuor
5	quinque
6	sex
7	septem
8	octo
9	novem
10	decim
11	undecim
12	duodecim
13	tredecim
14	quattuordecim
15	quindecim
16	sedecim
17	septemdecim
18	odeviginti
19	undeviginti
20	viginti
21	viginiti unus
22	viginti duo
23	viginti tres
24	viginti quattuor
25	viginti quinque
26	viginti sex
27	viginti septem
28	viginti octo
29	viginti novem
30	trigenta
40	quadraginta
50	quinquaginta
60	sexaginta
70	septuaginta
80	octoginta
90	nonaginta
100	centum
101	centum unus
150	centum quinquaginta
200	dudenti
300	trecenti
400	quadringenti
500	quingenti
600	sescenti
700	septigenti
800	octingenti
900	nongenti
1000	mille

Ordinal Numbers

1st	primus
2nd	secundus
3rd	tertius
4th	quartus
5th	quintus
6th	sextus
7th	septimus
8th	octavus
9th	nonus
10th	decimus
11th	undecimus
12th	duodecimus
13th	tertius decimus
14th	quartus decimus
15th	quintus decimus
16th	sextus decimus
17th	septimus decimus
18th	duodevicesimus
19th	undevicesimus
20th	vicesimus, vegesimus
21st	vicesimus primus

22nd	vicesimus secundus		**90th**	nonagesimus
23rd	vicesumus tertius		**100th**	centesimus
24th	vicesimus quartus		**101st**	centesimus primus
25th	vicesimus quintus		**150th**	centesimus quinquagesimus
26th	vicemsimus sextus		**200th**	ducentesimus
27th	secesimus septimus		**300th**	trecentesimus
28th	vicesimus octavus		**400th**	quadrigentesimus
29th	vicesimus nonus		**500th**	quingentesimus
30th	tricesimus		**600th**	sescentesimus
40th	quadragesimus		**700th**	septingentesimus
50th	quinquagesimus		**800th**	octingentesimus
60th	sexagesimus		**900th**	nongentesimus
70th	septuagesimus		**1000th**	millesimus
80th	octogesimus			

BIBLIOGRAPHY

Abbreviations (from James Savage, *A Genealogical Dictionary of the First Settlers of New England*). Available at <www.prenticenet.com/roots/ library/savage.htm> and <http://home.earthlink.net/~anderson207/ SavageAbbrev.html>

Abbreviations Found in Genealogy. Available at <www.rootsweb.com/~rigenweb/abbrev. html>

Abbreviations Used in Genealogy. Available at <www.uq.net.au/~zzmgrinl/ abbrev.html>

Abbreviations Used in Genealogy. Available at <www.rootsweb.com/roots-l/abbrevs. html>

Abbreviations Used in Genealogy. Available at <www.obcgs.com/abbrev.htm>

Acronym Finder. Available at <www.acronymfinder.com>

Acronyms and Abbreviations. Available at <http://mel.lib.mi.us/reference/ REF-acronym.html>

Acronyms Used in the Computer Community. Available at <www.freewarehof.org/acronyms.html>

Association of Professional Genealogists. *Abbreviations, Acronymns, and Postnomials.* Available at <www.apgen.org/resources/aa.html>

Association of Professional Genealogists. *Directory of Professional Genealogists*, 20th Anniversary Edition, 1999-2000. Compiled by Kathleen W. Hinckley. Denver: The Association, 1999, pp. 11-12.

Census Abbreviations. Available at <www.seark.net/~sabra/abbrev.txt>

Census Abbreviations. Available at <http:// frontierfolk.org/cens-abr.htm>

Census Abbreviations. Available at <www.got-genealogy.com/abbreviations.html>

Census Abbreviations. Available at <http:// homepages.rootsweb.com/~angels/census_ abbrev.htm>

Census Abbreviations Used in Soundex. Available at <www.seark.net/~sabra/ sxabbrev.txt>

Census Search. Available at <www.censussearch.com/terms.html>

The Chicago Manual of Style. 14th ed. Chicago: University of Chicago Press, 1993.

Cyndi's List of Genealogy Sites on the Internet: Dictionaries & Glossaries. Available at <www.cyndislist.com/diction.htm>

DeSola, Ralph. *Abbreviations Dictionary.* 6th ed. New York: Elsevier North Holland, 1981.

Edmonds, David, ed. *Dictionary of Abbreviations.* Edinburgh, Scotland: Chambers, 1995.

Emery, Ashton. *A-Z of British Genealogical Research.* <www.genuki.org.uk/big/ EmeryPaper.html>

Evans, Barbara Jean. *A to Zax: A Comprehensive Dictionary for Genealogists & Historians.* 3rd ed. Alexandria, Va.: Hearthside Press, 1995.

Family History Jargon. Available at <www. vellum.demon.co.uk/guide/fh11.htm>

GenDocs—*Genealogical Abbreviations and Acronyms.* Available at <www.gendocs.demon.co.uk/abbr.html>

GenDocs—*Abbreviations Used on Census Returns, England, and Wales, 1841–1891.* Available at <www.gendocs.demon.co.uk/abbrcen.html>

Genealogy Abbreviation List. Available at <www.niagara.com/~hanam/abbreviations/abbreviations.txt>

Genealogy Abbreviations. Available at <http://homepages.rootsweb.com/~sam/abbr.html>

Genealogy Abbreviations. Available at <www.netscope.net/~tchs/hist/gene.html>

Genealogy Dictionary. Available at <http://home.att.net/~dottsr/diction.html>

Genealogy Macedonia. U.S. Census Abbreviations. Available at <http://geneamac.dhs.org/reference/CensusAbbreviations.php3>

Genealogy Quest. Available at <www.genealogy-quest.com/glossaries/ abbrev.html>

Glossary of Internet Terms. Available at <www.matisse.net/files/glossary.html>

Harris, Maurine and Glen Harris, comps. *Ancestry's Concise Genealogical Dictionary.* Salt Lake City: Ancestry Publishing, 1989.

Hinckley, Kathleen W. *Alphabet Soup: Understanding the Genealogical Community.* Available at <www.genealogy.com/33_kathy.html>

Mayberry, George, comp. *A Concise Dictionary of Abbreviations.* New York: Tudor Publishing Co., 1961.

Netlingo. Available at <www.netlingo.com>

Schwartz, Robert J. *The Complete Dictionary of Abbreviations.* New York: Thomas Y. Crowell Co., 1955.

Smith, Juliana Szucs. *The Ancestry Family Historian's Address Book.* Salt Lake City: Ancestry, 1997.

Sperry, Kip. *Reading Early American Handwriting.* Baltimore: Genealogical Publishing Co., 1998.

UK Genealogy: Common Acronyms & Jargon. Available at <www.oz.net/~markhow/acronym-uk.htm>

United States Postal Service. *Official Abbreviations.* Available at <www.usps.gov/ncsc/lookups/abbrev.html>

ABOUT THE AUTHOR

Kip Sperry is an Associate Professor of Family History at Brigham Young University, Provo, Utah, where he teaches American genealogical research methods and sources, American and English paleography, and computer genealogy. He is a Certified Genealogist℠ (CG℠), Certified Genealogical Instructor℠ (CGI℠), and an Accredited Genealogist℠ (AG℠).

Kip is a Fellow of the American Society of Genealogists, National Genealogical Society, and Utah Genealogical Association. He has received the NGS President's Citation, NGS Distinguished Service Award, NGS Award of Merit, Utah Genealogical Association Annual Award, UGA Distinguished Service Award, GENTECH Certificate of Appreciation, and two first-place Excellence-in-Writing awards from the International Society of Family History Writers and Editors.

He is the author of *Reading Early American Handwriting* (book and VHS video), *Genealogical Research in Ohio*, and other works. His articles have appeared in *Ancestry* (Magazine), *The American Genealogist*, *The Genealogist* (American Society of Genealogists), *National Genealogical Society Quarterly*, *The New England Historical and Genealogical Register*, and other publications.

Kip is a lecturer at national, state, and local family history conferences and seminars, including National Genealogical Society annual Conferences in the States; Federation of Genealogical Societies annual conferences; Brigham Young University, Laie, Hawaii; BYU Campus Education Weeks, Provo, Utah; Ricks College Education Week, Rexburg, Idaho; BYU Annual Genealogy and Family History conferences; National Institute on Genealogical Research at the National Archives; Salt Lake Institute of Genealogy, Salt Lake City; 1980 World Conference on Records, Salt Lake City; and others.

He has served as a trustee for Board for Certification of Genealogists, National Genealogical Society council member, National Conference Chair of four NGS national conferences, director of BYU Annual Genealogy and Family History Conferences, and National Conference Chair for GENTECH 2000 conference in San Diego. Biographical sketches appear in *Directory of American Scholars* (Gale Group, 2002) *Who's Who in the West*, 23rd edition (1992–93), *Who's Who in Genealogy and Heraldry*, 2nd edition (1990), *Contemporary Authors, New Revision Series* (Gale Research Co.), and other works.

Printed in the USA
CPSIA information can be obtained
at www.ICGtesting.com
JSHW060044150824
68134JS00031B/2633